DO YOU COME HERE OFTEN?
THE MEEKSVILLE CONNECTION

The Ups and Downs
of a Sixties Rock Band

Robb Huxley

Silver Tabbies Publishing

ISBN-13: 978-1512369243

This book is edited from content currently available on Robb's web site www.robbhuxley.com. The same content has also been serialised in the Joe Meek Society's exclusive for members magazine *Thunderbolt*.

It is the first time it has been available in book form.

This book is dedicated to my wife

Efrat Vahab Huxley

Robb Huxley

Miami Florida 2015

+++

ACKNOWLEDGEMENTS

Robb wishes to thank:

Pete Holder, Dave Watts, John Davies, Roger Holder, Mick Holder, Sonia Watts and Sandra Holder (Diamond Twins), Rob Humphreys, Mandy Rogers, Stan Solomon, Bill Gozansky (photography) and Richard Wasley for their assistance in helping to remember the way it was...

Also:
Colin Kilgour for his general help with the book preparation.

David Peters for his photos of Joe Meek in 1966.

Robb also acknowledges the help and encouragement of his late sister Georgina Huxley Taylor-Spicer.

A special thank you to Dave Watts for the invaluable information from his Diary from 1966.

A very special thank you to Rob Humphreys of Silver Tabbies Publishing whose dedication and untiring energy have made this book a reality.

CONTENTS

ILLUSTRATION INDEX

FOREWORD

From recording with Joe Meek, backing Billy Fury, encounters with The Kray Twins, summer seasons on a variety bill with Marty Wilde and Adam Faith to bleak journeys for remote gigs. All the highs and lows of a recording and touring sixties rock band are vividly detailed.

Robb was a member of three groups, all of them managed by legendary producer Joe Meek. This is a fascinating insight into the world of sixties music. Robb shares memories of Joe Meek's recording techniques and much more. Major label recordings were issued by The Saxons and The Tornados but hidden gems lie in the legendary Meek Tea Chest Tapes.

Robb's recollections of sharing the bill with other groups and established old school variety artistes at summer season shows are numerous and insightful. Illustrated by many photos this is a rollercoaster read hurtling through the heady days of sixties groups and jam packed with reminiscences.

The title of the book is from "Do You Come Here Often" the single by The Tornados which was acclaimed to be the first openly gay pop record release by a UK major record label.

Rob Humphreys, Joe Meek Society

ROBB'S BACKGROUND

Growing up in Gloucester.
Robb gets his first guitar and works as a stage-hand.
Leaves Grammar School with no qualifications.
Gets a job at a department store and makes his first public appearance as a singer at the works party.
Robb joins his first band, The Vendettas.

*In the photo my grandfather (Robert Huxley 1st)
is sitting in the front row last person on the right.*

I was born in Gloucester England December 1945. My father worked as a carpenter at the Gloucester Wagon works and played piano in the local pubs on the weekends to make extra money. We were a working class family, we were not exactly poor but as my dad used to say we certainly were not rich. My grandfather was a career serviceman in the Royal navy. His rank was chief petty officer torpedo man instructor. He played in the naval brass band and also sang and played the mandolin.

In the early 1930s he took his own life when having only two years left to finish his 20 years service. He was Robert Huxley the first, my dad was Robert Huxley the second, and I am Robert Huxley the third. In 1995 0n a visit to England to attend a Tornados reunion held at the King of Clubs in Gloucester, I spoke with my father's cousin, Trevor Fry. Trevor had done extensive research into the background of the family tree, and after a meeting with Gervas Huxley, came to the conclusion that we were fourth cousins to the famed writer and philosopher, Aldous Huxley. Huxley became very famous in the sixties, when his novel *Brave New World* was widely read and acclaimed. Jim Morrison of The Doors was said to have taken the band's name from Aldous Huxley's book *The Doors of Perception*. As a kid I remember watching him on the B.B.C.'s talk show called *The Brains Trust*. That had to have been in the fifties. Of course, at my age I didn't have a clue what they were talking about. My mother Joan Beryl White Huxley often used to say that we bore a resemblance to Aldous, and that my father and I came from outer space! I obviously didn't get to meet my grandfather, and my dad has now passed on but I am sure my musical inclination came from them. My maternal grandfather William White played piano, organ, and melodeon, which is a type of small piano accordion. He played it very well, and I still have his instrument to this day.

At the age of eleven I passed the eleven plus exam and attended Sir Thomas Rich's grammar school in Gloucester which was and still is a very good school. I sang in the school choir for the five years that I was there. Around the age of 12 or 13, I became mesmerized watching the new rock shows on the BBC on Saturday nights. The first being *The Six Five Special* with Lonnie Donegan and Don Lang and His Frantic Five. Later followed by *Drumbeat* and *Oh Boy!* These shows featured artists such as The John Barry Seven with Vic Flick on guitar,

Cliff Richard, Marty Wilde, Adam Faith, Vince Eager, Billy Fury, Dickey Pride, The Kalin Twins, Joe Brown, Roy Young and Wee Willie Harris. My father was quite disgusted by my addiction to those shows but he, or I for that matter, could not have known that in a few short years I would be appearing on stage alongside of many of those artists.

Along with my love of these shows I also fell in love with guitars. I used to browse the magazines with guitar ads that proclaimed, "Play and be popular everywhere" and showed pictures of acoustic guitars. As I had no money I had to be content by visiting the only local music store, in the town centre. It was called Hickies. I never went in the store; I just stared through the window at the glossy electric guitars, dreaming that one day I would own one of them. Two of my school-mates Jimmy Brown, and Alan Keeling owned guitars, but neither of them could play. I used to love hanging out at their homes so I could get my hands on them and try to strum a little. Alan Keeling had a nice Hofner acoustic and after getting a feel of it I knew I just had to get my own.

Every morning before school I used to deliver newspapers for Jack Keeling (Alan's dad), for a few shillings a week. It was getting near to Christmas and I had saved up one Pound Sterling which seemed like a lot of money then. I had seen this acoustic guitar in a second hand shop on sale for two pounds and ten shillings and asked my parents if they could give me the balance so that I could buy the guitar for Christmas. As my father had paid for me to take piano lessons when I was twelve, and in which I failed miserably, he declined saying that after a week the guitar would be thrown in the corner of the room and the whole thing would be a waste of money. My mother replied say-ing that if he wouldn't give me the money, she would, so thanks to her I bought the guitar.

I had a little money left over and went to Hickies and bought a teach yourself guitar book. The guitar was really a piece of shit but it meant the world to me at the time. My dad even helped me tune it to the piano.

From that time on my parents didn't see much of me as I was con-stantly upstairs in my little bedroom twanging away.

Robb at age 14

Dave Nash, one of my school mates came to me one day saying that he had got a Grundig tape recorder. As we both sang in the school choir we liked singing and music and thought we could sing like The Everly Brothers and Buddy Holly. I used to take my guitar over to Dave's house and we would record songs. Dave was also interested in playing drums and he had bought a pair of drumsticks. We would set up the mic close to the floor and he would drum on the carpet and I would sing and play the guitar. We did "Peggy Sue" by Buddy Holly, which I thought came out pretty good. We also used to put on The Everly Brothers and sing along together with them. We could knock off the harmonies quite well for a couple of fifteen year old kids.

Robb & Dave Nash

One December just before Christmas, Dave told me that we might be able to get a job working as stage hands at the local Regal cinema. In those days they always held pantomimes there over the holidays. We decided to go up to the Regal to apply for the jobs. We told them we were both sixteen years old. They decided to hire us and told us to report to the cinema at eight o' clock on Monday morning. We were both very excited especially me as I was very interested in every thing to do with entertainment.

We spent that Monday meeting the stage manager, Owen, and his assistant whose name I have forgotten, and unloading the stage scenery and all the equipment from a train at the local station. I was totally in my element, working in this field, although I must say that the spicy language and bawdy conversations that came from Owen and his assistant, took a little getting used to, but it was really just a part of growing up and being involved with adults. Dave and I worked a lot of hours that week and when we got paid at the end of the week in cash, I got home late and my parents were already in bed.

I remember pulling all the pound notes from my pocket and showering them all over my parents' bed. I had made eleven pounds and that seemed like a fortune to me at the time. Looking back it was a great experience that gave me a look into the world of entertainment. I witnessed the whole procedure from start to finish; which included rehearsals with all the entertainers while carrying out the scene changes. One day I brought my guitar to show the A.S.M. who told me that he could show me how to play. He proceeded to slacken off the two lower strings as he said I didn't need them and basically played the guitar like a ukulele. Featured on the bill at that Christmas pantomime was a group of five singers called The Dallas Boys. One of them had a big old Hofner jazz style electric guitar which he played in one of their numbers called "Scarlet Ribbons." I noticed that he had not slackened off his two bottom strings, so I decided to ignore the advice of the A.S.M. and continued to play with six strings, thank God.

Dave and I worked the afternoon shows with Owen the stage manager, setting up and breaking down the sets and taking care of the props. For the evening show we were joined by some older guys who joked around with us and teased us from time to time. One thing that they were serious about was telling Dave and I to watch out for Owen as he, as they put it "Liked Boys." Sure enough they were right. Owen made advances to Dave and I behind the sets or when the curtains were closed. We made a special effort to keep away from him, especially back stage and we tried not to be caught alone with him. Taking everything into consideration I really enjoyed working at the cinema during the school holidays. It gave me a look at what it might be like to work in show business. On the last night of the show I was lucky to get a kiss from one of the dancing girls that I had become friendly with over those few weeks. As she was walking out of the stage door we said goodbye and she held me and kissed me on the lips. She had to be a couple of years older than me so it was quite a thrill. The worst part was that I knew I would never see her again. We shared one kiss and it was all over.

Robb around the age of 16

During the next year and a half my school work got progressively worse and at sixteen and a half I left school, and just like George Harrison, I didn't get any G.C.E.s. Having left school with no qualifications it wasn't easy to find a job. I went for a few interviews at various factories but I was told that I was not suited to do factory work and that I should look for work as a salesman. After a while I gave up looking for work and was lucky to be able to borrow Alan Keeling's Hofner Congress guitar to practice on. I kept it for over a year until he came and asked for it back. At the same time I borrowed a Dansette record player and a collection of Buddy Holly records from my friend

Kenny Reece who lived next door. As I was not working I had plenty of time on my hands and spent hours and hours playing along with the records trying to figure out the chords and licks. I guess it was Buddy Holly who helped me learn to play the guitar. Although I had only a very limited chord vocabulary I started to write my own songs. This was one of the first.

Once I had a pretty little girl,
She said that she loved me,
And that we'd be together forever,
Everyone knew it was plain to see.
But there came an unhappy day,
When a new boy came to town,
He went and walked away with her,
And then I wore a frown.

That was my first effort using about two and a half chords. The months passed by and no work was to be found, but my musical education and knowledge were improving.

Dave Nash came around to see me and told me that he had just come back from Liverpool. He had got a job at Wall's Ice cream factory as an apprentice electrician and had been attending a training program at Lever Bros. for a few weeks. He told me that he had been to a club called The Cavern and had seen this group there called The Beatles. They used to play there at lunch time. Dave said that they were a great group and were sure to be famous and that everybody loved them up in Liverpool. Then he pulled out a postcard size publicity photo of the band showing John Lennon, Paul McCartney, George Harrison and Pete Best all dressed in leather jackets, complete with all their autographs. At this time they did not have any records out so I had not heard any of their music but I had this strong feeling that Dave was right and that they would be big one day. It would be very nice if Dave still has that photo, I have had no contact with him for over forty years. In the 1980s I used the memory of this chance meeting with Dave Nash as part of a song I wrote about my first knowledge of The Beatles. I featured this song called "Always Remember" on my solo album *Churchill Gazoombah and The World is Mine*.

One Friday afternoon I walked into the local youth employment office and was told a job was available at the Bon Marche which was the local department store. The position was for a trainee buyer in the carpet department. It was not very appealing to me but I thought I would have to check it out as I couldn't just live at home depending on my parents. Anyway I went over there right away and was interviewed by Mr. Herbert the personnel manager. He was very impressed to hear that I attended Sir Thomas Rich's Grammar school but on learning that I had failed all my G.C.E.s he was not so impressed. He asked me why I had failed and I answered by saying that I didn't try hard enough. He then went on to enquire about my interests. My reply was that I loved music and singing and that I had sung in the school choir. Mr. Herbert then told me that if I would join the Bon Marche choir that he would give me the job based on one month's trial. I consented and went to the choir practice the following Monday night. That was the only time I attended. The thought of singing "Old Macdonald Had A Farm" with a bunch of old fogies was definitely not my scene. Anyway I still got the job and apparently my disappearance was never missed by the choir.

I guess that things really started happening for me one day when I sat at the same table as Phil Preest in the staff cafeteria. Phil was a management trainee and a year or two my senior. I overheard him talking to another young salesman about a band he was getting together to play a set at the staff Christmas party. He played piano and had a friend who played guitar, and some other guy to play the drums. I eagerly told Phil that I could sing and that I also had a Hofner Colorama electric guitar together with an eight watt Selmer amp. Now that I was working I persuaded my dad to cosign for me to buy the guitar and amp from Hickies on the Hire Purchase. Phil said OK and told me to come to a practice at the Bon Marche on the following Thursday afternoon. In those days the store closed on Thursday afternoon so everybody was off. With my guitar in one hand and amp in the other and wearing my grandfather's jacket which I liked because it reminded me of the kind that the Teddy Boys wore, I caught the No. 9 bus at the end of Clegram Road where I lived and set off for the rehearsal. Phil was there together with a guitar player and two guys that would be singing. I was very anxious to get up and sing but Phil said I should sit down and wait my turn. The first guy got up and sang "A Mess Of Blues" by Elvis Presley and although he had all the moves he couldn't really sing very well. The second guy sang "Let's Twist Again" by Chubby Checker and sounded like he was singing in a pub after drinking about fifteen beers. I could see the look of disappointment on Phil's face. Next an Asian girl got up and sang "East Of The Sun." She was OK but I knew I could out perform all of them. Meanwhile Phil was getting more despondent. Finally it was my turn and I can only imagine what Phil was thinking, after the disappointing performances of the other singers. He asked me what I knew, and looking on top of the piano I spotted a pile of sheet music which included some Buddy Holly tunes. "I can do these" I said, and we chose "Rave On." We went into the number and I really belted it out. The look on Phil's face changed drastically, and he broke out into a huge smile and asked me what else I could do. From that moment on I was the singer.

Well, Christmas soon came around and we played at the party.

First public appearance in 1963

I wore my black suit with a black shirt and a black Teddy Boy bow tie. I even bought some black clip on shades to wear over my Buddy Holly glasses.

I even wrote a special song for the occasion called "The Bon Marche Blues"

Well it's the same old tale week after week
Gotta get my hair cut gotta look so neat,
And when I press my trousers and I polish my shoes,
I got the Bon Marche blues.....

All the employees gathered around when we played the set and we really went down great. The following day at work I was approached by all kinds of employees, especially girls, saying how much they enjoyed my singing and how good I was. Was this fame at last?

A short time later Phil Preest came up to me in the staff cafeteria and told me that he had a band that was playing down in the Forest of Dean. They were playing at the Courtfield Arms in Lydbrook

Phil asked me if I would like to sing for them, they were called The Vendettas and they played every Sunday night. I would get paid ten shillings for the evening. I was delighted and immediately said "Yes."

That Sunday Phil picked me up in his mini van and we drove down to the Forest to his parent's house and ran through the songs on the piano. I also brought my guitar and amp as Dave Wynter who was the guitar player wanted to use them. Then we picked up Fiddy Laine the drummer. The Courtfield Arms was a country pub with an upstairs room and bar with a small stage where we set up our gear. We used the 8 watt Selmer amp for the guitar, and I also sang through it with a mic that Phil brought along. There was also a piano there. The band started off with some instrumentals and Phil could really knock out "Nut Rocker" by B. Bumble and The Stingers. I was very impressed and couldn't wait to get up and sing.

When the time came I got up and sang "A Whole Lotta Shakin' Goin' On" and the locals loved it. I also did some Marty Wilde and Cliff Richard songs and of course a good measure of Buddy Holly. During the break people came up to me and bought me drinks. They wanted to know all about this new singer. So this was my first paying gig and my second appearance. As Phil drove me home late that night I had a great feeling of happiness inside knowing that I was beginning to do what I had always dreamed of doing: sing and play in a band.

As the weeks went by we continued to play in the Forest. People had begun to hear about us and our audience grew. Sometimes other musicians came to jam with us. I remember the time that a guy showed up with an upright bass. This was a real treat as we had no bass player. Eddie Cochran's "C'mon Everybody" that we did sounded very good. At the end of the evening, Fiddy Laine the drummer raved about how good we sounded with a bass player. He mentioned that his cousin, also called Fiddy, a family nickname, had an electric bass and could come to play with us. A week later we had a bass player.

We got a few other gigs. One was at the Bristol Hotel in Gloucester. They had a music room upstairs and they held dances on Saturday nights. This hotel was only two blocks away from where I lived and at one point in the evening when I was on stage singing a "Whole Lotta Shakin' Goin' On", my dad appeared in the doorway and stood watching my performance. When the break came he walked up to me and said "Well I've seen it all now!" Then he broke into a big smile and we walked to the bar and he bought me a pint of beer.

We also played a gig for the Bon Marche at a club somewhere. Some of my friends from school came to hear me sing. Towards the end of the night a fight broke out and one of my schoolmates got hurt. Somebody was smart enough to turn out the lights and that ended everything. There were always fights in those days; you could always guarantee at least one or two.

HICKIES

HICKIE & HICKIE LTD.

52-56 SOUTHGATE STREET

GLOUCESTER

Mr R Huxley 7 Dec. 1962

Gloucester

Hofner Colorama II 37 16 0

Selmer Amp 265 31 10 0

69-6-0

Dep 12 0 0

57 6 0

2041

7-12-62 19 £ s. d.

Received with thanks from

M Huxley 12

For HICKIE & HICKIE LTD.

06764

Receipt for my Hofner Colorama/Selmer amp

Robb on the roof of Bon Marche

ROBB GAYLE & THE WHIRLWINDS

In which Robb meets the Holder brothers at the Courtfield Arms in the Forest of Dean.
After his audition Robb joins The Whirlwinds.
First contacts with Joe Meek.
Whirlwinds go to R. G. M. Sound for audition and experience Meek's recording techniques.
First recording sessions at Holloway Road and Robb's harrowing experience with Joe.
Robb and Pete Holder write their first song together and record it at R. G. M.

Joe announces a name change for the band.

Whirlwinds (L-R)
Robb (Gayle) Huxley, Pete Holder, Roger Holder, Brian Peachey

Meanwhile life at the department store went on the same. I worked in the bargain basement carpet department and spent most of my time sweeping the floor or talking to the female sales assistants. One of the salesmen in our department was a man who lived in Dymock which is a small rural area just outside of Newent, where Joe Meek, the independent record producer grew up. His name was John Devereux and he had a house on an acre of land. He had a Guernsey cow and made his own butter, and he kept bees which provided him with honey. He knew that I was singing with The Vendettas in the Forest and told me that his neighbours the Holder brothers had a dance band and that they were very good. He suggested that I should contact them because they might be looking for a new singer. I was quite happy being with The Vendettas and didn't give it much thought. When it became clear to John that I had made no attempt to get in touch with them he told me one day that they would be coming down to see me at the Courtfield Arms that Sunday.

Well, Sunday night came and we were playing our usual gig to a full house. During the break three guys came up to me and introduced themselves as Roger and Peter Holder with their older brother Mick who was their manager. They told me that they had a band called The Whirlwinds, that they had the same gear as The Shadows, Fender guitars and Vox amps, and that their singer Max Swift had recently quit the group. They asked me if I would like to come to a practice session. I was quite impressed with their story, especially the part about the gear. I figured if they could afford Fender guitars they must be pretty good. They bought me a pint of cider and I agreed to go along to the practice the next week.

Roger Holder picked me up at 7 o'clock that Tuesday outside of Moreland's match factory which was on the Bristol Road near to where I lived. He had a mini van and showed up with his girlfriend. I had to sit in between them on the emergency brake as there were only two seats in the front of the van. Roger was a real fast driver and we soon got to Newent and shortly to Dymock. We turned into a small country lane at John Devereux's house and followed it until we came to a farmhouse called the Welsh House. Adjacent to that building was an old barn and as we got out of the car I could hear faint sounds of electric guitars and drums. We entered the room and sure enough there were the Vox AC30s and Fender Strats. Roger introduced me to rhythm guitarist Pete Awford and drummer Brian Peachey. Brian, I recognized at once as he had attended the same school as me but was a little older. Of course Pete Holder was there and he played lead guitar on a custom left handed Strat. Mick Holder the manager and younger brother Derek were also there. We decided to start with "How Do You Do It" by Gerry and The Pacemakers, followed by various numbers by Cliff Richard, Buddy Holly and Elvis Presley. I remember we also did "This Time" by Troy Shondell and "Please Please Me" by The Beatles. Having got these songs down everyone was pleased with the way things sounded and I was asked if I would join the band as lead singer. I was happy to accept their offer and agreed to join, explaining that I would have to honour a few gigs with The Vendettas if that was OK with them. That was no problem so we went on to discusses the format of the band. The Whirlwinds played a lot of instrumentals such as "Apache", by The Shadows, "Telstar" and "Riding The Wind" by The Tornados and Pete Awford also sang a few numbers, so it was agreed that I would come on to do the other vocals after they had played the opening numbers. We also talked about getting me a special shiny suit to wear. So all in all the first rehearsal went along very well. Later that night as I got into bed in the little back bedroom in Clegram Road I thought to myself "What name goes with The Whirlwinds?" I knew for sure that Huxley wouldn't fit but just as I was drifting off to sleep; it popped into my head, Gale, no Gayle, yes Robb Gayle and The Whirlwinds.

When I woke up the next morning I knew that I would have to speak to Phil to let him know that I would be leaving The Vendettas. He knew that The Whirlwinds had come by to the Courtfield Arms to see me so I hoped that he would be expecting to hear some kind of news. He took it OK when I saw him at tea break but he asked me to honour a few gigs we had that were coming up. I told him, no problem. In the meantime I continued to rehearse with The Whirlwinds. A couple of weeks later we were ready for our first gig. We were booked to play at Staunton village hall. Roger picked me up and we drove out to Staunton. We walked into the hall and I looked up to see the gear set up on the stage. Pete Holder and Pete Awford were getting in tune and Brian Peachey was finishing setting up his drums. I sat down and talked to Roger's girlfriend while they all got in tune. The hall started to fill up as The Whirlwinds came down off the stage to put on their brightly coloured jackets. Each band member wore a different colour, and together with those sunburst Stratocasters they really looked cool. They started their set with "Apache" by The Shadows, all doing the same moves together and holding their guitars high in the air. I had never seen them in their stage clothes or playing live before and I was impressed. I was just dying to get up on stage and sing with them. When Pete Holder looked down from the stage and gave me the nod I knew it was time for me to go up. They started the intro for "Baby I Don't Care" and I grabbed the Vox Reslo mic and walked on stage. Dressed in my black suit (the same one I wore to work every day) and my Buddy Holly glasses, I started to sing and perform all those great songs of that time. None of us ever got paid any money. It was all invested in the band to buy equipment and clothing. A few weeks later we all went to a tailor in Gloucester and got stage suits. The band would be wearing identical dark suits and I had a blue shiny suit which was made out of "Lurex" as lame would be too expensive.

As the weeks passed by we continued to rehearse and play at various locations in Gloucestershire. We built up a repertoire of all the hit songs of that time, particularly hits by The Beatles, Hollies, Kinks, The Rolling Stones, The Shadows and many more. Pete Holder would go into town to buy the records, and then he would work out the chords and lead parts and write out the lyrics. As I was the lead singer it was my job to learn the melodies and the lyrics. Usually this was easy for me as I heard the songs on the radio all day long.

One night at band practice rhythm player Pete Awford announced that he would be leaving the band as he was getting married. His future wife insisted that she did not want him to continue playing in the band. Roger Holder said that there was a rhythm player who lived in Stroud, which is a town near Gloucester, and that he was willing to play with us. His name was Dave Prosser and at the following rehearsal we auditioned him. He was an OK rhythm player and we decided to have him join the band, although he didn't really have too much stage personality. He inherited Awford's Stratocaster and Vox amp. For my part I also continued playing my Hofner at home while the other band members had no idea that I could even play an instrument. As I had been highly influenced by Buddy Holly and later by John Lennon I secretly wished to sing and play the guitar at the same time. So one night at practice I showed up with my guitar. I told the guys that I would just like to use the guitar here and there in a few numbers. In a way I felt more comfortable when doing Beatles and group songs as many bands were not featuring lead singers anymore, and the singing was being done by more than just one singer. The songs were featuring more harmonies and the vocals were done by more of a combined effort. Singers like Cliff Richard, Adam Faith and Marty Wilde were on the decline as the groups were taking over the music scene. So I gradually started featuring my rhythm guitar playing in certain numbers at the venues. At a subsequent practice, Dave Prosser did not show up. Roger and Pete told me they were not picking him up as it was bothersome to drive all the way to Stroud twice a week. Besides they liked the way I played guitar and wanted to let Prosser go and have me take over the rhythm guitar spot. I of course turned down the offer thinking that I was not good enough. The Holders assured me that I was, and anyway they said that they were unimpressed by Dave Prosser and that if I took over the position I would get the Fender Strat and Vox amp to use.

That was all it took, and hearing these words from them I immediately agreed. So Roger drove over to Prosser's house and took back the Strat and the stage suit, which then made us a four piece band and more in line with the current trends. It was like a dream come true for me to have a Fender Stratocaster. It felt so heavy when I put the strap over my shoulders and tuned it up. I proudly showed it to some mates of mine who were starting a band. They had built their own guitars out of some cheap kits using Rosetti pickups which were really poor quality. I remembered how they had sneered at me one time when I showed up at one of their practices, hoping to join their band, and how they had laughed at my little piece of shit, acoustic second hand guitar that I showed up with. Now they were staring with envy at the 1962 Strat in the tweed case with blue plush lining. I was ecstatic.

There was news on the horizon. The Holders told me that they were going to rent Newent Memorial Hall and hold dances there every Friday night. Their mother would make sandwiches and sell soft drinks while the band would provide the music. The hall was just a stone's throw from the house that Joe Meek was born in and very close to the George Inn, the local pub. We had posters printed up announcing Rock and Twist To Robb Gayle and The Whirlwinds from 8.30 till 12.30. Admission was five shillings. As four hours was a long time for one band to play we decided to become the resident band and booked other bands from the area as guests.

Whirlwinds at Newent Memorial Hall 1964

The first night we appeared at Newent Hall we broke all records for attendances of any kind of functions that were previously held there. At the same time we were to be booked to play at the Gloucester Guild Hall which was a very nice venue in the city centre. A week or so before that appearance they wrote in the *Citizen*, which was the local newspaper that the Guild Hall was to get rocking. The significance in this was that previous dances that were held there used the old fashioned type of dance bands and that the attendances were so poor that it was a possibility that the venue would be discontinued. Furthermore in a subsequent news article in the *Citizen* William Dicey wrote that the dances would be doomed to fail as Robb Gayle and The Whirlwinds were not exactly a household name and that surely a more established group that the public were familiar with would ensure a more successful evening. Well, Dicey was wrong. That night was a huge success. The conventional band started off the evening and we closed it. Towards the end of our set I took off my guitar and ended up rolling all over the stage which caused a big sensation. We also broke all attendance records in the Guild Hall's history. We appeared at that location many more times in the future months.

Poster from Newent Memorial Hall

Whirlwinds set list 1963

Another significant occurrence at this time was that the Holders had heard from Arthur and Eric Meek, Joe Meek's brothers that Joe would soon be coming down from London to visit his mother in Newent. The Holders knew the Meek family very well although they had not met Joe at that time. Roger told me that he and Pete would visit Joe when he arrived and that we could possibly get an audition with Joe at his studio in London. The following week at the Tuesday practice Roger told the band that he had met Joe over at the Meek's house. Joe had come down with Heinz Burt, the bass player of The Tornados, as Heinz liked the country and loved to go fishing and shooting. Roger said that there was something special about Joe, something magical; there was a certain look to his hands. Pete said that Joe told them that when we were ready, to call him and we would set a date and go up to Holloway Road to do a recording audition. We were of course all very pumped up hearing this great news.

Around this time Pete and I discovered that we both liked to write songs. I guess we had a kind of closeness, we are the same age and our birthdays are only a couple of days apart. We had both written a little, so we decided to get together and see what would happen if we tried to write together. We were really influenced by the way the music scene was changing when bands were writing their own material, just like Lennon and Mc Cartney. I remember when I first heard "Love Me Do" and "P.S. I Love You"; I said to myself 'That's what I've wanted to write'. We never knew who wrote the songs for Adam Faith, Cliff Richard, Eden Kane or Jess Conrad, but we knew who wrote "Please Please Me" and "Don't Let The Sun Catch You Crying". Pete would come over to Clegram Road for writing sessions. We would sit in the little back bedroom and play our Strats through my little 8 watt amp and compose songs, writing out lyrics on scraps of paper.

Certain changes had also occurred with my job at this time. I was told that I was to be transferred from the bargain basement carpets to the carpet department up on the furniture floor and that I was to be enrolled in the technical college to take certain courses to aid in my career in retailing. My new boss would be Mr. Dyer, who turned out to be a real OK guy. All the salesmen on that floor knew me mainly from the Christmas party when I sang with The Vendettas. John Devereux, the man who put me in touch with The Whirlwinds, always maintained that it was he who arranged my promotion by talking to Mr. Dyer. On days when I was going to practice out at the farm I would take my guitar into work with me. I would stand behind the carpet display, together with a few of the older salesmen and the sound of voices singing "Autumn Leaves" could be heard drifting through the carpet dept. late on a Wednesday afternoon. Mr. Dyer tolerated this. It was OK because he said that I kept the employees happy.

One night on the way to practice Roger told me that Mick Holder, our manager, had telephoned Joe Meek and Joe had invited us to come for an audition on the Thursday of the following week. This was very exciting news, so at practice we really worked hard on perfecting our repertoire. Besides the excitement I was suddenly faced with the problem of getting out of work on Thursday, but after a little thought I decided that I would have to go sick on that day. After all this was what I most wanted to do in my life so what the hell?

Quite early on Thursday morning the guys came to pick me up in the group van. Mick Holder was driving while the rest of us talked with excitement about the forthcoming audition. We had our gear stashed in the back along with Brian's Trixon drum set.

When we drove into London it was a little difficult to find our way around but after asking a few directions we finally made it up to Holloway Road at around 10 am. At the address we had been given we found a leather goods shop with all kinds of handbags and suitcases displayed in the window, and at first we thought we had arrived at the wrong address; but when we saw another entrance door to the left where the walls had been written upon with all kinds of graffiti displaying the names of Heinz, The Tornados and various other bands and singers, we knew we had to be in the right place. Above the shop there were three floors, so as Mick opened the door we were faced with a flight of stairs that led up to a door at the top. We arrived at the top and Mick knocked on the door. Somewhere in the distance we could hear the sound of music. Yes it was the Joe Meek sound. The door was opened by a young good looking guy, who we later found out was Terry, Joe's office assistant, and almost immediately after that appeared someone who I guessed must be Joe Meek. He was about 5 foot 8 inches tall, medium build, and was wearing a blue mohair suit. He had on a white shirt with a black tie and wore pointed black shoes. His hair was combed in a neat quiff. He smiled when Mick Holder introduced us and I remember he had a certain look in his eyes when he spoke to you. I think that I will never forget the way he looked at me the first time that I met him. He was very happy to receive the fruit that his mother had sent him, and then said that we should bring up our gear. We carried our amps, guitars and drums up the stairs and then got a look inside as we placed the gear down on the floor. There was an office space with a desk with a red telephone on it. As I stood there I noticed that the cradle of the phone was cracked and broken just like someone had slammed the phone down in a fit of rage.

Joe Meek at the control panel in his studio (c) David Peters

Upon the walls there were glossy photographs of bands and artists especially Heinz and The Tornados also Cliff Bennett and The Rebel Rousers, The Cryin' Shames, The Puppets, The Aristocrats, The Outlaws with Richie Blackmore, Houston Wells, Glenda Collins and Screaming Lord Sutch There was a door that led to Joe's living quarters and a twisting flight of stairs which led to the next floor. We could hear Joe rewinding a tape of some recording upstairs, it sounded quite loud. Terry then motioned that we should take our equipment up the next staircase. As I rounded the top part there was a landing with a bathroom followed by a room where I could see Joe standing over two tape machines. He had now finished rewinding the tape and was listening to some recorded number looking towards the ceiling and clicking his heels together with the beat of the song, occasionally bending over to make some adjustments, turning some knobs on various control boxes. Behind him were two large speakers and a huge amount of reels of tape piled up on the floor with bits of tape everywhere. Right at the entrance to the control room, which had no door, was the doorway to the studio which had a concertina style door. The studio itself was the size of a sitting room. The windows had been blocked off, the walls soundproofed and there was a grey carpet on the floor. A Lowry organ was placed against one wall and an upright piano stood up against the wall adjacent to the control room. I remember running my fingers over the keys and noticed that they gave out a magical tinkling sound when the hammers struck the strings. We later found out that Joe had pushed thumb tacks into the hammers to create this special sound. In another corner of the room was a heavy duty folding screen, the kind you would undress behind. A large old BBC mic covered with yellow foam rubber, was behind the screen. Adjacent to the screen was an area for the drums. They were to be set up behind a couple of heavy screens which were about five feet high. As we started bringing the gear into the studio Joe stopped what he was doing and entered the room telling us where to set up the amps. The two Vox amps were set side by side with the bass amp set up a few feet away.

As Brian Peachey was setting up his drums Joe set up a few mics and told Brian to take the front skin off of the bass drum. Joe then appeared with some old pillows and blankets which he used to bury the mic inside of the bass drum. He also mic'd up the amps covering them with blankets. Meanwhile Roger, Pete and I were getting in tune. Joe fiddled about a little with the control knobs on our amps and paid special attention to Pete's Swissecho unit. Joe proceeded to walk back and forth to the amps and the drums and then to the control room and back until finally he said." OK just play me some songs that you play on stage." Joe had positioned me behind the screen with my guitar as I was the singer, so I had to look around the side to see Roger and Pete and say "Let's do "Rave On". I couldn't see Brian at all. We proceeded to play six or seven songs for Joe to hear and from time to time he would open the concertina door and stick his head into the room asking what other songs we had. The audition came to an end and we put down our guitars. For some reason I was overcome by a kind of depressing feeling that I couldn't explain. There I was with The Whirlwinds in Joe Meek's studio in London and it didn't feel good. I wasn't very happy with the way we had played and I felt that we were just not good enough. Joe set the tape to play the recording for us to listen to and the band followed him downstairs. I sat on the stairs looking miserable and dejected just fearing the worst. Even listening to the recordings didn't help. I thought we sounded terrible. Presently Roger Holder climbed up the stairs towards me and said "What are you looking so sad for? We've got a recording contract."

I stood up and followed Roger down the stairs. I began to feel better but my head was spinning; I was thinking and wondering what would happen next. Downstairs Pete, Brian and Mick were talking with Joe while a girl called Pip, who was Joe's secretary, handed out recording contracts to us. We all signed the contracts without reading anything. We were all so exited, who could even think about having to read all that text? When it seems that you have the chance of doing what you've always dreamed of doing, you just do it. In those days, who wouldn't do it? You never thought about the business side of it, you just wanted to sing and play music and be famous, and if you made some money, well that was the icing on the cake. We all shook hands with Joe and just before we left he handed us an acetate. On the label was written "It's Raining". Joe told us he wanted us to copy the song and the next time that we came up to London we would record it. He put it on the little record player in his living room and we stood there and listened to it. It was a pretty good recording, well performed by some unknown musicians and typical Buddy Holly style.

We packed up all the gear, said goodbye to Joe and got on the road back to Gloucester. We decided that we would spend some of The Whirlwinds' savings on a steak dinner and stopped at a classy restaurant. The proprietors and waiters assuming that we could not afford to eat there quickly informed us of the minimum charge. It felt good to know that we could afford it and that we were celebrating our success in getting a recording contract.

Over the next few weeks we continued to play our gigs, work at our jobs and learn the song that Joe had given us on the demo disc. It didn't take us very long at all to get the song off; we just basically learned it like we learned the other songs and instrumentals that we copied from other bands, to use in our repertoire. Before too long we were back at Joe's studio recording "It's Rainin". I remember Joe set up a mic close to my guitar and told me to play close to it. He wanted to hear the sound of the pick as it scratched on the strings. We soon got the backing track down and Joe said that everybody should go downstairs except for me as we were going to put on the vocals. Joe told me to stand behind the screen where the big mic was and to sing very close to the mic, and to smile at the same time. There was a small speaker hanging on the wall behind me from where I could hear the backing track. I sang the song through a few times and thought that I was singing it pretty well.

At about half way through the third or fourth time the music stopped and everything went very quiet. Suddenly Joe appeared behind the screen telling me that it sounded pretty good and that in another take or two we would have it down. Before I knew what was happening Joe put his arms around me and pulling my face to his. He kissed me on the lips, pushing his tongue into my mouth. I was completely taken by surprise and felt myself go totally limp and powerless just like an antelope which has been overpowered by a lion and knows that there is nothing else to do but lay down and die. He proceeded to ask me what kind of trousers I wore on stage and started pulling at the fabric near my crotch and fondled me. In his soft voice he asked me if I wanted to make it in the business. I told him that I did but I was not like that. He looked at me and said "We're all like that in this business". A thousand thoughts went through my mind. I knew that I couldn't use violence against him as that would probably just mess up the band's chances of making it, and then it suddenly became very clear to me that the rumours that I had heard with regard to Joe Meek being queer were really true. He asked me to fondle him and I did it automatically without thought or feeling. Suddenly there was the sound of someone coming up the stairs. It was Terry, Joe's assistant, or maybe boyfriend. Joe walked away from behind the screen saying that we would do another few takes. I still don't know how I was able to sing knowing what I had just been through. Two more takes and it was over. Joe came in and said "We've got it, that was the one." He asked me if I would come to spend a weekend with him. We would write some songs together. He said he would pay for my train fare. I explained that my job at the Bon Marche required that I work on Saturdays so it would not be possible.

We walked downstairs to see the rest of the band filling out forms regarding each member's life lines. They handed one to me, to fill out. I remember Roger Holder making a comment to me regarding the fact that I had been alone with the great Joe Meek upstairs recording a song and that how jealous they were. If only they knew what I felt inside at eighteen years old, the shock and complete realisation that I had been involved in a homosexual experience. It was a secret that I kept inside me for many years; I also remember that when I was filling in the replies to the questions on the Life Lines sheet, against DISLIKES I wrote "Being left alone."

Over the next few weeks we continued to play our local venues and with a few write ups in the *Gloucester Citizen* newspaper, our popularity began to grow. Pete Holder and I were really keen on writing our own songs. One day after I left work I boarded the bus from Gloucester to Newent with my guitar in hand and headed out for a rehearsal at the farm. I got off the bus in Dymock at the beginning of the lane that led to Aylesmore Farm. Upon arrival Roger Holder told me that we would be rehearsing in the farmhouse sitting room instead of the barn, as it was very cold that night. Roger and Pete had brought all the gear over from the barn and as I entered the sitting room I saw Pete standing at the mic with his guitar, and he was singing the first few lines of a song that he had just started to write. It sounded something like The Beatles and I could hear Pete singing "Please, please, please, please, tell me, what am I to do?" I rushed to get my guitar out and play along. This was a very exciting moment and in the space of an hour we had finished the song. When Roger and Brian came in and played along on bass and drums it sounded even better. We thought we had a hit on our hands or at least it could be used as a B side for "It's Raining", so we decided that Mick Holder should call up Joe Meek and tell him of the new song that we had written. By the time that the next practice rolled around we already had heard from Joe. He told us to come up to Holloway Road and he would listen to it and maybe we would record it.

At that session Joe set up the mics and gear in the usual way, trailing all the wires underneath the concertina door into the control room. We played the song through a couple of times, singing along, and I guess Joe liked something about it as he said "OK let's put down a backing track." We did this with Pete and I singing along, just mouthing the words with no sound coming out so that we all knew where we were. After this session we always made a point at rehearsals to play only the backing tracks, thus getting used to being in the recording mode. It helped us no end, in being prepared, when we went to future sessions. After Joe thought that we had a good backing track down it was time for the vocals. This time I was not so afraid, knowing that Pete and I would be singing the song together behind that screen. This situation would not provide an opportunity for any of Joe's advances. Pete and I finished the vocals after a few takes. We all gathered around near the doorway to the control room and listened to the track while Joe moved to the beat of the song, clicking his heels together. We thought it sounded great with all those high falsettos and Beatle style harmonies. As we were leaving in the early evening Pete asked Joe if he would make us a tape of "Please Tell Me" and "It's Raining" to take home with us. Joe said that he would, but under no circumstances should we let anybody listen to it. He mentioned that there were many people out there waiting to steal your ideas. He said that he had some editing to do on the songs and that we should call in about a week. Maybe he would have some news of a release date for us. As we were shaking hands Joe handed Pete two more acetate demos saying "Take these back down to Newent with you and listen to them and learn them. Call me when you're ready and you'll come and record them."

We listened to the songs when we got back home. They were decent songs and we went ahead and learned them. One was called "Baby Baby I Got Eyes For You" and the other, "Don't You Know?" We had no idea who wrote these songs or where they came from and didn't care really; we were just following Joe's instructions, doing what we were told. This was OK but inside of me I knew that I really wanted to record and release our own music. I believe that Joe could have personally written or co-written these songs. Joe basically wanted the whole thing. He wanted to create the group, write their songs, produce their records and sell millions of copies; which he did with The Tornados with "TELSTAR"

One night at practice Pete told us that he was going to visit Joe for the weekend to write some songs. This of course sent a lot of thoughts running through my brain. I presumed that Pete had no idea of what might occur if you happen to be alone with Joe. He and Roger had always disbelieved any of the rumours that circulated about Joe, and always defended him; and anyway Joe and Pete had never been alone together as far as I knew. It was a tough situation for me to be in as I could not warn Pete without revealing the story of what happened to me, and I was too ashamed to do that. I just had to let it go and see if anything would happen. By the next time we practised Pete had already been away for the weekend. Roger Brian and I were waiting at the barn when Pete showed up with his tape recorder. I looked at his face to see if there were any signs that could tell me anything. I felt he had a different look on his face. Roger said that Pete and Joe had written two songs together and that they sounded real good. One was called "Clickette Clack", and the other "How Will I Know". Pete was singing and playing on the demo with a drummer and the songs did sound very good. Pete never really talked about what it was like to be up in London with Joe, probably because nobody asked him.

At the next session we recorded "Baby Baby I Got Eyes For You" and "Don't You Know." Joe had invited a guy who played sax and piano. He was a good musician, better than us, but I felt unhappy with this situation as we had no sax player or pianist in the band, and how could we possibly play the song live without those instruments? I remember the session went quite well. Joe could have brought in this extra musician to enhance the band as he may have thought that our sound was not adequate enough to create what he was hearing in his head; or maybe he was just giving the musician a session to make a little money. I believe I may have sung on the two tracks. The only way to know would be to dig them out of all those years of tape stored in England. I'm sure they must still exist.

At the end of the session we sat around talking with Joe and the conversation got around to discussing the possibility of what might happen if we had a record released. Joe said that if we got a hit we would all have to leave our jobs and move up to London and play as professionals, and wanted to know if we would do this. Of course we all said that we would, although we felt a little concerned about Brian Peachey our drummer as he had a good job and may not have wanted to take a chance. Joe said that we may have to think about changing the name of the band as he thought that Robb Gayle and The Whirlwinds sounded like they could be a skiffle group. We tried to come up with a few names but nothing sounded exciting until we found out the Holder brothers had traced their family tree back hundreds of years and discovered that they were descendants of the Vikings from Scandinavia. One of their ancestors had actually founded the place known as Holderness on the east coast of England. We thought about the Great Danes, the Norwegians, and suddenly someone mentioned The Saxons, which sounded very appealing. We thought it was a good choice as the current trend with bands was to have names like The Beatles, The Hollies, and The Searchers so we decided to become The Saxons. Joe said he would pay for us to get some sharp stage suits made and we should have our hair bleached blond. In fact he insisted that the next time we would come to record we should all be blond.

So that was the end of Robb Gayle and The Whirlwinds. We were now to become an all blond band wearing Beatle style suits, writing new songs based around Saxon themes and stories of the old days and even maybe wearing authentic Saxon clothing on stage, complete with helmets and horns!

Letter from Joe to Mr & Mrs Holder

First photo - Pete Holder
Second and Third photos - the original Whirlwinds before I joined the band. (L-R)
Pete Holder, John Creese, Pete Awford and Roger Holder.
Fourth Photo features myself and John Creese has been replaced by drummer Brian
Peachey.

ROCK 'N TWIST

DANCE

DALE RIVERS & FABULOUS RAMRODS
with
ROBB GAYLE
and the WHIRLWINDS
at
Newent Memorial Hall
on
FRIDAY · 14TH · JUNE

Admission   5/-

THE SAXONS

The band turns blond and Joe threatens to fire drummer Brian Peachey if he doesn't comply.
Robb and Pete begin to write songs with Saxon themes.
Recordings with Joe and personnel changes in the band.
Mick Collins joins as new drummer.
"How Will I Know" recording session with drummer Bobby Graham (RIP) using two drummers.
More personnel changes as drummer John Davies replaces Collins.
Pete and Robb write "Saxon War Cry" and Joe records it with battle sounds.
"Song of the Sun God" recording session using the Fifth Man organ guitar that Joe was working on.
Release of "Saxon War Cry" on Decca c/w "Clickette Clack"
Joe Meek places a phone call to Aylesmore Farm which will change The Saxons' lives.

Roger, Pete, Robb & John

On the drive back to Gloucester we talked excitedly about Joe's new instructions to us. I asked how we would be able to bleach our hair as I was sure we all would be too embarrassed to go to a ladies hair salon with all the women customers around. Roger and Pete came up with the suggestion that we should go over to their cousin who owned a salon in Stroud and she would probably agree to colour our hair in the evening when there would be no other customers there. At this point, drummer Brian Peachey chimed in saying that he would definitely not colour his hair. He was a redhead and that's the way he said he would stay. We warned him that Joe would be really pissed off, but Brian insisted that he would not go along with the plan.

The Saxons in 1965. (L-R) Pete, Robb, Roger and John Davies

About a week later Mick Holder drove over with Roger and Pete to pick me up, and we made our way over to Stroud for our appointment at the salon. Looking back I can't believe that we never considered what we were really doing. Remember that this was 1964 and it would be deemed quite unusual and even looked upon as being effeminate or gay to do something like this; but I guess we didn't care about that, when you are doing something that you always dreamed of doing you will do almost anything to make it happen. I remember when they applied the bleaching solution to our hair it burned like hell. Roger had to take a couple of aspirins to take the pain away. Then they distributed it through the rest of our hair and we sat and waited. Then it was washed out and I looked in the mirror. It looked like somebody had poured a bowl of Bird's custard over my head. My hair was yellow! Just as I was about to freak out I was told not to worry as a toner had to be put on to make the real blond colour. After that application was done and my hair washed again it looked better. Roger Pete and I looked at each other with disbelief, we were all blond. All in all we took it very well, this was just something you had to do in show business and I guess we felt kind of special.

Special, that is, until the next morning when I woke up and my mother brought me a cup of tea in bed and almost spilled it over me in shock. "Oh Robert" she cried, "What have you done?" I also remembered that I had to go to work and face everybody there! I didn't have enough courage to get on the bus as I felt so self conscious about my hair and thought for sure that people would be staring at me; so I just decided to walk to work. Of course when I arrived on the carpet department my boss Mr. Dyer freaked out and the whole place went into an uproar. My salesmen friends couldn't take their eyes off me they were all in shock. This was close to forty years ago and they had never seen anything like it. The next thing I knew was that the Floor Manager, Mr. Robinson came to take a look. I can't remember if he said anything to me, I just remember him standing there and shaking his head in disbelief. The news about the blond bombshell on the carpet department must have spread through the store like wildfire, as during the course of the day a constant stream of employees filed past the department and stared at me. Many of them were girls and the sound of them tittering could be heard from time to time. This was a day I think I shall never forget, however the excitement gradually subsided over the next few days giving me the courage to ride the bus again and the feeling of being special returned and outweighed the feeling of embarrassment.

The first time that we played in Newent Memorial Hall the locals were very surprised to see this almost all blond rock group with a red headed drummer, that were now called The Saxons. During the break girls came up to us saying how much they liked our blond image and how cool we looked and how come the drummer was not blond too? Pete Roger and I knew inside that there would be trouble when we showed up for the next recording session and there was trouble.

Mick Holder rang Joe to arrange the next session. Joe suggested that we should go up to London soon for a weekend to record a few songs. I don't remember how I got the Saturday off work. It could have been a holiday weekend. Joe said that he wanted us to record "Clickette Clack", a song that Pete had written with Joe. At the end of Mick's conversation with him, Joe asked if we had coloured our hair and how it looked. Mick said we looked great but didn't have the nerve to tell Joe that Brian was still a redhead. At the rehearsals we tried to persuade Brian to do his hair but he outright refused.

When we arrived for the session we walked in and Joe greeted us with smiles of happiness. He looked us right in our eyes and in his soft voice he said "It looks great." Suddenly he looked at Brian and realized that Brian had not coloured his hair and his voice changed to a hard edged scream and he shouted out "Why didn't you do your hair?" Brian replied meekly saying that he didn't want to. Joe virtually screamed at Brian telling him that if he didn't do his hair today he was out of the group. At this point Brian consented. By a stroke of luck some of the band would be staying at the home of some friends of the Holder family that night and Mrs. Lucas used to be a hairdresser and could do the job.

We put down most of the backing track that day and in the afternoon Brian left for his hair appointment with Roger and Mick as they would be staying at the Lucas house. Pete and I would be staying at Joe's. I was not thrilled about this and at first I refused to stay the night. When Mick and Pete asked me why, I couldn't tell them what had happened before so I just told them that I was worried about all the rumours that we had heard about Joe. It was Pete who basically put my mind to rest by telling me that we would both be sleeping downstairs in the living room on the sofas, and did I really think that Joe was going to creep in, in the middle of the night and jump on me? I took his point and agreed to stay.

Robb – Saxons 1965

We went down the road to the Chinese restaurant a place where we would eat at, many times in the future. We talked to Joe for a while until he went up to the studio and was fiddling about a bit working on some recorded music. After sometime the music stopped and we saw nothing of Joe for the rest of the night and guessed that he had gone to bed. At sometime during the night I was woken up by the sound of the door rattling and someone clambering up the stairs to Joe's bedroom, but as it was dark I could not see who it was.

Pete and I were woken up that morning by Lionel who was Heinz's road manager. He wished us good morning and went upstairs returning shortly with Heinz Burt who was the original bass player of The Tornados. He greeted us with "Hello lads" as he combed his pure white hair and put on his jacket. Pete and I must have looked like a couple of junior Heinz's sitting there on our sofas. Can you imagine how it must have looked? Heinz the "White Tornado", as he was known, carrying on a conversation with two blond Saxons. Joe really had a thing for blonds! Just then Joe appeared saying good morning encouraging Heinz and Lionel to get going as Heinz was to appear in Scotland that night.

Around 9.30 the guys showed up. It was Roger and Mick with Brian the new blond Saxon with his hair looking like the colour of aluminium. Apparently it had been quite hard for Mrs. Lucas to get the colour right due to Brian having coarse sandy red hair. Anyway I suppose it was good enough for Joe as he was quite happy now. It was really funny to see Brian with the ruddy complexion that he had together with his metallic hair. Joe mentioned that he wanted to do some overdubbing before Pete and I put on the vocals. Pete was to do the solo guitar and Brian was to overdub the bass drum. Joe went over to the big vocal screen and tore a hole in the covering. Then he proceeded to push a mic into the gaping hole and covered it up with the fabric. Brian was then told to beat on the screen with his hand together in time with the bass drum. Joe came in a few times and scolded Brian for not being in time and to keep it simple. I don't think that Joe really liked Brian that much; in fact that was the last recording Brian did with The Saxons at R.G.M. Sound.

When the overdubs were complete Pete and I put on the vocals. We used to do it like the early Beatles. We would both sing the lead vocals incorporating the harmonies over and over again until Joe thought we had "One" in the bag. Sometimes the more we redid the vocals the worse it got and we would make mistakes or go flat. Joe would stick his head around the door and shout at us saying "A kid of three could do this." Then he would smile and say "Well maybe a kid of four." We would all laugh nervously until he would give you that special look and say "I think we'll get it this time", and usually we did. We would then overdub the vocals a second time being very careful to keep spot on with the previous track. Sometime later when we heard the completed track as it came out on the record it sounded different. This was because Joe had deliberately sped the track up slightly. He maintained that it gave the track a punchy sound. He had also overdubbed a metallic clicking sound with the drums to sound like high heels clacking on the side walk. It was a "Clickette Clack" sound. Joe came up with the spelling but I thought it should have been "Clicketty Clack."

As usual at the end of the session, after we put the gear away, we stood around talking with Joe and as always the conversation would end up with Joe explaining to us that if we had a record out, and it was a hit, we would have to leave our jobs and move to London. As usual we all replied saying that we would, but at the back of our minds we never felt really confident that Brian would turn Pro.

Pete Holder had come up with a design for stage suits. The jacket in particular had a special look to it, especially the collar. It was similar to The Beatles' suits. When Joe saw the design he offered to send us over to Dougie Millings, who, with his son, was famous for making the best stage wear for show business. Joe also said that he would pay for the suits.

We arranged to see Dougie on a Sunday. This was convenient for us as none of us was working that day. Dougie being Jewish didn't work on Saturday which was the Sabbath. We used to leave Gloucester real early on a Sunday morning, usually a little rough as we had probably played on Saturday night till one in the morning.

When we arrived in London we headed straight for Lyons Corner House to eat a great breakfast and drink that great coffee from the "Bottomless Cup." At our first appointment with Dougie we showed him Pete's sketch, and Dougie said "OK" and began to show us fabric swatches. Dougie told us that The Beatles had been there a few days ago and had chosen a certain fabric for their suits. When we saw the sample we all immediately agreed that we would choose that fabric.

Robb – Saxons 1965

I remember going to the toilet at Dougie's only to hear Dougie say to me "You just took a piss in the same place as John Lennon." I felt proud and special. After we got measured, Dougie told us to come back the following Sunday at 10am which we did. The suit jackets were partially made, we put them on, Dougie made a few chalk marks here and there, and that was that. Mick Holder who used to drive us everywhere, laughed and said that we had to drive almost three hours just for a couple of chalk marks; but on the following Sunday the suits were finished, and boy did we look sharp. The suits fitted us perfectly and we looked just like the "Blond Beatles." From that moment on whenever we played on stage we looked great. These four blond guys called The Saxons wearing Beatle suits. We even bought four matching pairs of brown Beatle boots to go with the suits, along with shirts and matching ties.

Roger picked me up one night for practice and we talked about the prospects of turning Pro. On the way out to Newent we discussed Brian and remembered the times that he had told us that he wouldn't leave his job to play music full time. Roger then told me that he had spoken to Mick Collins, the drummer of probably the best group in the Gloucester area, and as his band the "Beatniks" had disbanded, he was ready to join The Saxons and had no objections to turning pro. Roger said we would break the news to Brian that night.

It was a weird practice that night. When we all arrived we started to practice "How Will I Know", the other song that Pete had written with Joe. Pete and I devised an intro to the song and by the end of the night it was sounding very nice. After we put our guitars away Roger again questioned Brian about turning Pro. Out of the blue Brian said that he had thought about it and had decided that he would, if we had to. This took us all by surprise and Roger blurted out that we had already spoken to Mick Collins and that he was ready to join the band and to turn Pro. At that point I guess Brian realized that he was out of the band and began to pack up his drums and load them into his car. It was kind of sad, but at the same time it was kind of exciting know-ing that we were going to have a great new drummer. Brian was OK though. I remember that he used to play for the school rugby team, like I did. He was able to break up a fist fight between Roger and Pete at a band practice one night. They were fighting over a disagreement that they had about a certain chord in a song. It was A major! Brian was the guy who first took me out on a pub crawl when I was 18. Brian and I together with a couple of his friends drove to half a dozen pubs, one after the other, downing a pint at each pub. Brian was OK but I got real sick and threw up with my head hanging out of the car window. Brian thought it was hilarious and had a real good laugh. I had a hangover for a week. My dad kept telling me to go and have another beer and I would feel better but I just couldn't bring myself to do that. Knowing what I know now, my dad was right. I watched the tail lights of Brian's Morris Minor 1000 disappear into the darkness as he pulled away from the Welsh House. That was forty years ago.

Brian Peachey died of a heart attack while at work in June of 2006 just a matter of days before the opening of the Joe Meek Exhibition in Gloucester. I was hoping that I might have met Brian there but it was not to be. Brian was 62.

Luckily, Mick Collins was able to fit into Brian's stage suit quite well. He showed up for the first practice and set up his black pearl Premier drum set. His dad was a professional drummer. We had seen Mick play with the Beatniks who were a great group back then. We had played a few gigs with them when we invited them to play with us at Newent Memorial Hall. Things sounded great right away. His drums sounded different to Brian's set; more professional, crisper, he had no trouble with any of the songs, but his hair was jet black, dead straight and combed to the side. We were already dreading what Joe would say, after experiencing his outburst with Brian, but we tended to ignore it and to really enjoy playing with a first class drummer. We kind of accepted Mick with his black hair and I don't think that we ever asked him to go blond. It was a good contrast, in fact when Mick joined the band we were featured in an article in the *Gloucester Citizen*. The caption beneath the picture showing The Saxons read "The black sheep in the fold." It did look kind of special; three bleach blonds and a black haired drummer, better that is than, three bleach blonds and a red head! Mick soon learned our repertoire so we began playing gigs almost immediately. I remember the audiences freaking out when Mick would play his drum solos. They would stand around and watch. He seemed to play effortlessly like a jazz drummer.

The Saxons playing live in High Street, Tredworth, Gloucester on Easter Monday 1965

We started to rehearse "How Will I Know?" with Mick. We told him that we would be going up to Joe's studio soon to record it. When Mick Holder called Joe to let him know that we were ready to record and that we also had a new drummer, Joe surprised us by saying that he had hired a session drummer to play at the session; but he also told us "Bring Mick along, maybe we'll use two drummers."

At the session we introduced Joe to Mick Collins. Joe seemed to approve of Mick and said nothing about Mick's hair. When we lugged the amps and drums upstairs to the studio we saw this guy setting up his drums. He introduced himself as Bobby Graham. We set up Mick's drums across the room directly facing Bobby's set. Joe and Bobby agreed that Mick would play the straight beat and that Bobby would create all the fill-ins. We started running through the song so that Bobby could get acquainted with it. Mick of course knew the song and played very professionally together with Bobby Graham.

He never took his eyes off Bobby and laid down a good basic beat while Bobby seemed to be having a hard time with the song. At one point he turned around to me and told me that he had been at an all night party and had got really drunk and that it was taking him a time to get into the song. I think that Joe may have heard him say that because he came into the studio and complained to Bobby about his playing with words like "I'm paying you for this fucking session so you'd better get into it." After those few inspiring words from Joe, Bobby did get into it and put in some nice work; although I do believe that Mick Collins was just as good as Bobby Graham. After the backing track was completed Bobby Graham left. Joe made several comments to us regarding his disappointment with Bobby's performance. He was apparently pleased with Mick's drumming and it looked like he had taken a liking to Mick. Pete and I then proceeded to put down the vocals. This we did after a few takes and listening to the play back made my hair stand on end. The song had a haunting kind of sound to it and I believe that it was the best recording that we had done so far. This was the one and only time that Mick Collins recorded with us at Joe's studio. Much to our disappointment "How Will I Know" never got to be released as The Saxons until it came out on a Joe Meek's Gems album compilation in the late 1990s. However the song did get released on a B side recorded by the Honeycombs. We were not impressed by their rendition of the song. They had this silly intro sounding like the beginning of "Telstar", which I'm sure must have been Joe's idea and to cap it all when Pete Holder bought the record just to see his name on the song writing credits, he found that Joe Meek had taken full credit for writing the song and Pete's name was not on the record at all.

Not long after we had returned from the "How Will I Know?" session, we featured a local band from Cheltenham to appear with us at Newent Memorial Hall. The band's name was Tony Faye and The Fayetones. This was a notable occasion as it was the night that Mick Collins decided to tell us that he was leaving the band. He told us that he had given some serious thought to the matter and knowing how much the rest of us wanted to turn pro, he had changed his mind and in fairness to us he felt that he should be up front with us. He explained that he had a good job working for the government and could not throw that away.

The significance with The Fayetones was that they had a young drummer who was well accomplished and by a stroke of luck was a natural white blond. Mick suggested that we should approach him to join The Saxons. He was a good young drummer and his blondness would fit in with the band's image. Knowing there was basically nothing that we could do to change Mick's mind we decided to take his advice. Mick Holder got hold of John the following week. John agreed to come over to a practice session and subsequently joined the band. He was a good drummer and fitted in with the band real well. We didn't need that much practice as he knew most of our repertoire, the stuff he didn't know he picked up right away and best of all he was willing to turn Pro, in fact all that he wanted to do was play for a living.

He had no job that would pull him away from his ambition but unlike the rest of us he said he would have to be paid some money as he did not have a job. We agreed to his request, after all we had got exactly what we were looking for a good blond drummer who would turn pro. John Davies was about sixteen years old at that time and had just got out of Cheltenham Grammar school. That was the same school that Brian Jones of The Rolling Stones attended. Luckily Brian Peachey's Beatle suit that Mick Collins had worn for a short time fit John Davies pretty well.

Now we were complete. We had an all blond band and only Roger, Pete and I had to get our roots done every few weeks. We were playing twice a week for the most part getting more and more popular and in demand and getting to know our new drummer. John seemed a bit serious at the beginning as he listened to jazz and Bo Diddley. I always thought that John's head was somewhere else and not really into pop music. As a drummer there was never any problem with his playing. I can never remember him making a mistake. He was a very consistent, good drummer, and probably still is. Any time that we were working on original songs he would come up with good solid drum parts. He had a bizarre sense of humour and could be extremely funny. Sometimes he and his cousin Graeme would talk together in high squeaky voices for weeks. They even had me doing it in the end.

One night at practice as John and I, followed by Roger and Mick Holder walked in through the doorway at the barn we witnessed Pete Holder as usual messing around with his guitar and echo chamber. He had apparently been working on something and began to play this line of a melody over a few times. We all agreed that it sounded a bit weird but on the whole it was really quite commercial, especially with the heavy echo. We didn't really pursue the tune much that night but a few days later Pete and I got together and wrote the whole piece. We had no idea what to call it. We thought about some thing spacey like "Journey To The Stars" but we really couldn't come up with a title.

At our next practice we showed it to Roger and John and each player came up with their parts. Roger put in a good bass line and John came up with some nice drum parts. When it was finished we were excited and Mick Holder decided that he would call Joe with the news. Not long after that we were on our way up to Holloway Road with our new drummer and a couple of good songs as well. When we arrived Joe was in a happy mood and was very pleased to meet John Davies.

The rest of us were of course relieved that we did not have a hair colour to contend with. As we were setting up a pianist that Joe had hired for the session entered the studio. Joe introduced him as Peter London and he was a blind guy. We couldn't help feeling a bit disappointed as we didn't really want to record anything that we couldn't reproduce on stage. We started to run through the instrumental and I called out the chords to Peter London. He had a heavy London accent and in no time at all he said "OK I got it" and he really did. We were amazed at how quickly he picked the tune up. Joe's head popped around the door and he was beaming, and we proceeded to record the tune. We put the whole thing down pretty quickly and Joe had Peter London over dub the bridge on the Lowry.

The Saxons. (L-R) Roger Holder, Robb Huxley, John Davies, and Pete Holder

We listened to the play back and Joe had made a good sounding recording with some great sounds on the drums. As we had recorded the instrumental fairly quickly Joe asked if we had any other songs. We had rehearsed a song that Pete and I had put together and pre-pared it for recording. It was called "Your Eyes Tell Me." We played it through and Joe said "OK let's record it" and we began to call out the chords to Peter. He suddenly put in this intricate arpeggio line which totally knocked us out. After two times he had it down perfectly and it was amazing to see his fingers flying over the keys. We decided to take a break when the track was completed and said goodbye to Peter who was leaving. When we got back from the Chinese, Joe was work-ing on the instrumental which was really starting to sound great. Joe asked us the title but we had no idea what to call it. We talked a little about the name of The Saxons and came up with "Saxon War Cry" We thought it would be good to have the sound of a battle going on for the beginning so Joe made us gather around the mic telling us all to scream and shout. After we had done this a few times we listened to the playback as Joe faded the screaming into the tune. It sounded incredible whatever Joe had done with the voices and he fairly jumped into the air, laughing and saying "It sounds like fucking thousands of them!" We didn't get to put the vocal on "Your Eyes Tell Me", but some years ago I did get to hear the original backing track which does still exist on the "Tea Chest Tapes."

We were all very excited that evening as we stood around talking to Joe. We were really hot on The Saxons image. We talked about riding in a Chariot through the streets of London to advertise our hopefully forthcoming release of "Saxon War Cry." We also discussed the idea of wearing studded leather tunics along with helmets and horns. We were all coming up with ideas and you could feel the excitement, especially in Joe. We talked about writing pop songs built around Saxon themes. Songs that came out of that idea were "Castle On The Mountain" (the original backing track still exists), "The Wedding Of Cedric The Saxon" (never recorded), "Song Of The Sun God" (Backing track still exists) "The Lady In Grey", instrumental recorded at the Holder's farm on Pete's Telefunken tape recorder. We actually took the tape to Joe for him to hear. He quite liked it but he was most interested to know if that was a real owl that was hooting at the beginning of the piece. Actually it was me trying to whistle like an owl.

"Song Of The Sun God" turned out to be an interesting project. It was a composition that evolved out of our association with Joe. By that I mean that Joe's influence upon us was mainly in an instrumental vein, which was probably due to his desire to create another "Telstar" and our desire to be a vocal group like The Beatles. So Pete Holder and I came up with "Sun God" which was tied in with this new Saxon image. It originally started out as an instrumental but ended up as a vocal. In the song we were asking the Sun God to bring us home safely that night after a huge battle that we would be fighting that day. At the session after we had played the number to Joe he got quite excited and suggested that Pete play an organ guitar that he was developing together with the Watkins electronic people. So after we had finished the basic backing track Joe brought out this weird, little guitar that looked like it could have been home made and plugged it into Pete's amp. Immediately all kinds of crackling and sizzling sounds emanated from the instrument and one could almost expect to see sparks flying and smoke pouring out. Joe did not seem to be bothered by this at all and proceeded to fiddle about with some wires and controls on the guitar. We stood around wondering what was going to happen next afraid that the whole contraption would suddenly explode. Pete had a look of amazement on his face. On one hand he was feeling very honoured that he was to use this great new invention that Joe had been working on and on the other hand he looked concerned that he might get electrocuted at any moment. Pete was able to get most of the lead melody down after a few takes. Sometimes the guitar gave out a sputter or two here and there, but we finally got one down, although right at the very end of the song the last extended note burst into a crackle and Joe seeing that we were disappointed by this told us that it was nothing and everything would be alright. I believe that had we ever got round to finishing that track Joe would have probably disguised that crackle with some effect that would make it sound like something strange and would not be seen as a mistake on the recording. The whole thing probably would have turned out to be beneficial to the song and be just another spark of genius from Joe Meek. If anybody is curious as to the sound that the organ guitar produced I remember that it sounded similar to the Clavioline a small keyboard attachment that was used on "Telstar." To my knowledge it was only ever used on that track. I have never heard any body else talk about using it. Sometime later there was an article in the *Melody Maker* concerning some new gear that Watkins was coming out with. It talked about a new professional thirty watt amplifier with a built in echo unit and that the teething troubles with the organ guitar they called the Fifth Man were over and the instrument would be on the market shortly. Joe's name was mentioned in connection with some of their affects units. Today the Fifth Man is regarded as a "Turkey" that was technically perfect but commercially disastrous. I guess that's why I never remember ever hearing about it.

Roger Holder came to pick up John and me for practice one night and told us that the Holder family in a combined effort had made these Saxons tunics and helmets with horns. Roger and Pete had driven over to the slaughter house and bought some horns and cow hide for the trim. They also called up their neighbour, Terry Biddle-combe who was a champion steeple chase jockey. As Tom Holder, Pete and Roger's dad, had courted Terry's sister before he was married, the two families were well acquainted. They asked Terry if he had any Jockey skullcaps and they wound up getting four of Terry's caps. Actually they are more like crash helmets. They fitted the horns on to the skull caps and used the cow hide which they had decorated with studs for the trim. Mrs. Holder along with some of her son's girl-friends had made tunics for us from leatherette. Pete and Roger's were beige and John and I wore the dark brown ones. They laced up at the neck and we also wore wrist supports that matched the tunics. Not long after that we decided that we would take some publicity photos dressed in our Saxon gear. Once again the talents of the Holders came to surface. Mick Holder would take the shots and Pete would develop the prints. We did the photo session out at Aylesmore farm.

Aylesmore farm – The Saxons publicity shot

We took shots of us crawling up a rise, Roger threatening me with a sword and ended up riding around in a chariot that the Holders had come up with pulled by one of their horses. Mick Holder took a cine film of this which I believe has been lost over the years. During this photo shoot I was having a problem with my eyes and soon found out that I had a detached retina in my left eye. In those days they didn't have the modern methods that they use today and so I was in hospital for over a week. I remember that the nurses giggled when they found out that I was not a real blond. Upon my release I was told by the doctor that I was not allowed to shake my head or bend and lift heavy objects for a while. This meant that I was going to get about six weeks off of work. Also I was not allowed to sing. When things got back to normal I found that I had trouble hitting certain notes and that my voice would go weird at times, but this soon passed and we soon returned to our two gigs a week routine. Suddenly out of the blue we heard from Joe that our recording of "Saxon War Cry" was to be released on Decca. On the "B" side would be "Clickette Clack." Of course we were thrilled and couldn't quite believe it after nothing had happened with our other recordings. Anyway it was true and Joe gave us the information of the release date which was June 16th 1965.

We had a write up in the local newspaper *Gloucester Citizen* which announced that The Saxons would be awaiting an answer to their War Cry. I believe that we were the first entertainers from Gloucester to get a record released. I am not aware of anyone from Gloucester who has accomplished this since, although there may have been but I have been away from Gloucester for over thirty years so I could possibly have missed someone. Joe told us to look in the *NME* around the time of the release date as there would be an advertisement in the middle pages of the newspaper together with a picture of the band. Well Joe was right there it was right smack bang in the centre pages The Saxons "Saxon War Cry" C/W "Clickette Clack" on Decca Records, but who the hell was this band they featured in the picture? They looked like a bunch of bankers who were playing in a traditional jazz band. It was certainly not The Saxons clothed in their Saxon outfits. We were devastated and even quite embarrassed that people would think that this bunch of squares in the photo was The Saxons. We called Joe immediately and he had seen it too. He said that there had been a mistake at the *NME* and the editor had apologized to him. Later on Joe remarked that he believed that the paper had done this on purpose as they wanted to screw him up. *The Citizen,* Gloucester's newspaper did a review of the single and said that we sounded like The Tornados but it was worthwhile listening to the B side which was a catchy vocal that sounded promising. This basically confirmed what we were thinking which was that instrumentals were on the way out and that vocals were definitely in, and that, coupled with the horrible publicity shot we knew that it was doomed to fail. I for one knew that I would never listen to, and definitely would not buy a record recorded by the bunch of bankers in the picture. About the only thing that we benefited from this whole fiasco was that we were able now to be billed as Decca recording artists with a single out called "Saxon War Cry", which we proudly had printed on our business cards. I guess that we all felt pretty good that we had a record out and the gigs were coming in very regularly from all areas around Gloucestershire. We looked good on stage dressed in our Beatle style suits. The girls were crazy about our blond hair and we were working pretty much every weekend, Fridays and Saturdays. Saturdays were usually tough for me as we always played till late on Friday nights and I had to work in the department store on Saturdays. So when I got out of work at 6 pm I had just about enough time to have a cup of tea and leave for the gig. One gig that we played at was at the Warwickshire Agricultural College for girls. The school was basically this big old rambling mansion and at the end of the evening, after we had put away the gear in the van we started to talk with some of the girls there. They told us that the place was haunted and that a ghost of a lady wearing a grey dress was frequently to be seen wandering the corridors at night. Pete Holder and I were inspired by that story and wrote "The Lady In Grey" instrumental together. We recorded it at Aylesmore farm on Pete's Telefunken tape recorder using the Swiss Echo unit as a mixer, which was Pete's idea. Pete and his brothers had saved up the money to buy the recorder by allowing the public to gather daffodils on their land and charged sixpence a bunch. At Easter time Daffodils grow in abundance in the Newent area to such an extent that they turn the country side yellow. We took the tape of "Lady In Grey" to Joe for him to hear and I think he quite liked it; after all we were just knocking off Joe Meek. At that gig at the college I remember that drummer John Davies had been talking to a girl there and as we were leaving and were walking out to the van she called to him from an upstairs window. John asked "What's your name?" She replied "Debbie" Debbie Simons." They went on to get married and had two daughters. We were beginning to become celebrities in and around Gloucestershire. Everyone in the small town of Newent knew The Saxons, especially the Holder brothers, who were local lads, and lived a stone's throw away from Newent in the area of Dymock, their parent's farm being a mere 300 yards from the birthplace of Dick Whittington who as a boy ran away to London and wound up becoming the first Lord Mayor of London. We were also gaining popularity in the surrounding counties, with some of our gigs being played further afield.

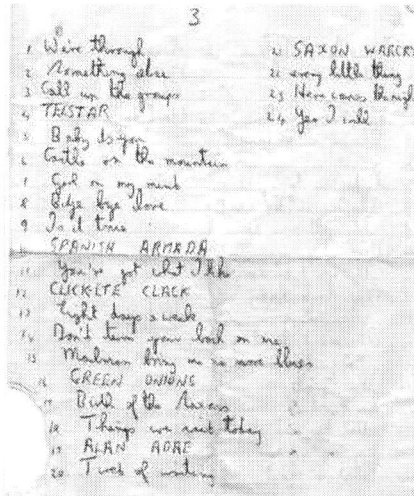

Saxons set list 1965

We were asked to judge bands that were competing in talent contests. I didn't find this too appealing as sometimes it was embarrassing to judge bands that knew The Saxons. We knew these bands too and it was hard to choose one over the other. Whatever decision we made would be wrong as you could always depend on offending somebody. We pretty soon stopped judging contests just like we had stopped entering talent contests. After we had entered a talent contest at the Malvern Winter Gardens and Pete Holder broke a string right in the first number and all these other bands had brought their own fans by the bus load we realized that we didn't stand a chance; although we did get a scream or two when I appeared on stage wearing my shiny suit. I remember some band from Birmingham won by getting the most votes from the audience. They played one of their own numbers and said that their style of music was called the "Brum Beat." In the six months that passed from June 1965 when "Saxon War Cry" was released, till the end of the year, The Saxons continued to improve as a band, looking and playing better on stage, writing more music, and generally getting prepared for a career in pop music. At my day job I was doing fine and received a special award from the managing director of the store for the good results I had achieved in my college exams. This must have been an unusual experience for David Pope the Managing Director, as only a few weeks before, he and a group of directors from other stores walked in and caught me and a friend of mine from the carpet department playing ten pin bowling. We were supposed to be cutting lengths of carpeting but as we were finished with that, we had made a large ball out of all the sticky tape that we had taken off the rolls of carpet and made ten pins which we had cut from the heavy duty cardboard tubes that the carpeting was rolled around. I was about to bowl down the ball when they all walked in. Jesus Christ I just stood there knowing that we had been caught and held the ball in my hand behind my back. Mr. Pope walked up to me and held out his hand. I promptly placed the ball in it. He tossed it once in the air and caught it, passing it back to me. "You'll have to do better than that" he said and turned round and walked away with the visitors. I never heard any more about it but a short time after that I was transferred to the linoleum department, which I took as a demotion and was pretty upset about. My ex boss Mr. Dyer said that it was because of my eye injury and as I was not allowed to lift heavy weights I was being transferred. Meanwhile it was heavier to lift the huge rolls of linoleum on to the cutting machine than to lug the rolls of carpet around. I eventually found out that a salesman from the furniture department had asked to be transferred to the carpet department and that's why I got moved. This all happened a few months before Christmas and the January sale was coming up. This was always a great event with customers lining up outside the store and then rushing in to be the first to get the best bargains. There would often be fights between the lady customers over who got to a certain item first. You could often see two ladies tugging on a rug or a piece of carpeting.

Sometime during the last week of December 1965, on a Monday afternoon a lady from the furniture office told me that there was a phone call for me. This was very strange because I had never received a call at work before and I didn't know what to expect. It was Roger Holder. "We've just got a call from Joe Meek" he said "He wants us to be in London next Saturday, we're going to be The New Tornados and you'll have to leave your job. We're turning pro!"

Saxons Midland & Royal gig

THE TORNADOS CHAPTER ONE

In which The Saxons leave Gloucester to become The Tornados.
They meet up with Dave Watts and perform their first Tornados gig.
Upon their return from Scunthorpe Joe throws a temper tantrum and
fires the band.
The New Tornados start to rehearse and to perform gigs.
Joe plans out the direction and future of the band.
Robb escapes another uncomfortable situation with Joe.
The creation, recording and release of "Pop Art Goes Mozart "/ "Too
Much In Love To Hear."
The Tornados get into the cabaret scene with The George Cooper Orga-
nization providing the venues.
Tornados go to Spain.

THE NEW TORNADOS
COLUMBIA RECORDS

(L-R) John Davies, Robb Huxley, Pete Holder, Dave Watts, Roger Holder

Note: I am using the name NEW TORNADOS as a way to differentiate the TORNADOS group that was born out of The Saxons with the addition of Dave Watts, from any other Tornados group that was created by Joe Meek, including the original Tornados. Although Joe stated that we were to be called The New Tornados and that name was printed on a publicity photo – see page 59 – we were never billed as, or appeared as, The New Tornados. The two singles that were issued in 1966 were released under the name of The Tornados. Although I refer to the group as The New Tornados, we were always billed as and were known as THE TORNADOS

ROBB HUXLEY.

Friday 31st December 1965 was to be the final engagement that we played as The Saxons. It was to be held at Church Stretton, a small town in Shropshire near the Welsh border. It was a very memorable occasion as we knew that at the end of the following week we would be driving up to London to embark on a career in music as The Tornados, later to be known as The New Tornados. It was a great gig. We all felt excited and confident and as the curtains opened for our set, we saw in front of us, lines of girls screaming, and pushing to get as close to the front of the stage as possible. We must have looked great dressed in our suits with our blond hair. The following Monday morning at work I walked into my boss's office and broke the news to him that I would have to leave at the end of the week as I was turning professional. A little later that morning I was told to report to Mr. Robinson's office. He was the manager of the furniture floor. Mr. Croft, the manager of my department was also there. Mr. Robinson asked me if I could give them a little more notice as we were just going into the January sale. I told them that it was impossible and as I left the office Mr. Robinson said in a sarcastic tone "I wish I could turn professional." I felt elated as I was finally going to do what I had always dreamed of, and in a way I was getting back at them for the demotion I had received when they transferred me to the lino department. At the coffee break many of my friends gathered around me to ask me how I felt about leaving my job for a career in music and wished me all the best of luck. One friend of mine by the name of Richard Wasley reminded me of the time we had taken a trip up to London and we paid a visit to the Two I's coffee bar. This was a place where many of the British rock stars such as Cliff Richard, The Shadows, Terry Dene and many others started out. He reminded me how he had persuaded me to get up and sing with the band that was playing there. It was a great thrill for me to have sung a song there and Rich Wasley told me that he always believed that I was meant to be in show business. He actually went on to be an actor.

(L-R) Don Gapper Robb Huxley (Playing Alan Keeling's Hofner
guitar which was borrowed for more than a year)
Derek Gapper and Richard Wasley

That first week in January was a busy one. I purchased a big green suitcase in which to pack everything that I was going to take with me to London. My Dad gave me a spare electric razor that he hoped would come in useful for me. Joe Meek had called the Holders to tell them that we would be able to stay at a flat that he rented which was a few doors down from the studio in Holloway road. He also said that we should arrive at the studio at 10am on Saturday morning where we were to meet up with a keyboard player, rehearse with him and then drive up to Scunthorpe to play our first gig opening up for Heinz and the Wild Boys.

Friday came around and it was the usual opening day at the Bon Marche for the first day of the January sale. The warning buzzer was sounded throughout the store signifying that the doors were being opened and that the lines of women shoppers who had been waiting patiently in the cold outside were rushing into the store to the various departments to get the first chance at the great bargains that were for sale. The carpet and linoleum departments were usually high on the list and soon we were surrounded by hordes of lady shoppers screaming and shouting for the attention of the salesmen. At around 3pm I was told to report to the personnel office as they wanted to settle up with me and pay me my wages. This being done I returned to my department and continued to work and stayed until the store closed at 7pm. At around 6.30pm my ex boss Tony Dyer came to wish me luck and praised me for working till the end of the day saying that most people would have left after getting paid and would not have cared to stay. All I had to do now was to get home and finish my packing and look forward to Saturday morning.

Bright and early on Saturday 8th January 1966 Mick, Roger and Pete Holder arrived at 40 Clegram Road, Gloucester. Mick Holder was coming along as our road manager and driver. I gave my mum and dad a big hug and a kiss, threw my suitcase and guitar in the back of the group van along with the rest of the gear and took my seat next to Pete.

So the great day had finally come and I felt a feeling of nervous excitement in my stomach as we drove over to Cheltenham to pick up our drummer John Davies. John informed us that he had made arrangements to stay with his cousin Graham who lived and worked in London and would not be staying with us at Holloway Road. On the way to London we talked about what it was going to be like to meet this keyboard player who was to be the new member of our band, or should I say Joe Meek's new creation of The Tornados.

Terry answered the door when we arrived, telling us to bring our gear up to the studio and to set up just like we would for a session.

We were about half way through setting up when Joe suddenly appeared in the doorway followed by a guy with straight black hair, wearing a big furry overcoat that made him look like a grey polar bear. Joe introduced him as Dave and he would be our keyboard player. Before we had a chance to extend our hands to say hello, Dave Watts pulled out his hand from behind his back saying he was sorry he couldn't shake hands with us as he had got into a fight at a pub last night and had taken a swing at a guy and had missed and hit the wall. His right hand was covered up with a white bandage spotted with a few traces of blood. Joe took over the conversation at this point telling us to start rehearsing all The Tornados numbers that we knew and by taking some numbers from our repertoire and putting them together with some songs that Dave would do we would come up with a set list to play that night at Scunthorpe. As we finished to get set up, Dave took off his huge coat and took a seat at Joe's Lowry organ. Well he wasn't such a big guy after all in fact he was quite skinny although he was about five feet ten inches in height. Dave immediately burst into this jazzy piece of music throwing in all kinds of jazz chords and intricate progressions saying that this was a piece by the Graham Bond Organization. He proceeded to suggest other songs by Nina Simone, Georgie Fame, Zoot Money and Brian Auger most of which we had never heard of before, although John Davies did seem to know a lot of what Dave was talking about, and seemed eager to play that music whatever it was. But first we had to rehearse The Tornados hits. Lucky for us we had played many of their numbers in our sets when we were The Whirlwinds and The Saxons and as Dave had a pretty good knowledge of the material we soon got the numbers down with Dave chiming in from time to time criticizing our chords. "Don't put in that silly fat A man, make it a Major seventh and follow it with a sixth". We could see that Dave was quite an accomplished musician and it seemed that he was already assuming a leading role in the band. Joe would stick his head around the door from time to time to check on our progress and at one point said that we should wind things down and get ready to leave for the evening's venue which was quite a distance from London. We also had to drive down to Bromley to Dave's place to pick up his Hammond organ which he assured us, in a whisper, would sound much better that that piece of shit Lowry that Joe had in the studio

Joe wished us all good luck as we left, asking us to try to contact him by telepathy from Scunthorpe when we arrived by tapping on the dressing room wall sometime during the evening and he would let us know if he received the vibrations in the flat. He said he would expect to hear a tapping on the wall. We all bundled into the van downstairs and drove down to Dave's parent's house in Bromley. Dave had a large speaker cabinet with a 100 watt amplifier and a Hammond M100. The speaker weighed a ton and the organ was bulky to handle and after a heavy struggling session we were mortified to find out that we couldn't fit Dave's gear into the van no matter how we tried. The back row of seats would have to be removed and we had neither the tools or time to do this. Dave said that somebody should call Joe and tell him of our dilemma and Pete Holder was elected to do this task. Joe didn't seem that worried and told us to return to the studio and pick up the Clavioline which he had there. The Clavioline was a small keyboard attachment that was played together with a piano. It was exactly the same model as my dad had and played in the pubs with. On the way back to the studio Dave complained and assured us that he would not play that little Mickey Mouse organ. He began to throw a feeling of depression over the whole scene with negative talk of how this was not going to work out. On arrival at Holloway road Mick Holder ran up the stairs with Dave and they returned with the little keyboard. We set out on our journey to play our first professional gig and I must say it felt terrible and depressing. Dave kept on about how he would not play that Clavioline and seemed to be trying to influence us not to show up for the gig. He even persuaded us to stop for a Chinese meal and after we ate he suggested that we call up the venue to tell them that we had broken down in the van and would not make it. My level of enthusiasm was at about minus 100 at this point as my first day as a professional musician was turning out to be a complete disaster. Mick Holder was delegated to make the phone call. Mick spoke to the promoter and was told we had better find a way to get there or he would sue us for every penny we had. Hearing this we all piled back into the van. The spirits must have been against us that day as if things weren't bad enough, as we were travelling through Lincolnshire we suddenly became bombarded by some very strong winds. Mick Holder could hardly keep control of the van and we almost got blown off the road. We ended up arriving late for the gig. Heinz and the Wild Boys had just finished their set. We were supposed to open for them but due to our late arrival they had to go on first. We were hoping that the Wild Boys would have an organ that we could use but they didn't and that sealed our fate. Dave refused to perform and we decided that we would just go on and do our Saxons show as The Tornados. We rushed to set up our gear and put on our Beatle suits. We still looked good and played a reasonably good set. Just over a week ago we had played the same set as The Saxons and now we were doing exactly the same thing only now we were called The Tornados. To me it seemed like a lie but the audience didn't seem to care or know the difference. We told the crowd that the organ had fallen off of the van and was broken. Throughout our set Dave Watts stood and watched from the audience. I guess he was weighing up this new set of Tornados that Joe Meek had come up with. With our first professional gig over we returned to London.

We dropped off Dave Watts and John Davies and made our way back to Holloway road and wearily climbed the stairs up to the flat at about nine in the morning, only to find out that there were not enough beds for us to sleep in so I wound up sleeping on the floor under the dining room table. As I was so tired I had no trouble falling asleep. There was absolutely nothing to eat in the flat and there was nowhere open to buy anything all we had were a couple of pints of milk that Mick got from somewhere and that was our breakfast. That Sunday afternoon Mick, Roger, Pete and I took a walk down to Charlie's restaurant which was a small establishment a couple of hundred yards down the road from the flat. It was kind of a grubby little place but the food was good and I enjoyed a beef curry which I devoured with relish as I was very hungry. There was no television in the flat so we wiled away the rest of the day and evening playing our guitars and chatting.

At around ten o'clock Monday morning a knock came at the door. It was Terry saying that Joe wanted to see us up at the studio. We all got ready and made our way up the stairs to Joe's place where Terry told us to wait in the office where we all sat down. Joe appeared and looked his usual self but there were no smiles or congeniality. He came straight to the point, asking us why we had not used the Clavioline in our act on Saturday. Seeing that Joe was very aggravated we started to explain that Dave did not want to use it and was embarrassed to play it. Joe's voice started to rise in pitch and his face began to turn red and he screamed that the Clavioline was good enough to use on Telstar which sold a million copies and it was for sure good enough for us to use. Waving his hands frantically in the air and looking like he was about to explode he screamed "You can all get out of here and fuck off back down to Gloucester!" He then abruptly turned around, stormed out of the office and seeing a tray with cups and a coffee pot picked it up and hurled it against the wall smashing it to pieces. He then strode into his living room and slammed the door behind him.

The room was then filled with a deathly silence. Nobody spoke, we couldn't, and we were all in a state of utter shock. We couldn't even look at each other; we just stared at the floor in disbelief. Our professional musical career had lasted only fifty hours! Now it was all over, forcing us to have to return to Gloucester in shame, humiliated and completely broken. We had never seen this side of Joe Meek before and after the harrowing weekend that we had just experienced it can be imagined the feeling of utter despair that we all felt inside.

I guess that we should have all got up and left, but we couldn't move we just sat there for what seemed like forever in total silence; the three Holder brothers and me. Eventually Mick Holder managed to get out a few words. "Maybe I should go and have a word with him?" he asked. We all nodded in agreement. It was the only chance that we had. Mick stood up and left the room. We heard him knock gently at the door and heard Joe's voice saying "Come in." Roger, Pete and I continued to sit in complete silence and the waiting seemed endless. Somewhere in the back of my mind I felt that everything would be OK or maybe I was just hoping that it would be. Even in that utter silence no sound of conversation could be heard from the other room, so we could not ascertain what our fate might be. After sometime we heard Joe's door open and Mick appeared in the room.

We all looked up waiting to hear what Mick had to say, fearing the worst but hoping for the best. Adopting a very serious tone he said, "Well, he said he's going to give us one more chance." It was as though the whole world had suddenly become a much friendlier place. A feeling of complete relief poured over us as we all melted inside. Mick continued to say that we must always follow Joe's instructions if we were to be a success, and that the only reason that we were The Tornados right now was because Joe had fired the previous band that had disobeyed him deciding to only keep Dave Watts on as organist. Joe told Mick that he liked us as we were from the same part of the country as he was and thought that we deserved an opportunity to make it in the business.

Looking back it was kind of unfair that the four of us had to bear the brunt of Joe's wrath. He may have admonished Dave at some other time and John Davies only heard about it from us and was not there to experience it first hand. However the memory of Joe's outburst always stayed with me throughout my association with him. There was always an eerie feeling whenever you were around Joe especially at the sessions. It seemed that at any minute he could suddenly burst into a fit of rage. Whenever he was joking or teasing anyone and we were all laughing everything was fine.

The following two weeks were spent rehearsing with Dave Watts. The repertoire that we played in The Saxons changed vastly partly because Dave came up with quite a few numbers that he wanted to play and sing. One of the first numbers that we learned was "Wade In The Water" by the Graham Bond Organization in which Dave really excelled. We also got off a few numbers by The Four Tops, did a version of" Somewhere Over The Rainbow". Dave did Nina Simone's "I Put A Spell On You", "Midnight Hour" and we even played an instrumental called "Rinky Dink." Although we were now The New Tornados we really felt that we wanted to be a vocal band just like all the other bands that were big at the time. Instrumental bands were becoming a thing of the past and were definitely not in. We always had to play "Telstar" as we were riding on the coat tails of the original Tornados and we dealt with their other hits by combining them all into a medley. We still had our blond hair except for Dave whose hair was dark brown. We did a few gigs here and there over those first few weeks. At some venues we were confronted by promoters and fans who claimed that we were not the real Tornados and if we were, where was Heinz and Clem Cattini?

One Sunday morning a knock came at the door, it was Terry with a message from Joe that I was to go up to the studio as Joe wanted to see me and wanted to talk to me. A sick feeling developed in my stomach as I was overcome with dread at the thought of being alone again with Joe. I turned round to Mick saying that I was not going up there. I was still hiding my shame from the first episode with Joe, and still could not bring myself to tell anyone what had happened. Roger and Mick wanted to know why I was refusing to go up to Joe and all that I could say was that I had heard stories about Joe. Roger tried to assure me that Joe was not like that and I had no choice in the matter, I had to go. Pete however remained silent as I believe that he knew what I could be in for. The next few hours were unbearable for me. It was almost like being on death row awaiting execution. Throughout my time with the band I always assumed the position of being the head cook and bottle washer, but due to my highly nervous state I made the worst meal that I had ever made and totally cremated the food much to the complaints of the guys. It was fine for them; they didn't have an appointment to see Joe. I resolved to make the best of the situation and although I was very nervous I decided that yes I would have to go. I would just keep strong thoughts in my mind of my girlfriend that I had left down in Gloucester and hope that some-how I would be able to get through the ordeal. Two o'clock came around and I got ready to report to Joe. He opened the door and smiled when I arrived and escorted me into his living quarters where we sat down on that old floppy sofa together. He had turned on the television and lowered the lights. He went on to tell me of all the great plans that he was making for the band and how he wanted to change my image by possibly using a different hair colour. He also said that one of the main reasons that he had taken us on as The Whirlwinds in the beginning was because of the way that I could sing like Buddy Holly. Then we got around to the type of clothing he wanted me to wear and when he asked me to stand up so that he could check out the pants I was wearing I knew what was coming next. When he started to fumble around with the zipper I knew that this would have to be the time that I would have to be strong and not give in as I did before. "I thought that we were just meeting here to talk, Joe" I blurted out and he stood up and said "O.K", and without any further attempts to approach me showed me the door and I was out of there in a flash. The thousand ton weight that had been on me was gone and I could breathe again. The Holders wanted to know the details of the visit so I just told them about the image change that Joe wanted me to undertake. I did not mention anything about the attempted advances that Joe had made. "See, we told you that there was nothing to worry about." Mick said.

After all these years, looking back it wasn't so bad. Joe had not been forceful with me and politely gave up his attempts at my request. His demeanour was soft and non aggressive. He could have tried to rape me but didn't. He was basically a soft, loving and caring person inside; the complete opposite of his other unpredictable sometimes even violent personality. That was the last time that I was ever in that kind of a situation with Joe. I have never held anything against him for what he did or tried to do. I have seen various big stars in the music business poking fun at Joe's homosexuality on various TV documentaries. His memory does not deserve that. In this modern age with its tolerance towards gays and gay issues, actions such as Joe's would go virtually unnoticed.

We had a meeting one day up at the studio with Joe where he proceeded to outline a plan to us of what his intentions were with regard to the direction of the band. "Firstly we must take some publicity photos." he said. Dave asked if we could abandon our stage suits in favour of mod gear which most bands were now wearing. Anyway we didn't look so professional anymore with the four of us wearing our Beatle suits and Dave dressed in his own different suit. Joe agreed with the idea and fronted us some money to visit Carnaby Street where we bought some brightly coloured hipsters with wide belts, some floral shirts and snazzy ties. We still wore our Beatle boots though. Joe also made an appointment at the hairdressers for me and instructed them to dye my hair black. All this being done and me with my freshly dyed black hair, which Joe paid for, we were sent to a photo session with a photographer that Joe had arranged. We drove over to the Photographers studio which was also his residence which he shared with a friend. They had a big Old English Sheep dog which padded softly around the place. The whole atmosphere and feel of the place was arty and bohemian. I saw a definite similarity between our photographer and David Hemmings who played a mod photographer in the movie *Blow Up* which had just been released, so everything felt very hip, modern and exciting. The photo session was held at Highgate Cemetery. The reason for this was, as we had no particular ideas of a theme for the shots, the photographer suggested the cemetery as he thought it would be an interesting location and would provide some unusual shots. We all agreed thinking that Joe would probably dig it as we knew that he had spent time in graveyards with his portable recorder in the past, hoping to get some supernatural recordings. When the photographer asked the name of our band and was told that we were The New Tornados he wondered what had happened to the Old Tornados. "They are all dead" we joked. "Well here you all are," said the photographer, "You are paying your final respects to your dead predecessors, the Old Tornados." We all thought that this was very appropriate and proceeded to pose around various grave sites looking very sad and forlorn. Highgate cemetery was a very creepy place to be in, and by the end of the session we thought that we had taken some excellent shots that really would enhance the image of our new band.

How wrong we were.

A few days later Joe called a meeting at the studio. On the desk in the office were the contact sheets and a few samples from the shoot. Joe picked them up and tossed them carelessly back asking whose idea it was to shoot the session in the cemetery. We could see that he was displeased so we nervously replied that it had been the photographer's idea and we feared another outburst. "This is not what I wanted" he stated, "It should be nice, simple, publicity shots featuring your faces and not a bunch of people staring at a grave." He went on to say that the dead should be left in peace and not used in such a fashion and furthermore he would call the photographer to complain and would also refuse to pay for the session.

The next session was held up at our flat on Holloway Road with a different photographer. We posed in front of the wall in the living room with the wallpaper as a back drop. A few days later at another meeting to review the shoot Joe was angry again. "Look at your faces" he said "You all look so miserable." and he had drawn big smiles on our faces with a pen. "This is how you have to look if you're going to make it in this business." The publicity photo sessions were abandoned for sometime and no further attempts were made until we started in the Night Club business.

In reflection I feel that the photo session in the cemetery was somewhat indicative, as it was an example of the way things were changing, particularly in the direction of psychedelia where it would be the in thing to freak people out and to look weird. Obviously Joe had this clean cut, all smiling, good boy image in his head, just like Brian Epstein had with The Beatles, but somehow he failed to realise, or refused to accept the radical changes that were taking place in music and art in the mid sixties.

Dave Watts introduced the word "brown" to us as a derogatory term to address anything that was not "hip" or "in"; something that you might refer to as being square. So you could be a "Brown Band", wear "Brown Clothes", play "Brown Music" or just be "BROWN." Joe's desirable image of The New Tornados made us look like a "Brown Group" and with all the bands like Pink Floyd, and The Yardbirds beginning to get big on the scene with the "New Music", we were just in that same old rut that was fast becoming history.

Joe said that we should go over and pay a visit to the George Cooper Organization as they were to be our booking agency. We were introduced to George Cooper who, from behind his desk said in a very heavy London accent "Well boys, we'll see what we can do for you, we'll get you some work and we'll see how it works out." We then got to meet George's associate Harry Dawson. Harry would be in charge of getting work for us. He hinted that there might be a chance to get us some gigs in the cabaret field and also maybe some summer season shows. George Cooper handled many artists albeit many of them were on the decline. Artists such as Marty Wilde who had some big hits in the late fifties, but this was the mid sixties bordering on the psychedelic era and artists such as Marty, Adam Faith, Cliff Richard and many others were falling under the onslaught of the changing times and the new trend in groups such as The Beatles, The Rolling Stones, The Hollies and so on. Taking all these things into consideration at least things were getting a bit more organized and the general feeling of the band was improving. We were playing enough gigs in order that we could eat and none of us had to pay rent or utility bills so we were surviving. We might not have been doing what we all wanted to artistically but at least we were in the music business which sure as hell beat working in a department store or on a farm. Mick Holder was the only exception to this as he opted to return to Newent to work on the farm, we couldn't blame him as he had gone from being the manager of The Saxons to the driver of The New Tornados and that did not look like being a very appealing future for Mick.

Joe called us up to the studio one morning to tell us that it was time for us to put out a record and that he wanted to show us how we were to go about it. He said that he wanted to do a classical piece of music for the next Tornados release. He invited us into his living quarters where we sat down on Joe's old creaky sofa which when you sat down on it your knees came up to your chin. Joe stood with his back to us and put on a disc of a movement by Mozart. As the music played Joe clicked his heels and jerked his head in time to the music. We were in a state of surprise and things really got bad when Dave, unseen by Joe, stood up just inches behind him and frantically pretended to conduct the orchestra. This forced us into a state of almost not being able to contain our laughter and at the end of the piece when Joe turned around to see our reaction nobody knew what to do with themselves. We just hoped and prayed that he would say something funny so that we could release the laughter that was bursting to escape from us, but he didn't, so we all had to straighten up quickly. Joe proceeded to say that we should get some ideas from this piece, and take the gear up to our flat and create a new instrumental based on key parts of the song. We were all concerned about what we thought that Joe wanted to achieve. We had heard this Mozart piece a few times and with only the memory of this we were supposed to come up with a piece of music. "Don't worry lads" Dave assured us "I know what Joe likes." and we went on led by Dave to create this classical sounding instrumental based on something that Joe had played us by Mozart. We created it up at our flat in Holloway Road but the session ended when the Irish family that lived upstairs knocked on the door warning us that if we didn't shut up that they would call the police. Anyway to us it sounded like Joe would be pleased with it but we were wrong again.

The following morning we all met up at the studio and got ready to record. Joe hooked everything up and said "OK play it for me." This was tough for us as we could hardly remember what we had done the day before. Anyway we got into it when about half way through the recording he turned off the machine, walked into the studio with his hand in the air, "No, no, no, that's not what I meant." he proclaimed and led us back downstairs to listen to the Mozart record again. He played us a few specific parts saying that we should incorporate them into the tune. "You play this part first and then go into this part and follow it by this part and that's it." Joe explained. With Dave's leadership we got the main parts rehearsed. He perfected the melodies and helped us work out the chords and the bass lines. At one point in the recording Dave complained that due to the bad action on the piano he was not able to play a certain part correctly and was stumbling over some of the notes. If only he could play it slower it would be easier. With Joe's expertise he slowed down the speed of the tape so that Dave could play the melody line an octave lower at a much slower speed. Pete also played a lead part but at the normal register. This was all done on the second tracking. When we heard the play back, the piano part sounded great as it had adopted a special sound. Also Pete's guitar which was recorded slowly at normal register on a tremolo affect now sounded an octave higher resembling a mandolin Joe was obviously delighted with the results together with the praising that he got from the band, mainly Dave. "If anybody asks you how you got the sound on the keyboard tell them you used a Splatter Board." Joe announced with a big smile on his face. Joe also had John Davies turn his bass drum over flat on the floor so it resembled a timpani drum. He loaded it with echo and had John beat on it throughout the piece in certain passages that Joe selected. We even put in the typical last verse, Tornados style vocal backing track. In the end Joe had created the typical Tornados single with the typical "Joe Meek" sound, receiving credit as writer, Trad. Arranged Meek; which was exactly what he wanted. Using a band of musicians and using their ability to provide a way to create what he felt and heard in his mind, Joe Meek created "Pop Art Goes Mozart".

Joe asked us if we had anything for the B side. We had a song that I had started to write on my Dad's old, out of tune piano down in Gloucester and Pete holder helped me finish it off. It was called "Too Much In Love To Hear". We played it to Joe and he liked it but he said that it should be done in three four and not in four four as we were playing it. My immediate reaction was that Joe had no idea what he was talking about until Dave Watts said "Yeah man! That's it." and started to play the chords with what turned out to be a six eight feel. It seemed that like magic the song took on a completely different feel and appeal and all this had basically come from Joe.

I have read over the years many articles portraying Joe as someone who could not sing in tune and was tone deaf but I do not agree entirely with that. He had a vivid imagination and heard things in his mind that he could only bring to the surface with the help of others. If any one was singing off key he would know immediately and any one who was tone deaf would never have known this. Joe could sing but he was not a very good singer as he would often waver and go off key. Nevertheless he would stop the tape at once during a take and shout out "You're off key." and we would start the take again.

He was also very critical with regard to the attack and presentation of the vocal. He would almost always tell me to smile when I was singing and even to this day I employ that technique to my singing in certain songs.

"Too Much In Love To Hear" actually came out very well. Dave Watts put a very nice jazzy almost old world feel to his piano parts, Pete Holder put in a nice typical Shadows style solo and together with jazzy style drumming and a good bass line, I put down the vocal and played rhythm guitar.

So here we have the typical Tornados instrumental written by Joe Meek coupled with a perfectly acceptable vocal "B" side," Too Much In Love to Hear" written By Pete Holder and myself; showing how the music scene had changed and was still changing. We had the famous writer of "Telstar" consumed with the hope that he might create another "Telstar" with another of the groups that he had formed to be The Tornados. On the other hand we have the virgin pure recently "Turned Pro" Saxons, together with Dave Watts, a seasoned professional musician, all with their individual desires to be part of what was "IN", while masquerading as The Tornados.

When the record was released Joe sent a letter together with a demo disc to Keith Becket at *Thank Your Lucky Stars* in a bid to get The Tornados on the show. He illustrated that they say that every hit song has a gimmick which was really anyone's opinion, but he said our gimmick was the special sound on the piano which was achieved by using a "Splatter Board". He then went on to tell Keith that it was a chunk of gear, that was attached to the piano and that it looked like the inside of a grandfather clock that somebody had trodden on!

Joe also encouraged Becket to give the "B" side a listen as it was good enough to be an "A." Unfortunately Joe's efforts didn't pay off.

However there was a review made in the *Melody Maker* which was done by Steve Marriot of The Small Faces. Without reading the review we knew that we would get crucified. Here is Steve Marriot of the very popular and very "IN" Mod band The Small Faces reviewing an instrumental By The Tornados, that I'm sure he looked upon as a bunch of old "Brown" guys.

He seemed to like it in the beginning and even commented on the sound of what he thought was a harpsichord, and even said "That's nice." However after asking who the band was and being told that it was The Tornados, "It's the Massed Bands of The Tasmanian Air Force featuring Sooty on vibes" he joked and "A bad scene" and "Joe Meek should lose his echo chamber." He immediately put the 45 rpm disc on to the 78 rpm setting increasing the tempo to almost double the speed, saying that this was "Pop Art Goes Off Its Head".

Steve Marriot gave us a royal thrashing, which we were expecting anyway, but I believe that had he been played the "B" side "Too Much In Love To Hear" and not told who the band was till the record had finished, we may have avoided our thrashing. This was all part of the on going changes in the musical scene at that time.

Today, critics not influenced and unaware of those changes in musical history hold "Pop Art Goes Mozart" in high acclaim. It really was very good, even for that time. Joe's inventiveness with the play on words with the title, together with the conception of the music was great. Using his ability to cope with the problem when the poor action on the piano affected Dave's ability to perfect a passage, Joe was able to slow down the recording and by doing so provided this special sound that was created by the non existent "Splatter Board". The only problem was that this music did not fit in with the current musical trends of that time.

"Too Much In Love To Hear" is rarely mentioned or talked about, although I did record it again later in Tel-Aviv with an Israeli band called the Churchills. It reached number one on the Israeli charts in 1968.

One Saturday afternoon we made an appearance at the Marquee Club in London. It was just an appearance and we didn't get to play. Other bands would get to perform there but we just got our record played in the break and were paraded around on the small stage. It was more like a fashion show. The New Tornados all dressed up in their new mod gear. I for one was not happy with this and I felt rather embarrassed. How much nicer it would have been to be playing and performing some great vocal number instead.

We went on to another non playing appearance afterwards where we judged a beauty contest at a Fete in Lodden which was a small community in Norfolk. I gave a small speech saying how happy we were to be there and we basically stood around signing autographs.

We were to continue to appear and perform for charity throughout our career as The Tornados. Joe was a believer in doing this.

Later he wrote us in a letter that we should always be good and kind, as goodness and kindness was always repaid by goodness and kindness.

Tornados at Lodden Fete 1966. (L-R) Pete, Robb, Roger, Dave, John

We all met in the studio one afternoon and Joe announced that we were going into the cabaret business. He said that he wanted us to come up with an act that featured Tornados hits, night club music and comedy. Within a week he said that we should work on this act and then perform it for him at the studio. We immediately started on this project, drawing from our experience when playing in The Saxons. We used to play "Call Up The Groups" by the Barron Knights and at one time we had even made up Birth of The Saxons which was a parody on certain hit songs of the time directed at ourselves. We were basically poking fun at ourselves. We decided to do a similar thing with new songs and artists. We had The Spencer Davis group promoting the laxative Exlax with the hit song "Keep On Runnin'", Sandie Shaw singing about the brand new "Bra" she bought today. We even had the Walker Brothers singing "Washing up is so very hard to do, so make it easy on yourself, there's some Squeezy on the shelf". Marianne Faithful was singing "Yesterday" "Why he went all the way I don't know he wouldn't say I did something wrong now I'm in the family way". Within a week we came up with a set of music which we believed that, maybe Joe would like. This time we were surprised to find out that we were right.

We all met up at the studio to run through our new cabaret act for Joe to listen to. Dave sat at the Lowry organ, Roger, Pete and me stood in front of our amps each with a microphone that Joe had set up for us and John was over in the corner at his drum set peering out from behind the screens. We began to perform but Joe stopped the set and put his head around the door and said "What about the comedy?" At that point we started the comedy routine and played it through. At the end of the routine Joe virtually burst into the room with the biggest smile on his face, actually laughing out loud and clapping his hands with utter joy. We all breathed a sigh of relief. Any time that Joe burst into a room you never knew if he was going berserk and would scream and shout at you or what! We knew that we had pleased Joe and could all relax. We all felt good knowing that Joe felt good. Joe then proceeded to run downstairs to call up Harry Dawson at the George Cooper Organization to arrange for Harry to come over and see our cabaret act.

On the day of the audition Harry Dawson came over and sat in front of us up in the studio smoking his pipe and watched our complete cabaret act. At the completion Harry smiled at us saying "Very nice, boys." and went to talk with Joe in the control room. They appeared shortly with smiles on their faces and after Harry Dawson left Joe congratulated us telling us that Harry was very pleased with the set and that he would start to book us on the night club and working men's club circuit up in the north of England. These venues usually ran for a week at a time.

The first of these dates that we did was at the working men's club in Greasbrough. We were to be the supporting act for singer Kathy Kirby. In the mid sixties Kathy Kirby was recognized as the top British female singer. She bore a striking resemblance to Marilyn Monroe and was also famous for her glossy lips and her blonde hair. She had a big hit in the mid sixties with the Doris Day song, "Secret Love" and enjoyed much success on British television. She was known as the "British Songstress". In 1965 she had a hit in the States with a song called

"The Way Of Love" which received little attention in the U.K. Unfortunately she was to become another casualty of the onslaught of the Mersey Beat and the changing musical scene which we in The Tornados were desperately trying to fight against and hopefully to overcome by trying to persuade Joe to let us become a vocal group. This was to be a very new and exciting experience for us as we had always played dance halls and were now playing to sit down audiences.

As The Whirlwinds and Saxons our venues had been confined mainly to the south of England in and around Gloucestershire, but now as a professional band our travels took us further afield. Pete, John and I would usually travel to the gigs in the van with the gear and Roger and Dave would travel by car. We had not seen much of the north of England before and on our way up to Greasbrough which is situated near Rotherham in Yorkshire we noticed that the further that we travelled north the appearance of the towns and cities began to change. Everything began to look more industrialized and the buildings began to get blacker and blacker just as though they had been covered with a layer of soot. This basically gave me a kind of depressed feeling as I stared out of the van windows. This was a big difference from the green grassy hills dotted with quaint little villages with their little black and white cottages and village halls that we had been used to in the south. Another important thing we realized as we spent more time up north is that the further you travel north the stronger the beer gets.

When we arrived at the working men's club in Greasbrough, which in Old Saxon language means Grass or Grassy brook we found a hive of activity outside the entrance. As we approached the old guy that was on the gate directing the traffic asked "Are you artists, luv?" We were amazed by this as we had never been called "love" by a man before and found it quite amusing but soon got used to it in this new "Foreign Land" that we were exploring. The club had a large seating capacity inside but I remember the stage as being a bit on the small side. We set up our gear and made sure that everything was in good working order and went on to find a place to stay. We found rooms at some old Gothic looking hotel on the main street and were given some very good Northern hospitality such as tea and sandwiches by the proprietor and his wife. As it was a Sunday we did our show in the late afternoon. The place was hopping when we arrived and was full to capacity and the pints of Newcastle Brown were being downed with great fervour. We got dressed up in our new mod gear and took the stage to perform our first cabaret show. We ran through The Tornados hits and played "Pop Art Goes Mozart" together with our comedy routine and a few vocal numbers. In the middle of one of the vocals, some guy jumped up on the stage and grabbed my mic shouting "Stop, stop." Thinking that there was some kind of emergency we immediately ended the number while the guy shouted into the microphone "Hot pies are now being served!" He then calmly handed the mic back to me saying "Thanks luv." We all stood staring at each other with complete disbelief not quite knowing what to do. We had never been interrupted in the middle of a set before and we all found it embarrassing. Dave just counted the number in and we played it again wondering when the next interruption might come. Well we got to finish the set and we got a good reception from the audience. We got requests for an encore but not having any more material that was suitable for cabaret we just played "Telstar" again. We stayed around to watch Kathy Kirby's performance and she went over very well. The audience loved her and she received great applause when she performed her string of hits.

The week went on without a hitch. We were now starting to get used to this new musical scene that we were getting into. John, Dave and I had discovered Newcastle Brown Ale, which the locals called "A trip into outer space." We found their description of this beer to be quite true, and most nights we wound up banging on the big old door of the hotel at 3 o'clock in the morning, laughing and falling all over the place with some groupies that we hoped to smuggle into the hotel. The hotel owner got tired of this after a couple of times and ended up giving us a key to let ourselves in.

The cabaret work came in fast and furious. The George Cooper Organization had us working very steady. We would do a week of cabaret followed by a few weeks of "One Nighters" and then back to a week of cabaret again. The money was not that good but at least we were being seen around the country. We discovered that it would be more appropriate to wear stage suits for the Club and Cabaret circuit and to leave our "Mod Gear" for the "One Nighters". So The Tornados still had two personalities. We were the "Joe Meek created" instrumental group striving to break out and become a hit vocal group and a polished professional Night Club Act. In the clubs we performed with a smooth professionalism and at the dance halls we put on our Mod Gear and turned up the volume. We had a Club set and a Dance Hall set. Harry Dawson suggested that we should get stage suits and we paid another visit to Dougie Millings and got fitted for dark blue mohair suits which I believe that Joe paid for. We also attempted another photo session. This one was a success, as far as Joe was concerned. As the bulk of our work was to be Cabaret it was decided that we should wear our suits and look real sharp. So we ended up with the typical glossy black and white shots with everybody smiling and looking like such a nice bunch of blokes. This was perfect for the Night Club scene but definitely the wrong image for a band that was hoping to become a hit group and be a part of this new changing world of music. Anyway Joe finally got exactly what he wanted and was happy.

We found out from Joe that Harry Dawson had landed us a TV show in Barcelona Spain. We would fly over there for about three or four days and be part of a show featuring various artists. Harry said that the money was good and that it would be like a holiday for us. We would be booked into a first class hotel and have a few days to enjoy ourselves. We were obviously thrilled and after having to get John Davies an emergency passport we flew out to Barcelona. Harry Dawson said he would fly out there too and meet us there.

Well Harry was right about the hotel, it was a real nice place, much, much nicer than the seedy bed and breakfast places we stayed at when we worked the working men's clubs. We spent the first afternoon and evening checking out the area around the hotel and having a few drinks. John and I were really happy when we realized that drinks seemed to be much cheaper in Spain. The next day Harry Dawson showed up at the hotel along with his wife and two kids. Harry took us over to the TV studios where we were shown the set and we checked out the equipment. Dave was not too happy with the

"Mickey Mouse" organ but what choice did we really have? One by one the other artists arrived. They had a full orchestra of musicians for the singers. There was a black girl singer from England and also a singer from France called Christophe. They had each act run through their set. We were first and we had no problem with anything. It was easy for us, we didn't need any orchestra, we just played "Pop Art goes Mozart" "Telstar" and probably we did a vocal. Then the black girl did her set and in the last number she ripped off her skirt which took the orchestra and especially the conductor completely by surprise. They were all centering their attention on her and not on their music and with the conductor bending his head around as far as he could to get a good look at her, the orchestra practically fell into disarray. We were amused by this scenario as we were not shocked by her skirt coming off at all we just presumed that maybe this performance was unusual or maybe even not allowed on Spanish TV. Sure enough we were right, and much to the disappointment of the orchestra she was asked not to remove her skirt during the final take. Christophe, who we presumed would probably be the star of the show performed last. It seemed to us that there looked like there were problems from the start. We couldn't understand what every one was saying but when we kept seeing them go over and over the same song with the orchestra getting more and more annoyed, we figured out that Christophe was probably screwing up. He looked like he could have been stoned but who knows? In the end they looked like they all probably gave up with the rehearsal and we proceeded to do the actual show. There was no audience so I guess they added in the crowd sounds later. Every thing went fine. We did our set, the black girl did her set and kept her skirt on and Christophe was still trying to get his stuff down when we decided to leave. We couldn't stand the embarrassment any more.

Just before we left we were told that we could get paid so Dave and Pete went to pick up the cash which was in Spanish currency. Back at the hotel we met in Pete's room where we proceeded to split up the money. It did seem to be much more that we were used to getting paid and after taking out Harry's commission we divided up the balance of the cash between ourselves. We had no sooner done this when a knock came at the door. It was Harry Dawson coming to pick up his commission. We gladly handed it to him but were informed that Harry had to collect the taxes from us that were to be paid to the Spanish government. We doubted that very much but we ended up by handing over more of our money to him. It probably went into the pockets of the George Cooper Organization. We were green in the business and let them get away with it. Anyway our work was over and we still had a couple of days left to enjoy ourselves.

The following morning we hired a couple of cabs and along with Harry Dawson and his family we took a ride to the beach to spend the day there. We laid out in the sun which was a great luxury for us and from time to time John and I paid visits to a little kiosk on the beach which amongst other various sundries they sold wine on draught. It was hot so we downed the wine in large quantities much to the concern of the kiosk guy who continually laughed and pointed to his head signifying that we would get smashed on that stuff. Well we did, and when it was time for us to leave John and I were falling all over the place and with extreme difficulty we managed to pull our clothes on and stumble over to where the cabs were waiting. The drive back to the hotel was a complete blur for me and the next thing I remembered was that I was lying in a hot bath in the hotel room with John Davies. We were both laughing and completely out of our minds and at one point John got out of the bath and left to wander the corridors of the hotel, much to the disgust of some of the American guests there. When he returned John pulled me up out of the bath as I was sinking under the water. The bath actually straightened us up and after a meal at the hotel we decided to go out on the town again.

After a few drinks we wandered around and came across this amusement arcade which had what you might call a "Ghost Train" ride. As we were all in a jovial mood we decided to take a ride. Two people could fit in each car so Pete and Dave sat in the first car, followed by John and I in the second. Roger said he would not ride and waited for us at the exit. The ride started and Pete and Dave disappeared into the darkness, John and I followed shortly. It was a typical kind of Ghost Train you travelled in complete darkness and here and there you were subjected to various scary situations. Suddenly as John and I rounded a bend we saw a light up ahead which turned out to be a cluster of mannequins depicting some macabre scene. All at once somebody jumped out at us from behind the display making these ghostly sounds. It was Dave. He had jumped out of his car that he had shared with Pete and was now jumping into our car that had hardly room for two. Of course we were all hysterical until close to the end of the ride we were suddenly faced with a huge decline in the track which was followed by a very sharp turn. We all screamed as we hurtled down the track and when the car reached the turn it flew off the rails, there was a loud explosion and a huge electric flash and the three of us were thrown into complete darkness. This occurrence gave us a more serious outlook and we stopped laughing and started to be a little concerned about our safety. There we were in complete darkness not able to see how to get out or where we were. Somewhere in the darkness we saw a flash light and two of the proprietors of the ride approached us. We couldn't understand what they were saying but we could tell that they were really annoyed. All they could say was "Two no three, two no three." They led us out of the darkness and when we appeared from a hidden door somewhere, Roger and Pete were in fits of laughter. Roger could not understand what had happened to Dave as he saw only Pete emerge from the ride, and when the big power failure happened he expected that something weird had occurred. We tried to buy tickets to go on the ride again but for some reason they would not sell us and were quite happy to see us all leaving, stumbling and laughing down the street.

When we were doing the TV show we met an English guy there who had been living in Barcelona for sometime and he advised us that we should pay a visit to the Red Light district before we returned to England. He assured us that all the girls were clean and anyway the oldest profession was legal there and he provided us with details of how much to pay & etc. He told us that they all hung out in the bars. When I asked him how you knew who the whores were he told me that if they are in the bar they are in the business. So after our joy ride on the Ghost Train we all headed down to the Red Light District where we proceeded to check out the bars. We looked different to everybody else as we were wearing our new mod gear, clothing that was different to what guys were wearing in Spain and as we spoke no Spanish I guess that we were looked upon as some kind of tourist novelties. For us, the guys fresh up from the country, it was unreal. You walked into a bar and standing against the wall was a line of women. At one end of the line stood young chicks and as the line grew in length, you ended up with the big tough, heavy mommas. The young chicks were kind of nice to us, but the mature women teased us and called us babies. After a few bars and a few drinks, Pete and I got separated from the other three guys and ended up in a bar together and we thought "What the hell, let's do it." and after plucking up enough courage we took a girl each, and they were pretty nice looking girls and they led us upstairs over the bar to the rooms there. My heart was pounding as the girls took us by the hand and led us up to the top of the stairs where there was a small kiosk with a guy who took the money for the room. Before we could pay he demanded our passports, which unfortunately Pete and I were not carrying. And in broken English we were told" No passport, no fuckee, fuckee." Anyone could imagine how we felt. After we went through the whole thing we got refused at the end. Not to be outdone, Pete and I grabbed a cab and raced back to the hotel and with passports in hand made our way back to the same bar, where we fulfilled our desires, but not with the same girls.

All good things come to an end and it was time to return to England. We were picked up from the hotel by taxi. On the way to the airport Dave announced that he had to take a piss real bad and as the driver spoke no English we could not communicate with him. Dave decided to piss in an empty bottle of Johnny Walker whiskey that John Davies and I had just finished. When we arrived at the airport we had no idea what to do with the bottle of pee. We were immediately surrounded by a bunch of burly porters all ready to carry our suitcases and guitars into the terminal, which they did and after putting the baggage down for us on the conveyors they stood around as if expecting a tip. Dave, in one of his most memorable actions pointed to the bottle in his hand gesturing that he was giving them this bottle of whiskey as a tip. We all picked up speed to get out of there as the biggest guy of all bent down to pick up the bottle that Dave had put down on the ground for them. We saw them walking away with big smiles on their faces together with a lot of very excited conversation of their anticipated drinking party that they would be having. We were so glad to reach the safety of the plane as those guys could have killed us.

The next few months were filled with the usual gigs either doing one night stands or weeks of cabaret up north. We were getting more and more used to the life as professional musicians, getting used to staying in all kinds of places, most of them pretty bad, as that was all we could afford, and working and living together. We would still occasionally get people who questioned our authenticity as The Tornados and we were relieved when Joe announced one day that we were now The New Tornados, if anybody asked. Our publicity photos depicted us as The New Tornados but the two 45's that we had issued with Joe, "Is That A Ship I Hear" and "Pop Art Goes Mozart" were as The Tornados.

We began to discuss various ideas with Joe at our recording sessions. Joe was getting very hot on the idea of us becoming a comedy act. We toyed with the thoughts of making an LP all based on comical songs, and which Joe decided would be called "They're Not Just Pretty Faces." There would be spoken parts as well as music on the record. The closest that we ever got to that was on "Do You Come Here Often" B side of "Is That A Ship I Hear" At one point in the instrumental Dave Watts and I held a conversation just like we were at a club somewhere. We also put down a track which was based on the old country folk song "A North Country Maid" but in our version she was Sandra the Stripper who had strayed down to London and eventually died from pneumonia from standing around in the nude. That track (backing only) must still exist somewhere in those tea chests. We also thought of writing a song about flat hunting, as Joe just a few weeks before had told Roger, Pete and Me that we would have to move out of the flat on Holloway Road as he thought that he had carried us this far and now we should take care of ourselves. He actually gave the flat to Richie Blackmore and his wife as Joe said that they needed it more than we did. We had no problem with that and found a decent place at 75 Portland Road in Bayswater. We had told Joe the funny stories of our efforts in trying to find a suitable flat. We got several addresses and checked them out. Joe laughed when we told him of how we entered a street and how everything looked great but the further we drove down the street the worse the houses got and when we finally reached the building where the flat was located we found holes in the roof and rotting floor boards and God knows what else. Joe thought that we could get some kind of comical song and situation out of this. Looking back I think that it could have been a good idea and would have certainly been fun. I believe that Joe would have enjoyed it too as when he was a youngster he liked to dress up and perform in theatrics. Had he lived maybe we would have created an LP based on comedy or at least it could have been a concept album.

Sometimes at the sessions Joe would take a break and go downstairs for a while. He would leave us up in the studio and would be secretly recording our conversations. We would be there just sitting around talking about things. We were oblivious to this except for Dave who somehow knew what Joe was up to and by sign language and whispering we got the message. Dave took over the conversation and we all went along with it. Dave said that what Joe says is right and we all agreed just saying the right things to make Joe happy. When he returned he played the tape back to us and really got a big kick out of thinking that he had tricked us. He was giggling and totally enjoyed the prank. After he heard what Dave had said Joe proclaimed in a very happy voice of authority "Of course I'm fucking right." and followed it with a big smile.

Joe was very happy to tell us that he had heard from Harry Dawson, and that Harry was interested in booking the group to appear on the Big Star Show Of 1966, which was a summer season show held at the South Pier at Blackpool. We would also have to back the whole show. The three main stars were to be Marty Wilde, Billy J Kramer and The Dakotas and Adam Faith. Adam was to be the star of the show followed by Billy J Kramer and then Marty Wilde. Joe asked us if we thought we could do it and we said that we could so he arranged a rehearsal with Marty Wilde as a trial run to see how things worked out. Marty said that he would show us the songs. We met him one afternoon at a theatre to run through his set. It was a great thrill for me and probably the Holder brothers too as we remembered him from the first rock shows like "Drumbeat" and "Oh Boy" and he had some big hits such as "Donna", "Sea Of Love", "Endless Sleep" and "Teenager In Love". He was big and tall and wore these thick dark glasses and sported a fine toupee.

The Tornados at South Pier, Blackpool, Lancashire in summer of 1966.
(L-R) Dave Watts, Pete Holder, John Davies, Robb Huxley and Roger Holder

Marty was friendly and very comical. He used a Gibson acoustic/electric the same as John Lennon had used and he proceeded to show us the chords to the songs. It was quite easy for us as we had grown up listening to that music and had also played some of the songs before. So we had no trouble in learning his repertoire so our first rehearsal with him turned out fine.

At the rehearsal he was accompanied by his wife, Joyce, formerly Joyce Baker of the Vernons Girls. Marty and Joyce met on one of the shows promoted by Jack Good in the late fifties and early sixties. The Vernons Girls were a collection of girls employed by Vernons football pools in Liverpool recruited into being a choir that performed on a charitable basis at old people's homes. Jack Good gave them their break when he invited them to appear on his TV show *OH BOY*. They put out a number of singles in the late fifties early sixties. It was ironic that once Marty got married, and it was very well covered in the press with a picture of Marty and Joyce frolicking in a swimming pool on their honeymoon in some far off exotic island, that his career really seemed to taper off. But we cannot blame Joyce for this entirely. Although when a big singer got married it was usual that he might lose many female fans, Marty was also battling against the up and coming younger entertainers such as The Beatles and Rolling Stones who were appealing to the younger generation. It is notable how when John Lennon got married to Cynthia, Brian Epstein insisted the marriage be kept a secret as he thought that it would be bad for the group's image. Maybe Brian Epstein had learned from what he had seen happen to other singers and anyway he was very friendly with Larry Parnes. Marty liked The Beatles and at that time included their song called "Every Little Thing" in his act. Marty was also a very accomplished songwriter himself. Regardless of whether Marty had got married or not his bright star would ultimately have dimmed considerably just like other singers such as Adam Faith. In fact the show that we were going to back as The New Tornados on the South Pier, Blackpool in 1966, starring Adam Faith and Marty Wilde was a fine example of a show featuring artists that were on the decline. As The Tornados we were also a part of this waning group of entertainers who were making their way down the stairs of success. As we had been recruited by Joe Meek to become The Tornados we were on the way down and we had not even been to the top. Even so I would not have missed this opportunity for anything as I will always remember the thrill of standing on-stage beside these entertainers who had been to the top and had been performing on TV before my young eyes in days when I had not even touched a guitar. I guess that Marty was satisfied with our first rehearsal and so a second was arranged at the same location. This time we arrived early and having set up our gear decided to sit in the auditorium and wait for Marty to arrive. Soon he arrived and was accompanied by two very attractive girl singers. They were tall and wore mini skirts and high heels. Our attention was immediately captivated and we all got up and approached the stage led by

Roger and Dave. Marty introduced them as the Diamond Twins. So-nia and Sandra. Two very pretty girls medically identical but their looks were different. Sonia had brown eyes and dark hair while Sandra was blond with blue eyes. Born an hour apart and the only birth of their kind that doctors knew of at that time. Not only did they have great musical talent in their piano playing and singing abilities they were gifted with Perfect Pitch, which means that they could pitch any note that they wanted and it would always be perfectly in tune. In fact many times when we wanted to tune up our guitars we would say "Hey Son, give us an E", and sure enough it would be right on key.

The Diamond Twins would be appearing with us on the Blackpool show and agreed to also appear as Marty's vocal backing group along with Marty's wife Joyce. They also brought their musical sheets which they gave to Dave. These were the numbers that they would be featur-ing in their act and had been written out by their pianist for us. We concentrated on Marty's stuff that day and together with the three piece vocal backing by the girls, with occasional help from Pete and me things began to start to sound pretty good.

A few years later Roger Holder married Sandra and Dave Watts married Sonia. They are still married. What a musical combination. We have Dave, an excellent piano and organ player who could also sing and entertain, with Sonia, a great singer and accomplished pian-ist and Roger, bass player and vocalist with Sandra, a great singer and pianist. That's a whole lot of music right there.

Publicity photos 1966

(L-R) Pete Holder, Dave Watts, John Davies, Robb Huxley, Pete Holder, Dave
Watts, Roger Holder

(L-R) Pete Holder, Dave Watts, Robb Huxley, John Davies, Roger Holder

THE TORNADOS CHAPTER TWO

The Big Star Show of 66 Blackpool summer season with Adam Faith, Marty Wilde and Billy J Kramer.
The creation, recording and release of "Is That A Ship I Hear" and the truth behind the creation and recording of "Do You Come Here Often" the controversial, first ever openly gay. record release.
Opening night of Blackpool Show is a success for The Tornados.
Cooper organization is elated with Tornados performance

Photos taken on beach to publicise new record "Is That A Ship I Hear"
(L-R) John Davies, Dave Watts, Pete Holder, Robb Huxley (front) and Roger Holder

As a kind of a dress rehearsal we were invited to play with Marty at a charity performance at the Savoy Hotel in London. We played our set as The Tornados and then Marty came on with Joyce and the Diamond Twins and we ran through the set. Marty split up his set by doing a Medley of his hits and a few other numbers. Marty explained to us that he was tired of playing those old numbers and had combined them all into a medley to get them all out of the way so that he could get on with other numbers that he preferred to play. I remember he did a very good version of "You've Lost That Loving Feeling" which he featured in his act. The show went over very well. It was in fact a fund raising show for Israel. The audience was made up of wealthy Jews who were sending money to Israel to help with defence and to buy tanks. At the close of the evening when we were winding down the show many in the audience approached the stage with compliments to us on our playing. They said that we had put new blood into old veins. When we finished our last number for the evening and were saying goodnight the crowd started to ask us to play longer. As they knew that we had played for charity they swiftly came up with some donations for us and we got paid very nicely for playing the extra time. This was my first contact with anything to do with Israel. Little did I know at that time how much Israel would be part of my musical career and for that matter how much it would affect and influence the rest of my life.

Joe was very eager to get another single ready to be put out as our second single as The Tornados. He explained that we would be away for several weeks in Blackpool and as we were working seven nights a week there would be no time to record. So we all met at the studio to hear Joe's latest idea of what our next single should be. Firstly he told us that he had come up with this new beat that nobody else had ever done before. He played it to us on tape and it sounded like somebody banging on a piece of wood or a floorboard in the rhythm of "Bam, bam, bombom, bombom", "Bam, bam, bombom, bombom." The Tornados looked at each other with looks of amazement wondering what Joe could be up to now. We were afraid to think of what was to come next. Would we be told to go away and write a whole new instrumental on "Bam, bam, bombom, bombom," or what? Well fortunately not. Joe had a tune on tape. He played it for us and it was basically a melody that somebody was playing on the Lowry organ with some bass and drums in the background. On listening to it after many years I regard it as a good example of Joe taking a backing track of something and writing something else over it. As The Tornados we took the piece and constructed it as an instrumental, putting in the correct chords and making any adjustments that were necessary along with any suggestions that Joe had. At one point in rehearsing the number, as a joke we used the beat from "Hold Tight" by Dave Dee, Dozy, Mick and Titch in the modulation. It was an adventurous prank for us to play on him not knowing how Joe would appreciate it. He put his head around the doorway asking what "That" was, and as we started to explain that it was from Dave Dee he realized what it was and told us to leave it in. I think he got a big kick out of knocking somebody else off as he was always complaining that somebody was always knocking him off.

When we finally got the number down we started to record it. We put the basic backing track down with Dave playing the melody on the Lowry organ together with the bass and drums and rhythm guitar. When that was all put down and Joe was satisfied he told Pete to play the same melody on top of what Dave had played on the organ. At one point in the rehearsal with Pete Joe came into the studio and started to take a look at Pete's Swiss Echo unit. He told Pete to keep playing and then he left and came back with a screwdriver which he pushed into the tape mechanism of the echo unit causing it to make a kind of fluttering or shuddering sound on the melody. "Yeah that's it" he said and ran back into the control room while we all stood around in disbelief. Joe had created a sound that occurs when there is a malfunction with the echo unit and used it to create this weird Chinese sounding effect on Pete's guitar. Dave Watts showed his appreciation during Pete's take by pulling down his pants and mooning Pete while he was putting down the track. All this was unseen by Joe and we all fell apart in the studio unable to contain our laughter. Joe then instructed Dave to put in some fill-in bits on the piano which Dave did with little effort. The accompanying melody that he played behind Pete in the middle part was very good indeed. At the same time Joe had John Davies put on some tambourine and he had me shaking bells and dragging them across a Glockenspiel at certain parts of the number. So as our second single Joe had come up with this instrumental which we had helped him perfect and had no idea what it was to be called or anything about it. Then we came to the question of the B side. At this time what with our Cabaret shows and use of comedy and Joe's suggestion that we should put out a new album by The New Tornados which would be a collection of comedy songs, we decided to approach the B side with that in mind.

We met at the studio a few days later to record a B side. We really didn't have anything that we thought would be suitable for a B side and we were nervous as we did not know what to expect from Joe. Dave as always came up with an idea and started to play a kind of Jazzy swing tune. We were all standing around listening to Dave and talking about ideas for the number with Joe. I came up with something and Joe ridiculed me over it and I got kind of upset. Joe said that we should record the number and walked towards the control room. To show how I was pissed off at Joe for putting down my ideas I threw a minor temper tantrum throwing my guitar case down on the floor and slamming it shut. Joe picked up on it right away and strode towards me. He obviously knew why I was acting that way. "If that's what you're gonna do" he shouted "You can get out of here. Get out and sit downstairs." I put my Fender back in the case gently and disappeared down the twisting stairs like a sad little puppy with my tail between my legs. I sat down on a chair in the office area and listened while the band rehearsed the number and got the backing track down. When they had done that they tried to put on a guitar solo but Pete was not having much success. I heard footsteps coming down the stairs and it was Joe. He came up to me and in a very tender way said "Don't worry, I want you to come upstairs and put on a guitar solo." He went into the other room and came out carrying a cheap old beat up acoustic guitar, "You'll use this" he said with a smile and handed it to me. I climbed up the twisty stairs to the studio with a feeling of happiness knowing that I was back up in the studio again but at the same time I was horrified to think of what I was going to do with this piece of crap guitar. Luckily I had heard them playing the number over and over when they were recording it so I knew how it went. As I appeared in the studio Dave greeted me with "Here's Robbie. Are you gonna play a solo for us Robbie?" I guess they were happy to see me back and I was happy to be back. I tuned up the guitar to the Lowry and took a seat. Joe came in and started to mic up the guitar. He took the big old mic from behind the screen and positioned it close to the guitar. Throughout this he continually smiled at me and asked me if I was comfortable. I played along with the backing track and after a few takes Joe said "OK that's it" and we had a take down. It wasn't really much of a solo and was almost buried by the backing but I suppose that it served its purpose.

Joe said that he thought that we should put some funny talking on the track. We all bounced ideas around and finally decided that Dave and I should carry on a conversation together as if we were in a club somewhere. We would talk about fashion and chatting up birds, and be sure to mention something about the pirate radio stations. So Dave and I started to talk. We put on these real camp voices and by running through it a few times we got the idea of where we were going with it.

We imagined that we had just met at a night club, and we were chatting together. Joe suggested that I should ask Dave "Do you come here often" And that Dave should answer by saying "Only when the pirate ships go off the air." Dave came up with the bit about the pyjama style shirts being "In." Joe liked that very much and he really got excited when he told me that my reply would be that "Pyjamas are out as far as I'm concerned anyway." Dave and I came up with "Who cares? Well I know of a few people that do" and Joe chimed in with "Yes you would" which he instructed Dave to say in a very sarcastic way. So we had the first verse figured out. Dave and I presumed that we would be on the lookout for women so Dave said "Here's two girls coming now, what do you think?" Joe immediately told Dave not to say "girls" and just say "Here's two coming now, what do you think?" I of course replied with the corny line "Mine's alright but I don't like the look of yours", which must have been used at least a million times before and followed it with the equally hackneyed phrase "Well I must be off then, yeah you're not looking so good" which was used at least two million times. My reply to Dave's "I'll see you down the Dilly" was "Not if I see you first you won't", which Joe came up with and was also a very corny line. But in some way it all seemed to fit probably because it was all done "Tongue in Cheek." Dave and I practised with the two verses reciting the lines gradually getting the timing right so that the conversation was spread evenly over the two verses. Throughout the whole session and particularly during the recording of the talking parts Joe was totally happy, excited and smiling. We were not really aware at the time but Joe was really excited as he must have felt that he was in some way making a Gay statement by the way that he had Dave and I put on those camp voices and carry on that conversation. We had a ball doing it also. It was really like having fun, the pressure was off and we all had chances to be creative. Any time that you had that type of atmosphere in the studio with Joe it was always good and we enjoyed every minute of it whenever it happened. Dave and I never thought that we were portraying a couple of gay guys but at the same time if it came across that way it was OK, it was fun and we thought we were being cute. Joe's sole purpose in producing this single was to aim it at the pirate radio stations and try to get them to play it. He hoped that the success that the stations were having along with the controversy they were creating would rub off on The Tornados playing their new Joe Meek instrumental titled "Is That A Ship I Hear", and maybe become a hit. Time has shown that the original demo that Joe played us was called "Is That A Spaceship I Hear?" He also wrote to us when we were on the Adam Faith show saying that he had put seagulls on the number and was calling it "Is That A Pirate Ship I Hear?" This was the first time that we ever had any idea of what the title of the number would be. I don't think that we realised where Joe meant to go with this number at the time and anyway we were not interested in this kind of music as we were still hoping to win Joe over one day and get a vocal "A" side out. I guess we just put up with it and went along with it. We didn't have much choice anyway we were just an instrument of Joe Meek's creativity.

It has been written that Joe took a tape recorder into a men's toilet in a club somewhere and secretly recorded a conversation which he then used for "Do You Come here Often" This was absolutely untrue and was just another case of fictitious stories made up by people in order to present Joe as some kind of a perverted individual who when judged by today's standards would not appear to be so. He was just a homosexual and most likely bisexual and probably fought within himself to try to resolve his dilemma. Any time that he could creep out of his closet and create something like "Do You Come Here Often" and have a fun time doing it, probably brought him a great deal of satisfaction and release. To my knowledge this is the only track that Joe ever put out that had any noticeable Gay references. The Gay references also do really depend on the way that they are interpreted. As far as we were concerned we were looking for girls in a club. Joe was looking for something else.

Things were beginning to get into motion with the Blackpool show. Dave received a package from the producers that contained all the music sheets for the show. There were no sheets for Billy J Kramer as he had his own band, we already knew Marty Wilde's stuff and we met with the guitarist from Adam Faith's band who gave us some discs and showed us the basic songs on the guitar. We figured out Adam's numbers mostly from the records, just like we had done covering songs as The Whirlwinds. However there were all other kinds of musical pieces that we had to learn and rehearse, such as the comedians' numbers, pieces for the dancing routines, and also show production numbers. Dave took up the position as leader in the process of getting the numbers down, which was OK by us as Pete, Roger and I had some minimal musical knowledge but we could not sight read well enough. We could read chord symbols and follow bars so that's basically how we did it. John basically did what he wanted on the drums once that he knew the pieces but Dave really was the guy that made it happen as he had received musical training and could read the dots.

We decided that it would be a good idea to do all our rehearsals down at Aylesmore farm. We would all stay at the Holders' farmhouse for a week and we would rehearse over at the Welsh House just like we did as The Whirlwinds and Saxons. With the exception of Dave we all came from that area so it was nice for us to get home. John and I got to go to Gloucester and Cheltenham to see our folks. Everyone was excited to hear that we would be playing on this all star show in Blackpool for the summer. While we were rehearsing in Newent, Joe came down and we met together with him in Cinderford where we appeared with him at a fund raising fête for handicapped children. We had done one there before with him as The Saxons. Joe asked us how our rehearsals were coming along and mentioned to us that Harry Dawson had been calling up from the Cooper organization as they were feeling worried that we might not be capable of dealing with the task of backing the whole show. As far as we were concerned we thought that we were doing fine and let Joe know that George Cooper should not worry. Joe was also hesitant to tell us that the Cooper Organization had even got another band on stand by just in case we didn't work out. After Joe had made his speech we played a set and he proceeded to give out kazoos to the kids so that they could participate in the music. He also gave away demo discs and glossy promotion pictures of his artists. Joe brought his mother with him and she was obviously very proud of him. At the end of the day we got to make some money as we played at a dance that evening at Lister's Hall. At our appearance at the fête there was a youngster there who had a small cassette recorder and recorded the set. That tape surfaced over twenty years later and there are various copies of it floating around.

The Annual Fete for the Forest of Dean Society for Mentally Handicapped Children took place on June 11th 1966 and as the Blackpool show was scheduled to open on June 24th after a few more days we left for Blackpool. There was to be a week or ten days of rehearsals to get the show down. A few weeks earlier we had been working in Manchester and had taken a drive over to Blackpool to check things out. We took a look at the South Pier where we would be performing from the last week in June until the middle of September. The South Pier was the third pier to be built in Blackpool following the North and Central piers and was opened up in 1893 and featured two brass bands and a fifty piece orchestra together with a choir performing

Handel's Messiah for the visitors' entertainment. This was a far cry from the rock shows that would be held there in the mid sixties. It was originally called the Victoria Pier but was later renamed the South Pier in 1930. The Grand Pavilion situated on the pier could seat 3000 people and The Regal Theatre was located at the pier entrance. In later years the Regal was converted into an amusement arcade. In 1964 The Grand Pavilion was totally destroyed by fire. When we arrived at the pier in 1966 we were greeted by a brand new theatre that had been built in its place. We walked through the arcade and strolled along the pier and made our way to the theatre. As we reached the main entrance we were approached by a guy who asked us if we were in the "business", and after he found out that we were The Tornados, he introduced himself as being Al Paige, comedian and entertainer who would be appearing with us on the show. He took us inside and we met the stage manager Sid Raymond, who was busy with the stage hands organizing the sets for the show. We took a look at the dressing rooms that were situated off to the left hand side of the stage and we noticed that our name "The Tornados" had been placed on the door. We were next door to the Diamond twins and Marty Wilde and across from Billy J Kramer. Al Paige and fellow comedian Johnny Clamp were sharing a room and Adam Faith's dressing room was located on the other side of the stage along with the rooms for the dancing girls known as the Fox Miller Girls. On our way out Al asked us where we would be staying and as we had no idea he gave us the name of a real estate agent that specialized in finding accommodation for Show Biz people. We were able to find a nice fully furnished three bedroom house on Whitegate Drive to stay in.

The first day of the rehearsals we all met down at the pier and got the gear inside and set it up on stage in the rear. The Tornados would be on stage throughout the whole show as we were backing everyone except Billy J Kramer who had his own band. It was a good break for us as Billy closed the first half of the show which was followed by the interval. We set up our music sheets on stands in front of us and bit by bit the cast began to show up and congregate in their dressing rooms. The producer, John Lyndon summoned everyone to the stage and when we were all together he proceeded to give us a brief outline of the running of the show. We then started to work on the opening number for the show which was "Things Are Swinging" and it involved the whole cast. The dancing girls would start the whole thing off and at a certain point comedian Johnny Clamp was to enter the stage, walk up to the mic, and proceed to introduce the cast who would all line up at the front of the stage and when Adam was introduced as the star of the show he sang the number together with the rest of the cast.

Telegram from Billy J Kramer to The Tornados

John Lyndon had explained to Johnny Clamp the spot where he should make his entrance but Johnny couldn't get it right to save his life. He either came on too early, too late, and one time he came on in the middle of the dance routine and was dodging in between the dancers. We were virtually pissing ourselves and John Lyndon was getting really pissed off and began screaming "No, no, noooo" and things turned really bad and we kind of felt bad for Johnny. It was pitiful the way that Lyndon berated him and belittled him. So we said that we would give Johnny the nod when to enter the stage. He stood there nervously in the wings watching and waiting. We gave him the nod and he made a perfect entrance much to everyone's relief and proceeded to run through the spiel and introduce the acts. He ran through it too fast and by the time Adam came on, Adam had to stand doing nothing for half a verse until the music came back around again. John Lyndon started up on Johnny again saying that he was standing like he was working in a fish and chip shop and introduced the acts like he was calling out bingo numbers. He eventually got it down to a point where the producer was satisfied. As a band we really had no trouble with the music, the producer, or the artists. With help from Les Baguley, the Diamond Twins' pianist we were able to go through their set easily.

When it was our turn to do our set John Lyndon was eager to see what we had. He had seen that we were capable enough to be a good backing band but what did we do for our act? As always we started with a slightly shortened version of "Telstar" and featured a vocal such as "Let It Be Me". We did our comedy routine which got to be more elaborate and adventurous as the season proceeded. We basically poked fun at other artists through playing their hit, very similar to what The Barron Knights had done with Call Up The Groups. I was running all over the stage with my finger in my butt singing "Keep on Running" as if Spencer Davis had been taking Ex Lax for constipation. John Lyndon would not let us use the word "Constipation" so we had to cut it out. A week or so into the show we gradually reintroduced all the parts that were excluded from the show by the producer but from time to time Sid Raymond the stage manager would reprimand us saying "Do that again and you'll be off the show Cocker."

Before we left for Blackpool we had bought some stage props and items at the Joke Shop. So, when we did Marianne Faithful, Dave came out in a maxi skirt and a blond wig singing yesterday with a cushion stuck up his shirt to make him look pregnant, and lamenting "Now I'm in the family way." The funniest part was when Dave did Sandie Shaw. While we were doing the Walker Brothers' "Washing Up Is Very Hard To Do" Dave would dash off into the wings, pull off his pants and put on a small mini skirt (which I think he pinched from his sister) together with a blouse and a fake breast which displayed elaborate nipples covered by a Playtex bra.

As the weeks rolled on Dave would be sure to accidentally flash a nipple to the audience or letting them get a good look at his underwear and package that he wore under the mini skirt. We would all be having a good laugh and wonder what Dave would come up with next. He also had to do a quick change when he became Professor David Van Ripayacorsetsoff and came on to conduct the orchestra. He would be dressed in a black set of tails with boxer shorts and wearing a plastic bald wig with glasses and carrying a conductor's baton. We would actually piss ourselves when he would appear as he looked so funny and he would always try doing something unexpected to surprise us and make us laugh. One night he decided that he would stand on top of the stool that he sat on behind his Hammond to conduct the orchestra. As he began he started to topple and ended up falling off through the curtains and into the wings. The loud thump he made when he hit the floor caused the reverb unit to make a loud crashing noise like thunder which totally took the audience by surprise and caused a sensation. We all got a big laugh out of it and sure enough Dave was sure to fall off that stool every single night until the end of the season. If by chance the reverb didn't go off Dave would secretly give the Hammond a good kick to ensure the success of the effect. We would then go into "Wade In The Water" by Graham Bond and that was it more or less. Apart from the few bits here and there that Lyndon asked us to delete he was pleased with our performance and we were able to move on. We had a break at this point as Johnny Clamp did his spot and was followed by Billy J Kramer and The Dakotas so we were not required for this.

We went off to the dressing rooms and hung out with Marty and Joyce. It was always great to hang out and talk with Marty. He was funny and we had some good laughs. He told us that his favourite new word was "Flange" and he christened me with that name and throughout the season he always referred to me as Flange. At one point he did get serious and asked us to back him the best that we could as he thought, and had always maintained that he was better than Adam.

In fact he predicted that his act would look better than Adam's as The Tornados would be hidden behind a gauze curtain during Adam's act but in Marty's act we would all be up front together with him and with the Diamond Twins as back up singers with Joyce it would look and feel exciting, and it was. Marty's act was exciting especially for me as it was still hard to believe that there I was on the same stage playing alongside of Marty Wilde whom I had watched on the B.B.C.'S *Six Five Special* when I was just about thirteen years old. It was always a thrill when we opened up with "Jezebel." Marty sang it really well and he looked good as he was very tall and had a certain "Down to earth" attitude on stage which the audience liked. After he dispensed with his medley of hits he would use his guitar and we would all join him in "Every Little Thing" by The Beatles. It was a way for Marty to try to clutch on to the changing musical trends and keep up with the times. He told us that he liked The Beatles' songs and I believe that he really enjoyed singing that number. He closed his set with "You've Lost That Loving Feeling" by The Righteous Brothers, which he also did very well. All in all he had a good, tight, dynamic and exciting set and we had no trouble at all running through it at the rehearsals.

Adam's rehearsal went very well with us when we finally got around to it. In fact all the artist's acts that we backed went without a hitch. The only things that took more time were the dance routines and the numbers that certain artists did together. They would have to learn various moves and dance steps that were shown to them by the producer with help from Betty Fox and Shelagh Miller the choreographers of the Fox Miller Girls.

Just like Marty and Billy J Kramer, Adam did a medley of his hits. He also featured "Unchain My Heart" by Ray Charles, "Michael Row The Boat Ashore", "A Message To Martha, and a version of "When Johnny Comes Marching Home" which we started at a slow beat and each verse got faster and faster until it climaxed at the end. He also featured a joke in his act about a horse playing on a cricket team. We could see that Adam was pleased with our performance as his backing group as he popped his head behind the gauze curtain and said:"Thank you Lads" and followed it with a smile. Adam was very professional in the way he performed his act and always looked relaxed and comfortable. He got the audience to participate in "If I Had A Hammer" and had them going "Ooh, ooh, ooh, ooh"

Billy J Kramer's set was very similar to Adam and Marty's but he did not do a medley of his hits, moreover he just played the numbers as they were on record, and that was basically his act. Billy was friendly enough but The Dakotas were somewhat aloof. At that time they were comprised of Tony Mansfield (drums), Robin McDonald (bass) who were both co-founders of the band and Mick Green (guitar). They didn't make too much conversation with us and on stage they all looked rather serious, kind of staring into space and they did not move at all and just stood there like statues. Musically they were fine, especially Mick Green who played well and effortlessly but looked very stoic in his stance and attitude on stage. He didn't look at all happy and neither did the rest of the band.

The show opened up on Friday 24th June 1966. We had run the actual dress rehearsal on Thursday. Everything went very well with the exception of a few issues with Sid Raymond, the stage manager. As the opening of the show became imminent Sid was getting more belligerent and started to pick on members of the cast that were on the lower end of the bill. He particularly picked on Johnny Clamp and had a couple of goes at us from time to time about the volume that we played at and generally tried to exert his authority as stage manager wherever he could. In my opinion he did not do his job that well.

We were to play two shows a night and at the close of the first show, which went over very well and without a hitch with even Johnny Clamp being able to come in on time, thanks to us. We were highly congratulated by George Cooper and Harry Dawson when they came backstage to see us. They were actually quite ecstatic and even told us that we were the best backing band that they had ever used. They admitted that they had been worried about our ability to back the show and confessed that they had thought about having another band ready if we did not work out. Luckily all those concerns had now disappeared due to their satisfaction with our performance.

That Sunday Billy Fury and The Gamblers came into town to do the special show that we did every week. This was more of a rock show than a variety show and it was another chance for us to abandon our stage suits and don our mod gear. We cut out our usual comedy routine and adopted a rock band image. We were able to play a longer set and feature more rock songs. Marty Wilde also played the Sunday Show along with the Diamond Twins. Adam Faith had the day off and so did Billy J Kramer. We always enjoyed the Sunday shows as we could relax and play what we wanted. Al Paige acted as compére for the show. Once again it was a big thrill for me to be on the same stage as Billy Fury remembering that just a few short years ago I was a member of the audience and along with my sister we were screaming for "Billy." I had always been a big Billy Fury fan and still am to this day. I did not know it at that time but the following year 1967 would find me and some of the present Tornados performing as

Billy's backing group. Billy covered the second half of the show so we crept out into the auditorium to watch his performance. He was terrific.

We settled into the first week of shows quite well. The houses were pretty full each night and judging by the general feeling of the artists on the show we could tell that we were doing a good job. The Diamond Twins were going over well and they could really belt out their numbers. They had powerful voices and of course they were always on key! Their Pianist, Les Baguley seemed happy with everything and we began to build up a good relationship with him. We were starting to have some good laughs together. Marty was happy with the way his set was going over and as a matter of fact I don't remember him ever complaining throughout the season. Billy J Kramer was going down well and brought in a younger crowd. As Adam had appeared behind our gauze curtain each night at the end of the show and greeted us with a smile and a "Thank you lads" we presumed that everything was OK.

At the end of the first week Pete Holder went to pick up our wages from the theatre manager and continued to do so for the rest of the season. We were each paid thirty pounds a week. The critics from the local newspaper gave a very favourable review of the show drawing very special attention to The Tornados who in their words worked very well and hard throughout the whole show as well as doing their own spot featuring TV pop take-offs and some humour shock treatment. The shock treatment referred to a part of our act when we gave Pete this big build up for the song that he was about to sing and as he swaggered up to the mic and touched it with his hand a shower of sparks flew out from the mic and Pete collapsed onto the stage guitar and all as if electrocuted. Pete had bought this little device that you wound up and fit into your hand and when you released the pressure of holding it, it released these bright sparks. I think that Al Paige may have given us the idea. You were just supposed to be pretending to be getting small jolts from the "Electricity" but our scenario with Pete who was apparently getting knocked over by an electric shock proved to be too realistic and when some member of the audience wrote a letter to the newspaper that the South Pier was using faulty electrical equipment causing a member of The Tornados to get badly shocked, we were kindly asked to take it out of our act.

That Sunday Manfred Mann would open up their season of Sunday night shows. They were kind of aloof, to say the least. Nobody would acknowledge us except for Mike Hugg the drummer. Manfred Mann and Paul Jones minced around the stage while Jack Bruce, who must have been doing it for the money, was playing bass and was probably embarrassed, so he didn't speak to us. Their act was good, but mainly due to Paul Jones who basically carried the whole show as the rest of the band had little personality. They played at a surprisingly low volume but the kids that came to the Sunday night shows seemed to enjoy themselves. Even Sid Raymond didn't have to complain about their volume. He always had a go at us though. He knew that we really enjoyed the Sunday shows and that we liked to turn it up a bit, so he always had to say something.

As the first few weeks passed by we all settled in to the daily routine of the Summer Season Show. Roger Holder and Sandra from the Diamond Twins were going out together and it wasn't long before Roger moved in with Sandie along with her sister Sonia and their pianist Les Baguley. They shared a flat together. Dave Watts was also friendly with Sonia Diamond but their relationship took a little longer to blossom. We would get together on Sundays and I would cook Sunday dinner for 10 people at a time. One weekend Derek Holder brought my girlfriend Jenny up to stay with me for the weekend and we slept together down on the living room floor. She was a cute little Welsh girl but she was young and by the end of the weekend I knew that my affections for her were fading fast. She had acted like a little kid a couple of times, probably as she felt a bit inferior when the Diamond Twins were around. I told her I would see her in Gloucester after the Season was over but I never saw her again. She did come around to my folks' house when I was there. I had told my mother that if she should come around to tell her that I was staying out at the Holder's farm and would not be coming home. Poor little Jenny left in tears.

Eventually she married a guy in the Army stationed in Germany. She was always talking about him when she was going out with me so I guess she got what she wanted anyway.

As the show progressed we gradually became very relaxed on stage and comfortable with the artists that we were backing. We began to inject various embellishments into our music. In Marty's act Pete and I put in some nice guitar parts and the Diamond Twins together with Joyce provided great backing vocals. Dave Watts for some reason got very bored in Marty's act and used the time to practice all kinds of runs on the keyboard with no sound or sometimes at a very low volume. Sometimes when Marty was introducing the numbers, raving keyboard runs could be heard very faintly in the background. We would turn round slightly and see Dave freaking out on the Hammond all on his own, apparently oblivious to everything around him.

One of the dance numbers that the Fox Miller Girls did was "These Boots Are Made For Walking" by Nancy Sinatra. Sometimes when John Davies was in a mischievous mood he would count the number in at almost twice the tempo making the instrumental so fast that the girls were out of breath and almost falling over each other by the time we had finished the number. They would stumble off stage glaring at us. We of course thought it was hilarious.

The only real problem we had was with stage manager, Sid Raymond who was beginning to pick on us more and more. We were threatened so many times with "You'll be off the show Cocker" that we became more or less immune to it and began to bite back a little. One day when he raised the house mic barely past my navel when I was to address the audience I looked at him across the stage and asked him if he thought I was Jimmy Clitheroe! This got a big laugh out of the audience, which was nice, but we saw it was getting worse with Sid so on a subsequent phone call to Joe, Pete Holder complained to him about it. In one of his letters to us Joe mentioned that with regard to the Stage Manager, he had spoken to Harry Dawson about it. As a matter of fact Joe wrote more to us in Blackpool than at any other time.

SOUTH PIER THEATRE
SOUTH PIER   -   BLACKPOOL

EVERY SUNDAY
Twice Nightly

TOP STAR ATTRACTION
with
FULL SUPPORTING PROGRAMME

Billy Fury and The Gamblers
JUNE 26th

Manfred Mann
JULY 3rd, 10th, 17th, 24th, 31st

Small Faces
AUGUST 7th, 13th, 36th, 27th   SEPT. 4th & 11th

SOUTH PIER THEATRE
Manager Leslie Lightfoot
BLACKPOOL
Telephone 43096
COMMENCING FRIDAY JUNE 24th.
twice nightly
6·15 & 8·30
Prices
8/6. 7/6. 6/6.
Larry Parnes the George Cooper Organisation Ltd
presents
THE BIG STAR SHOW OF 1966
ADAM FAITH
BILLY J. KRAMER
AND THE DAKOTAS
AL PAIGE
DIAMOND TWINS
FOX MILLER GIRLS
JOHNNY CLAMP
THE TORNADOS
MARTY WILDE
Every Sunday from June 26TH · · 6 AND 8 P.M. · · Seats 9/6. 8/6. 7/6.
Top Groups including 5 Sundays July 3RD. 10TH. 17TH. 24TH & 31ST
MANFRED MANN
AND Big Supporting Company – Watch Details & Dates of Our Big Sunday Attractions !!

The DIAMOND TWINS

THE TORNADOS CHAPTER THREE

Personal letters from Joe to The Tornados in Blackpool.
An unprofessional end to the Blackpool show, the "Lawrence Of Arabia" recording session with Joe.
The Cooper Organization lands us a spot in the Mike and Bernie Winters Birthday Show in Coventry. Robb falls in love with dancer Jackie Grant.
The Aberfan disaster benefits show where The Tornados meet up with the infamous London gangsters Ronnie and Reggie Kray.
Ronnie Kray wants to take over The Tornados and send them to USA.
Robb has an unusual, revealing and scary séance with the dancing girls.
Bert Weedon jams with The Tornados and reveals financial improprieties by The Cooper Organization.
Tornados' practical joking on the Coventry Show results in some dire consequences. Robb turns 21 and Jackie Grant gives up the Ventriloquist in favour of Robb. The Coventry Show comes to a teary end.

Tornados in Newcastle.
(L -R) Roger Holder, Pete Holder, a girl I met that night, Robb Huxley, Dave Watts and John Davies in the foreground

Dear Tornados,

Just a line to wish you well I hope your OK, Peter tells me you are and the shows going very well. Harry Dawson is very pleased and I got a cheque for twenty pounds this week. It couldn't have arrived at a better time.

With luck the Telstar case could be over in November then I shall by your disc in. Harry Dawson has not been round to hear it I think I rave about every disc and this time he's only expecting a good one not a really great one. I think it's a sure hit this time, I hope so it would be wonderful for us all.

I've got Eric to bring mum up here next Sunday for the day, it will do us both good, I'm very run down with worry over the company and the muck Shanks has put me in, I can't really turn to any one except my folks and you but give me a few more weeks and I should be on my feet again.

I found the instruction book for the projector it could help you and the link with its tape machine you could have a lot of fun with it, with loads of sound affects, by time I want it back you'd be able to by a good Japanese one with built in sound everything, there about a hundred and fifty pound so you by it on the hire purchase.

That fête at Cinderford with you is the best time I've had this year it seems crazy to always be working and not even getting the money, still you live and learn, I think were destined to be a success together and must always stick together, and bring up the problems when they come along.

Although I had a go in the last letter we have a learned from the mix up, and everything you have done so far has been good and getting better, I can't ask for more.

Well I'll get a tape to you soon and the exact release date, if you have a séance try to get through to me, I'm up till about 1 each morning ask that I get three taps on the sideboard. I'll ask for the same, you must be sincere and believe, I'm sure this big company sort out is for the best and I'm guided in lots of things I do, not to be selfish is the thing.

My best wishes to you all, keep up the good work, God bless, Sincerely. Joe.

Joe's letter summed up what was going on in his life at that time, the summer of 1966. He was obviously in financial trouble as he stated that he was very happy to get the money from Harry Dawson. As his receipt of the cheque was apparently connected with Dawson's pleasure with our performance in Blackpool, it could be presumed that Joe was being paid some kind of commission with reference to the hiring of The Tornados for the season. Joe was not only the recording producer of The Tornados he was their manager and had full rights to the name and had total control of who was in the band and for the most part what the band recorded. He also dictated what clothes the band were to wear as well as each member's hair colour and so on. The Tornados were Joe's band. As the manager of The Tornados I guess Joe was entitled to get a percentage of what we made, although he never mentioned anything regarding that to us and as The New Tornados we never signed any kind of contract with Joe so it was never known for sure if Joe was getting anything from the Cooper Organization. On the contrary Joe was always offering to help us out financially if we got into a bind and on a few occasions did actually pay for some of our van repairs.

He was obviously hoping that the Telstar case was coming to an end and that it would be resolved in his favour. Then the royalties would be released and he would take some of the money to, as he put it, buy "Is That A Ship I Hear" into the charts.

Things were also getting pretty bad within his company as he complained that Shanks his partner had put him in a mess. We were actually quite touched when he included us among the very few people that he could turn to with his problems. It made us, in some strange way; feel rather close to him, even though we did not know him personally, that well. We had spent a great deal of time with him in the studio, but the only time we had ever done anything with him socially was at the Cinderford Fete. He, as he said, had the best time with us there, and we enjoyed it too. It was the only time I ever saw Joe outside of the studio.

He made reference to the movie projector that he had and was considering lending it to Pete. Joe was hot on the idea of making us more of a comedy group and urged us to try to come up with all kinds of funny situations that we could try to put on film and we could all write the music to go with it. Of course we were never able to accomplish anything in this field, but I have often thought that had Joe lived and reaped the benefit of the "Telstar" royalties, we could have quite possibly followed that road and maybe we would have produced some kind of comical music videos. With Joe's history of enjoying and participating in theatricals when he was a youngster, he probably would have found it very enjoyable and who knows he may even have developed a new facet to his career out of these pursuits. Joe was pleased with us and he made it clear in this letter. His reference to the seance and knocking three times on the sideboard shows that Joe was still very much into the spiritual side of things. We never held a seance in Blackpool, and Joe never ever referred to ever hearing any knocks on the sideboard, but he did mention to me once that sometimes he would wake up at about three in the morning and the table and chairs would be dancing around the living room. At the same time he told me that the flat was haunted and on one occasion he heard the steps of somebody walking around his bed. The spirit had apparently tripped over the cord of the electric fire that was plugged in and pulled it out of the wall. Joe said that's how he knew that it really happened as he saw the plug come flying out from the outlet.

After reading Joe's letter and feeling that Joe would benefit from a change by getting out of the studio for a few days, we decided that we should call him up to invite him to stay with us in Blackpool and come and see the show. As Pete was always the one who communicated with Joe on behalf of the band he called him up and made the invitation. Pete said that Joe sounded very pleased and happy and said that he would try to make it. About a week later another letter arrived from Joe. This time, it was more upbeat.

Dear Tornados,

I was great to be able to talk to you again, if only over the phone, you gave me a lift, with your kindness and sincere wish for me to spend a few days in Blackpool. I will do my best in the next few weeks, as I will not be able to take a vacation this year, and a few days with you all, I would enjoy, as I like you, and why I don't know I think you think something of me.

Well EMI has promised a top play on your disc, and the release date should be August the 15th, the delay has been over a big change around there, it could be better for plays from now on, I've put seagulls on the A side which is now called "Carry On Pirates" It will be flogged by the pirates of course.

I put a little more organ and gitar on it and cut out the verse we left for a mad gitar break, I couldn't find a mad guitarist to do it, the better side for your stage act is the B side it's just a bit to the same but the end talkie bit still makes me laugh, and after 373 plays, so it must be funny, who's counting, (Well some people do?).

Try and put some funny ideals on your tape machine to have a go with when your back in London. That Robb should have been a comedian, a churchyard attendant, or a carpet salesman, David should get a decent organ, John should not worry when I moan to much, or it will turn his hair white, and Pete and Roger, I'm frightened to say anything about or they'll set about me.

Once again I can't put into words my admiration for you all, I hope one day soon through all our efforts you will hit the top of the charts, and I know this must happen if you keep praying and stay as great as you are as people, then the tables will turn, and what a difference, all the digs will stop, but I was very pleased some one spit on the floor when your name was mentioned, it means you're a worry, your going over better, it's a strange world, keep together, look after each other, don't lissen to to many others with an axe to grind, and if anything should go to far wrong, I'll sort it out try to be nice to every one, pass the can on to me, I hope you won't spit on the floor, if you have to, do it in the wings or behind the curtains, I hope I'm not around.

Anyway I make a joke of a few things, but you know my heart is in my words to you, keep up the fine work. I know it's not easy, but it's worth it, don't forget my belief, the more good you can do for others, the more comes back to you one day, if it's only a thank you, from your friend God bless, sincerely, Joe

Joe was obviously in a different mood with this letter which was probably brought on by his pleasure in realizing that The Tornados cared enough about him to invite him to get away for a few days to relieve his stress. We can only speculate as to what that may have been like as Joe never did make it up to Blackpool.

He was apparently optimistic that things were going to go well with our new single as he assumed that the big shake up at EMI was going to provide more exposure for the disc. He had again changed the title of the disc to "Carry On Pirates" which was a play on the "Carry On" series of comedy movies that were popular in the sixties. For some reason unknown to us when the single came out a few weeks later it was called "Is That A Ship I Hear". We will never know what made Joe change his mind with the title. He may have thought that "Carry On Pirates" was too blatant or there may have been a copyright infringement with the "Carry On" part with regard to the movies. Anyway it ended up as "Is That A Ship I Hear." It was also notable that the titles of both the A and B sides of the disc were in the form of a question and were not accompanied by question marks on the record.

As far as the seagulls were concerned we did not see the connection and we thought to ourselves "Oh no, what is he doing now?" When the disc came out and was reviewed in the musical papers it was severely ridiculed with one critic asking sarcastically if seagulls were paid musician union rates for appearing on record! We laughed when we read the review but I think that it hurt us inside to realize that we and Joe were being made out to be a laughing stock in the music business.

Once more we see Joe in his theatrical personality pushing us in the direction of humour and entertainment when he mentions that the B side of the record would be better for our cabaret shows. He was probably right, but we never played it on our shows. Joe's reference to all the members of the band with his little funny remarks about us in some way suggests that he wanted to acknowledge us all and let us know that he appreciated us as individuals as well as a band.

We had told Joe sometime previously a story that may have come from Dave Watts that somebody somewhere had spit on the floor when the name of The Tornados had been mentioned. It must have stuck in his mind as he offered us some consolation by telling us that it was a good sign and that if we all stuck together it would be alright. If anything got to be too bad he would step in for us. He of course told us to be nice to every one and as in his previous letter; he ended it with words of encouragement for us to be humble and helpful to others as that would bring rewards in the future.

The final letter that Joe wrote us in August 1966 towards the end of the season was accompanied by the demo discs of "Is That A Ship I Hear", and some publicity photos that we had taken before leaving for Blackpool. Joe joked about the photos, suggesting that we go steady with them as they didn't drop out of the air; but knowing how Joe was in financial trouble and that he probably had to come up with the money to provide them, we understood what he meant. Of course we were very happy to get the disc of "Ship" but as we had no record player to play it on we couldn't listen to it. We ended up getting to hear it on a record player that Al Paige brought in. To be honest we thought that it was crap although we were reasonably pleased with the B side. Hearing it today without the influence of all the various changes that had, and were, taking place in 1966 it's really not bad, and was quite a good recording. It was certainly not hit material. It didn't seem to get a bashing on the North Ship as Joe had been promised. We could tell this as we listened to that station whenever we were driving to the gigs and that could have been hours and although we heard it a few times it really didn't get heavy plays. He also mentioned that he had written a letter to Harry Dawson to complain about Sid Raymond and wanted to know the results. Even on a short note as this letter was, Joe still ended up by assuring us that he was there to help us by offering to sort out any problems that might come up with the group van.

Meanwhile the show went on in Blackpool and the Manfred Mann Sunday shows came to an end. The following week would feature The Small Faces who were fast becoming a very popular and "in" group. It was about half way through the season and some nights the audiences were very small. Sometimes only a handful of people came to the show. There was a rumour that Billy J Kramer and The Dakotas were being fired from the show as they had come late one night to the show after a recording session in London. Well something definitely happened as they were suddenly gone and were replaced by the Lorne Gibson Trio. Not too long before this we saw Larry Parnes and Brian Epstein sharing a conversation at the end of the pier. Sid Raymond revelled in the whole thing and reinforced his threat to us that if we disobeyed we would be off the show just like Billy J Kramer. The show was losing money so it may have been a business decision made by Parnes and Epstein to replace Billy J Kramer with Lorne Gibson as the latter was more affordable. Anyway I'm sure that Brian Epstein had better plans for Billy. Sid Raymond strutted around the stage like a pompous ass rejoicing in the fact that somebody had been thrown off the show and that he was the God Almighty boss of the stage. This was all to be blasted into oblivion with the arrival of The Small Faces.

Dave Watts talked excitedly about giving it to Steve Marriott for making a joke out of "Pop Art Goes Mozart" in his review in the *Melody Maker*. Dave may have hinted on it when we got to meet The Small Faces but we never made a big deal about it because deep inside we knew that Steve was right for that time and place and the way music was heading. They turned out to be a likeable bunch of guys. Unlike Manfred Mann, they came up and talked to us and Steve Marriott seemed to have a certain respect for Marty Wilde. I can't say that we got that close to them, after all they were this big band and we were the latest incarnation of Joe Meek's "Tornados" with most of the band feeling dissatisfied with the musical direction in which we were being directed by Joe. All we tried to do to exonerate ourselves was to play what we thought was our best and most modern numbers. We would turn up the volume a bit, get "Telstar" out of the way, and do mostly vocals, with Dave also doing his raving version of "Wade In The Water." We also tried to wear the most hip clothing that we had to show that we were not really a "Brown" group.

It was really quite remarkable to meet the Faces for the first time and to see that they were all in fact quite small in stature. Not only that, they were also skinny and had these Mod hairstyles which after a while we began to adopt. They all came from the East End of London and were just a little younger than us. At that time their line up was Steve Marriott on guitar and lead vocals, Ronnie "Plonk" Lane on Bass and vocals, Ian McLagen, organ and Kenny Jones, drums.

The first Sunday Show with The Small Faces was August 7th 1966. The show went in the usual way with The Diamond Twins and Marty and when it came to our set we really let it rip to try to save face in the eyes of the Faces who were hanging around off stage during our set. Sid Raymond glared at us from the wings and we knew that the "You'll be off the show Cocker" threats would be on the agenda again. Sure enough as the Faces gear was being set up during the intermission Sid strode over to us and began to give it to us about the volume and came out with all kinds of threats. Half way through Sid's tirade Kenny Jones walked over to his drums, sat down and proceeded to batter the hell out of them at full blast. Sid's head spun around like a weather vane to see who was causing all the commotion and then he looked back at us, and we looked back at him with a "Well, what are you going to do about that?" kind of look. He strode over to the side of the stage where he always stood and stared at Kenny Jones but didn't say a word and after Kenny had been going at it for a good ten minutes he gradually started to pretend that he was unaware of it. We were in a state of utter rejoicing to see this scenario taking place with the great Sid Raymond being unable to do anything about it. Kenny Jones did the same thing during the intervals of all of the next six shows we played with them and we loved it.

When the rest off the band started to come on stage to pick up their instruments to get ready for their set we decided to go out front to watch the show. As we took our seats at the back of the theatre we could still hear Kenny walloping the drums behind the curtains and the sounds of tuning up. Suddenly everything went quiet and Al Paige came out to do the build up for The Small Faces. After his introduction Sid opened up the curtains and "Wham" here was The Small

Faces at full throttle. Steve Marriott was dancing around the stage and singing with that unique raspy soul voice that he had, which you could never imagine coming from a guy of his small stature, and we guys were enjoying the show and imagining the looks on Sid Raymond's face as he had to endure a Small Faces set at full volume. We loved every Sunday Show from then on as Sid never complained about our volume. How could he? He knew that the Faces were twice as loud as we were. On their third show with us The Small Faces hit #1 on the UK charts with their latest release titled "All Or Nothing". They were all in great spirits and looking for fun. During our set they opened up a case of champagne in the wings and engaged in a battle by popping the champagne corks across the stage at each other. We acknowledged them, they smiled at us, and we smiled back at them, and in a way it felt good that we were being included in their celebration. They also shot corks across the stage during Marty's set and he took it all in good fun. The Faces were enjoying themselves. We could see them guzzling from the champagne bottles. It was great that they were close to us on the side of the stage, they could just as well have been secluded in their dressing room like Manfred Mann would have been, but no, they were young down to earth guys, and wanted to have a good time with every one. When we closed our act we guzzled some champagne too.

We continued to churn out the show week after week and as the season wore down the audiences began to dwindle. On some nights, especially in the middle of the week, both shows were poorly attended and sometimes when the audience was particularly bad Adam Faith would appear behind our gauze curtain shaking his head and giving us a hard time about the way we had played his set. I guess he had to blame it on somebody, there was nobody else to blame it on except himself and he wasn't going to do that.

It wasn't very long before The Lorne Gibson Trio left the show for reasons unknown. However they were an interesting group. They had no drummer. Lorne played electrified acoustic guitar and sang and was accompanied by a lead guitar player and a bass player. They were really just the same as the Karl Denver Trio. Their music seemed like it probably came out of skiffle and was a bit like folk and country.

Most of the songs that they performed were of American origin. One night their bass player was unable to appear and Roger Holder stepped in for him. They wrote out the bass notes and set up a music stand and Rog did a very good job. Lorne Gibson was a nice kind of guy and his band were the same It was always nice when other artists were unaffected by their fame as it always made every one feel comfortable. The only person on the show that kept a polite distance from us was Adam Faith. I can't say that we knew him any better at the end of the season as we never had any conversations with him about anything. He was always secluded in his dressing room on the other side of the stage and never did anything with us socially.

Marty was different and although he had done more in show business than we could ever hope to do he was still basically one of the boys. We would all go out to the Indian Restaurant together and Joyce would insist that we put pineapple on our curries and the following day Marty would greet us with the words "My ass exploded at seven o' clock this morning." One night after the show he took us down to meet Tom Jones who was appearing at the North Pier. We stood around and talked for a few minutes and shook hands. Tom Jones had a cut on his forehead covered with a band aid and Marty asked him if he'd been fighting again, and Tom answered in his thick Welsh accent "No mun, I 'it me 'ead getting' out of the car." Marty and Joyce would come over to our place and I would make some food. One night I made some spaghetti and meat sauce. Les Baguley who had come over with the Diamond Twins was getting kind of drunk and when nobody was watching overloaded the meat sauce with Parmesan cheese and basically ruined the whole meal. Marty and Joyce didn't say anything but John Davies said that it tasted like shit and that he had thrown it out of his bedroom window. Sure enough there was a pile of it on the front lawn which was still there at the end of the season. Anyway we didn't hold anything against Les and after a few more drinks we wound up with him upstairs watching him jump up and down on the bed singing "We're gonna smoke some marijuana tonight!" But we never did. The season was beginning to wind down. Apart from the Sunday shows, which we always enjoyed, everything was gradually becoming the same old thing. Two guys by the name of

Mo and Jeff replaced Lorne Gibson and although they were decent guys they were nothing more than just an act you would see in a Working Men's Club. They were doing musical comedy with Mo doing the patter and the singing and Jeff backed him up on electric guitar. We backed them but they didn't want Pete and me to play as Jeff would be on guitar, so we just stood there and mimed while Roger, John and Dave played for them. At a point during their act Mo would always mention The Tornados as some of the finest musicians in the country. Pete and I got a big kick out of that as we weren't even playing. Mo and Jeff were about one rung on the ladder higher than Johnny Clamp. We would still hang out with Marty and Joyce in their dressing room from time to time. We would swap songs together on Marty's Gibson. Roger was always to be found with the Diamond Twins as he and Sandie had hooked up together. Pete and I got friendly with a couple of girls who were part of the Players No. 6 girls dancing group. There were four of them altogether and they wore these cute little outfits and danced on a show somewhere in Blackpool for the season. Pete got Judy and I got Vivian. We would meet at their place after the show and hold séances, smoke Players No. 6 cigarettes which were always in abundance and generally hang out with whoever was at the flat at the time. The only highlight towards the end of the season was when we rushed over to the Central Pier at the close of our show to catch the last two songs of the Yardbirds set. They were all wearing sharkskin suits with Jeff Beck on guitar and Jimmy Paige playing bass. They went over really well and we enjoyed what little we got to see.

Eventually the final night of the show came around, and on the second show of the night Sid Raymond and his cronies, the stage hands, did everything in their power to totally mess up the whole show. They completely decimated Johnny Clamp in his act by holding up a "Clap Now" sign to the audience at inappropriate times. At first Johnny was completely bewildered by this and couldn't make out what was going on as they pulled away the sign every time he turned around to see what was going on. Eventually he finally caught on and began to try to make fun of it all by throwing sarcastic remarks at Sid and his band of "terrorists." During our act everyone back stage decided that they would join in singing our vocal number "Let It Be Me" by the Everly Bros. on a spare mic and they made sure that they were all singing out of tune. They also let off some smoke bombs which they had stolen from our dressing room and persisted in walking across the stage in the middle of our numbers. During the Fox Miller girls dance number they continually kept pulling the girls off stage and holding them there until there was only one girl left on stage. Marty Wilde was somewhat spared in his act but did get his mic turned off here and there and was awarded a smoke bomb. Sid Raymond was acting like a big kid and was thoroughly enjoying himself until the second half of the show when Adam Faith refused to appear as he had come down with a bad case of food poisoning and was vomiting all over the place. Anyway that's what Marty Wilde reported when he was commandeered to take the stage before Adam's spot was due to begin and explain that Adam was sick and was unable to appear. I doubt very much if this was true and knowing that Adam Faith was a very proud and professional entertainer, he obviously did not want to be put through this embarrassing last show debacle. I can't say that I blame him really.

Looking back it was a shame that a show that started off as a really good show ended up like this. Some people thought that it was a great joke and real good fun but really it was a disgusting display put on by Sid and his Cohorts. Pete and Roger's mum Mrs. Holder and my mum Joan Huxley were present for the last show and reported that it was terrible and embarrassing to watch the show. So that was it, the Blackpool South Pier Show was over and instead of going out in a blaze of glory it fizzled out as a fiasco.

That night we said goodbye to every one on the show with the exception of Adam who had left the theatre. That was almost forty years ago and apart from members of The Tornados and the Diamond Twins I never got to see anybody from that show again, with the exception of Manfred Mann who we opened up for at a gig in South Wales. He was now "Manfred Mann's Earth Band" it was the early seventies and I was playing in the Israeli hard rock band "Jericho." Needless to say Manfred Mann was still stuck up and didn't speak to us this time either.

*Our rented house on Whitegate drive Blackpool 1966. (L-R) Mrs Nancy Holder
(Pete & Roger's mother), Georgina Huxley Taylor (Robb's sister), Robb Huxley,
Mrs Joan Huxley (Robb's mother)*

As we had worked for about eighty-three days straight without a
break we decided to take a little time off. Roger and Dave left together
for London while Pete, John and I went back to Gloucester and to our
respective homes to stay with our families. We kept in touch by phone
and a couple of times I would walk up to the top of the street to the
phone box, just past the fish and chip shop, out side of Wesley Hall
and call up Pete to find out where we would be playing at next. It was
nice to be home and sleeping in that little back bedroom in Clegram
Road where I had grown up. It was great to eat mum's cooking again
especially the Sunday dinner of roast beef and Yorkshire pudding. It
was always great to creep into the front room and raid my Dad's collection of home made wines. Roger and Dave were hanging out together possibly because of their association with the Diamond Twins
with Roger staying at Dave's place. From this point on we never again
rented a flat. We just stayed wherever we could. Between one nighters

Roger and Dave would drive to London and Pete, John and I would go to Gloucester. When we did venues of longer duration we would team up and find somewhere to stay together. As a rule Pete and I usually stayed together. In fact we did a lot of things together. We dated girls, sometimes even sisters together; we wrote songs together and went on holiday together. One time while in The Saxons when we had our bleached blond hair we caused a sensation on the beach in Nice. We had a lot of curious onlookers saying "Topless, topless" as they walked behind us. They couldn't see our fronts so from behind we probably looked like a couple of blondes sunbathing topless on the beach.

Before very long we were back in London again. Pete and I stayed with his girlfriend Judy from the Players No.6 girls and my girl Viv also a No.6 girl came over to stay with me. The Beatles album *Revolver* had just been released in August and we listened to it over and over and talked about how amazing it was and that they were sure to be getting high on something to be turning out this psychedelic pop music. Pete and I assumed that this was the reason although neither of us at that time had any idea what it was to get high. The most that we had ever done was have a few drinks. Pete called up Dave as Roger was staying over with him and Dave had come up with this idea to play the theme music to *Lawrence Of Arabia.* We all met up at R.G.M. and Dave demonstrated the piece to us and it was quite a simple job for us to get it down. Dave once again asked Joe if he could play the piece on his Hammond but Joe was still adamant that it should be done on the Lowry. I must say that Joe's basic attitude during this session was indifferent. It was just a straight forward recording without Joe coming up with any mind blowing effects or off the wall ideas. This was notable as after all, wasn't this just a typical Tornados instrumental? The reason for Joe's apparent disinterest may have been due to his distressed mental condition, he also had nothing to do with the writing of the piece, and who knows, Joe might have at last realized that this kind of thing was getting old. When listening to the recording today (it was never released at that time) it totally lacks any of the Joe Meek magic which leads me to believe that Joe probably abandoned it and did no further work on it. He was not excited about it at the session and it was basically recorded in a matter of fact way and really just sounds like a demo. However we kept it in our act right up to the end of The New Tornados and it was always very well accepted by our audiences and actually became a highlight in our act. At the same session we recorded a song that I had just written around the end of the Blackpool show. It was called "I Wonder Why?" We even put the vocals down and Dave Watts sang the lead on it. As far as I know it has never been found in the Tea Chest tapes but I guess it must still be there somewhere. I don't even remember Joe asking us what the title was.

Not long after that session Joe was excited to tell us that Harry Dawson had called to say that he had landed The Tornados a spot on the Birthday Show at the Coventry Theatre with Mike and Bernie Winters as headliners. The show would run for eight weeks, which was good steady work, and we were to be paid 50 pounds each per week. This was a good step up from the South Pier at Blackpool and would give us good exposure. We worked it out that we would play a shortened version of Telstar, do our comedy routine, sing a version of "Let It Be Me", by the Everly Brothers and finish with our new instrumental "The Theme From Lawrence Of Arabia." There would be quite a full orchestra and we would need to provide them with our "Play Off" music which was of course, a few bars of "Telstar." Being as the orchestra was available we decided that it would sound great to be accompanied by them in "Lawrence Of Arabia"; so Dave got together with Les Baguley, who had also moved into the Watts residence, and together they wrote out all the parts for the orchestra. We fine tuned and perfected "Lawrence" and the rest of the set that we would play when we did our various one nighters here and there. We also found out that we were to be featured in a dance routine with the dancers which made us all feel a little scared to say the least. They were rehearsing the dance routines at a studio in London and we were required to show up to rehearse our parts. Well it certainly was great to show up there and check out all the girl dancers. They were a very nice looking bunch for the most part and it was a pure pleasure to see them all prancing about in their skimpy leotards. The choreographer and head dancer was Johnny Webster who was accompanied by his brother Jimmy. The first thing that he told us was not to worry and we would not have to do any dancing. All we had to do was walk hand in hand with a girl, take our top hats off, bow and sing "Love And Marriage". We did the basic rehearsals with the girls and we were all relieved when it was over. Actually we didn't do a bad job. Full credit must be given to John Davies as he absolutely hated to do anything like that. We were sent over to outfitters in Leicester Square to be measured for the morning suits that we would be wearing in the dance or should I say walk routine. The actual suits that we would wear were chosen from suits worn in *My Fair Lady.* We arrived in Coventry about a week prior to the opening night of the show. It was a Monday and Harry Dawson told us that there was to be a press conference at the theatre that morning and that it would be good for us to be there as it would get our faces shown. Around noon time artists began to show up together with the press. We all assembled together and got acquainted which culminated in a group pose together which would be featured in the local newspaper together with a short article which basically advertised the show. The Tornados stood in a row with Mike and Bernie Winters in the middle while Bert Weedon and Stan Stennett goofed around with their instruments as Johnny Hackett and Kris Keo looked on.

The artists that showed up for the press were nice people. Mike and Bernie, although aware of their fame were unaffected by it and appeared friendly and talkative, Mike puffing on his pipe, and Bernie fooling around. They were obviously seasoned pros and remained friendly towards us for the duration. Bert Weedon was a charming and friendly character and above all a great guitarist. In the weeks to come we would hold jam sessions together with Stan Stennett and Bert. We always ended up with Bert teaching us some of those old Django Reinhardt numbers. Stan was also an accomplished guitarist and a good all round entertainer. Bert would always encourage us to take solos in the jams and even if we didn't have a clue what we were doing, if we only got two or three notes right Bert would say "Nice!"

As we had just arrived that morning in Coventry, we would need to find a place to stay. Pete and I noticed a small note on the bulletin board back stage offering accommodation.

We called the phone number and spoke to a guy who said he would meet us backstage at 4pm. His name was Peter and he had a three bedroom house. Pete and I could make ourselves at home and use all facilities for a fiver each a week, which we thought was a pretty good deal. It turned out to be better than we thought when we got a look at the house which was well furnished and equipped. It was definitely a bachelor's pad. Peter was an accountant who loved the theatre and also had a terrific record collection consisting of musicals, jazz and even a collection of Dylan Thomas works that were read by Richard Burton. He had a Welsh corgi that was unpredictable and possessive by the name of Shan. I think the dog was jealous of us and from time to time made a point of taking a crap in our beds if we forgot to close our bedroom doors. Although it did not appear so, Pete and I fancied that Peter was gay and when his blond, actor boyfriend came down to stay with him on weekends, that confirmed our suspicions. Peter was a nice mellow guy to be around, never came on to us but did decide that he would call me Robin which Pete thought was hilarious and constantly ribbed me about it, smiling and saying "Cheers Robin."

The following day would be first day of rehearsals. Roger, John and Dave had found a house and came by Roger's car. Pete and I always arrived in the Commer van. As we walked backstage the dancers were already running through their routines and the cast was milling around engaged in conversation. When Alec Shanks, the show director arrived we all gathered around as he outlined the format of the show and the rehearsal procedures. All the acts that were involved with the dancers were to be done first and run through correcting any mistakes. Our turn soon came around and by some kind of a miracle we managed to get through it with little or no problems. Shanks' only concern was that we were not singing "Love And Marriage" loud enough. By the end of the day all the dance routines and sketches had been run through and things were shaping up. It was already clear that this was a very different show compared to the summer season at the South Pier. It was a very professional affair. There were no "Johnny Clamps" on this show.

A full run through of the total show took place the following day, along with the Coventry Theatre Orchestra conducted by Bill Pethers. It was a dress rehearsal and all artists performed their acts under the scrutiny of Alec Shanks. We were very excited as we had never played together with an orchestra before. Dave was quite concerned as he had no idea how the parts that he and Les Baguley had written for the orchestra, were going to sound. We got through "Telstar", did our comedy routine, sang "Let It Be Me" and then under the watchful eye of Bill Pethers for the first time ever we played "Lawrence Of Arabia" with orchestral accompaniment. It sounded great and made a tingle go up my spine. Our "play off" music turned out fine, which consisted of a few bars of "Telstar" which the orchestra played nicely but which did make us smile a little. We had never heard "Telstar" played by a brass section before and we were amused by the sound of it. It was quite interesting for us to watch all the other acts run through their routines. Mike and Bernie were very funny and all the skits that they did either alone or with the help of some of the dancing girls came across very well. Bert Weedon's act was good and he played his music in a very pleasant manner. He was billed as the King Of The Guitar which was an appropriate title for him. One of his numbers that he played had over 2000 notes in it. He claimed that he held the record for playing the greatest number of notes in the shortest time.

He was probably correct about that as he did play incredibly fast and didn't miss a note.

Coventry Birthday Show artists. (L-R) Bert Weedon, Alec Shanks, (Producer) John Davies, Pete Holder, Stan Stennett, Adele Leigh, Dave Watts, Robb Huxley, Mike Winters, Roger Holder, Kris Keo, Bernie Winters, and Johnny Hackett.

1966 Birthday Show

JOHNNY HACKETT

JOHNNY HACKETT, a Liverpool ex-docker turned comedian, is a new name to Coventry, yet he is no stranger to television audiences due to his success on television in the BBC TV "Club Night" series. This Fernandel-like comic with tattooed hands and a permanent grin gratefully acknowledges the help he has received from his favourite Merseyside colleague, Ken Dodd.

"Doddy has encouraged me all the way," he says. "He's a marvellous person and as a comedian I admire him very much."

Married with three children, Johnny says that if he ever does earn a lot of money he'll buy an ultra-modern house for his family. But he's also made up his mind on another point—never to get conceited.

BERT WEEDON

BERT WEEDON has brought guitar playing to a fine art. Yet he began playing on a battered instrument he bought for fifteen shillings in Petticoat Lane when he was just 12 years of age! Bert had a classical training, yet he can play any type of music. He has topped popularity polls on nine occasions and is also a prolific composer.

Making his first appearance in a Coventry season show, Bert is a great favourite on television. Children love him too, and he was resident compere of ITV's "Tuesday Rendezvous" for five years.

His advice to guitarists? "Practise hard all the time, study music properly and when you play put everything you have into it."

THE TORNADOS

THE TORNADOS began their career as the backing group for Billy Fury and toured with him all over Britain. At a recording session, Joe Meek asked them to make a record for him—they made "Telstar" which rocketed to the top of the charts, sold over a million copies in Britain, and was a phenomenal success throughout the world. They estimate that the sale of their records has totalled five million pounds! They have made successful tours of Germany and Belgium and come to Coventry after a Blackpool season.

Page fifteen

Bob Williams had the strangest act. It was basically a performing dogs routine. As it happened his troupe of dancing poodles were in quarantine and could not appear. They were hidden away somewhere on the roof of the theatre. All he did in his act was to hold a conversation with this old looking Spaniel called Louie that literally looked as if he was on his last legs. The dog did absolutely nothing. He completely ignored Bob's orders and requests and appeared totally disinterested in anything. He basically looked like a canine that had just come back from the taxidermist. At the end of the act the dog just strolled off stage looking very professional and aloof. Bob was an American artist and had actually performed at the London Palladium with his partner Louie.

Johnny Hackett did a very professional comedy routine with his Liverpudlian style of humour. Stan Stennett did a musical and comedy set assisted by Kris Keo. Stan and Kris had been long time regulars on the *Black and White Minstrels Show*. They were followed by Adele Leigh whose act was comprised of a set of romantic numbers which she always performed flawlessly with her well trained operatic voice.

At the end of the first run through of the show the entire cast was instructed to gather in the foyer of the theatre for a meeting with Alec Shanks. He proceeded to inform us that the show was running way too long and either some of the acts had to be shortened or somebody or some act would have to be cut from the show. This was poorly received by the cast as nobody wanted to cut down their act. Mike and Bernie were obviously not going to be asked and so the problem was really put upon the rest of the cast. At one point the conversation got quite heated between Stan Stennett and Alec Shanks with Stennett basically telling Shanks that he had been thrown off better shows than this, and he was prepared to walk off. I was feeling worried about The Tornados as I half expected Shanks to criticize our act and when he brought up our name I expected the worst. He told us that our comedy routine was being cut out of our act to save time and that we should play "Telstar","Let It Be Me", and "Lawrence Of Arabia." On Saturdays when we did two shows we were allowed to play only "Telstar" and "Lawrence." We argued against this but we had no choice in the matter. Shanks told us that we had been hired as an instrumental group as a contrast to the rest of the show and that the comedy routine was not needed. On the Saturday shows that followed I made a point to get a little dig in and after we played the opener "Telstar" I would announce "Thank you very much ladies and gentlemen we would now like to finish with the theme from

"Lawrence Of Arabia." In a write up which appeared in the local Coventry newspaper concerning the show it was written that it was a pity that The Tornados spot was so short and that they were deserving of a longer set. Anyway nobody got thrown off the show and the acts were somewhat shortened so that the show ran for the correct length of time. On that Thursday we did the final dress rehearsal. This performance was attended by certain members of the public and all the proceeds were donated to a recently founded fund to aid dependants of police officers that had been killed when on duty. The next day being Friday was the opening night of the show. Everything went well without a hitch and we were all pleased with everything. It was really a great feeling to be appearing on a first class professional show.

One thing that we as The Tornados found out was that we had quite a lot of time on our hands during the running of the show. We were not required to appear on stage until the end of the first part where we did our routine with the dancers in the Love And Marriage sequence. We had plenty of time to put our stage make-up on and get into our morning suites. After the interval we were the first act on after the opening dance sequence and then we did not reappear until the finale where we had to stand on a staircase and wave to the audience. We were given straw boaters to wear and joined the cast in singing "Bye Bye Blackbird" to close the show. This was a much better deal for us as The Tornados compared to the Blackpool show where we had to be on-stage for most of the evening. This was less work and more money which we of course enjoyed.

We soon settled into the daily routine showing up at the theatre by 6pm. The show started at 7.30pm. and was over by 10. There was a speaker in every dressing room so that all the acts knew at what point the show was at. This enabled every one to be ready to take the stage at the time they were required. After about ten days on the show I was able to recite the whole show along with the acts as the sound was transmitted through the speaker. I knew all the punch lines and gags and each night I recited the whole show in the dressing room much to the annoyance of the rest of the group. In the end Dave Watts had to say "For Christ's sake shut up Robbie." and that kept me quiet for a while. There was a small private bar backstage for the cast to enjoy and we began to frequent it from time to time in between our acts. We would meet the other acts there and get acquainted swapping stories with each other. Mike and Bernie liked their whiskey and Mike loved to puff on his pipe while standing at the bar. From time to time some of the dancing girls would pop in for a drink and Pete and I, as always, were keeping our eyes open for nice looking ladies.

One evening during the interval Pete and I decided to go up to the bar for a lager and lime. As we walked in we noticed two dancing girls having a drink together. One was a brunette the other a blonde. I had actually been keeping an eye on the blonde one as she appealed to me and I often strolled backstage while they were doing their dance routines and watched her from the wings. She was a good dancer and I enjoyed watching her. Pete and I joined them at their table and we all chatted together. The brunette was Ann and the blonde was Jackie. Ann had been in the Tiller Girls and had also worked as an assistant for the famous magician David Nixon. She told us that she used to get cut in half by him in his act and said that he was a very pleasant person to work with. Jackie had also been in the Tiller girls and had done many shows with the Black and White Minstrels and had also danced at the London Palladium. She knew Stan Stennett and Kris Keo very well as they had all worked together before. Seeing that Pete was already making considerable headway with Ann to the point that he had asked her out and she had accepted, I had to make my move on Jackie somehow. I just virtually blurted out, "By the way I would like to say thank you." Jackie looked puzzled and asked me "For what?" and I replied "For saying that you'll come out for a drink with me." "I didn't say that I would" she answered and my heart sank. Then she smiled and added "But I will."

Once again Pete and Robb had scored a couple of girls together just like we had always done, and as always we used the Commer van to pick up the girls and take them out for a drink. It was a great evening sharing conversations about the business and various people in the business, and winding up at Peter's place where we were staying. Peter was a great host and made Pete and I and our guests feel at ease. He even had us all listening to Richard Burton reading *Under Milkwood* by Dylan Thomas. We dropped the girls off and I was surprised to find out that Jackie had her own caravan and car to tow it. She explained that she took it wherever she worked and always had a place to stay and saved a lot of money by not having to pay hotel bills. Her friend Glennis who also danced on the show was staying with her so we stopped in to say hello.

About two weeks into the show on Friday 21st October 1966 at around 9am a disaster struck the village of Aberfan in South Wales. A waste tip (slag heap) had slid down the Merthyr Mountain destroying many houses and virtually decimating Pantglas Junior School. The children were returning from assembly where they had just been singing "All Things Bright And Beautiful" when the disaster struck. There were 144 people killed with 116 of them being children between the ages of 7 to 10. There were also 7 teachers killed and only a very few children were pulled out from the rubble alive.

The following week we were approached by the Cooper organization through Bert Weedon and Stan Stennett who asked us if we would be willing to play at a benefit show in Cardiff for the victims of the Aberfan Disaster. They explained that we would be put up in a fine hotel and would get money for petrol. We of course consented and made our way to Cardiff that Sunday. Bert Weedon had just finished his set when we arrived and it wasn't long before we were playing our set. The theatre was packed with many celebrities and everyone was dressed to the hilt in tuxedos. As we played I noticed two sharply dressed men sitting together in the Royal Box. One of them in particular seemed to like us and gave great applause and acknowledged us with waves of his hand. I had no idea who these guys were but I presumed that they must have been somebody important to be seated in the Royal Box. We hung around the theatre for sometime talking to various people and had a few drinks from a case of wine that had been placed backstage by a sponsor of the show and eventually decided to return to the hotel for the night. As we were about to drive off a guy came up and asked us where we were staying and we told him The Angel.

At around 1am that morning when we were all sound asleep we were woken by the phone and Pete picked it up and found out that someone over at a local hotel wanted us to have a drink with them.

We all gestured "no" and Pete apologized and we all went back to sleep. A few minutes later the phone rang again and Roger answered the phone. He told us that these guys called the Kray twins said that it would be in our interest to go over and meet them at the Piccadilly Hotel. Dave was quick to explain to us that we had no choice, we had to go." You don't know who these guys are" he warned. "Remember those two guys in the Royal Box? They're the Kray Twins." "So who are the Kray Twins?" we asked. "They're the two biggest gangsters in London, like the head of the Mafia, they're the fucking Kray Twins, they'll kill us if we don't go over there, my dad used to be copper in London and I've heard about them, they could nail us to the wall if they wanted."

We were all out of bed and dressed and ready to go in two minutes flat, crowding into the elevator, pouring into the van and speeding over to meet the Kray Twins. When we arrived in the lounge, we noticed a large group of celebs gathered together near to the bar, and way over on the other side of the room sat the Kray brothers accompanied by Reggie Kray's wife who we later found out was Frances. We approached their table and introduced ourselves and were invited to sit down with them and have a drink. They introduced us to their older brother Charlie and a couple of their henchmen who were standing behind them. One of them had a big scar on the side of his face and looked real scary. After the drinks were ordered they passed out cartons of cigarettes to us and introduced themselves as Ronnie and Reggie Kray. Ronnie was definitely the talker and started up a conversation with us. He looked at us with a kind of leer, telling us what a great band we were and how good looking we all were. "You look lovely boys, just like The Beatles" Ronnie said while Reggie kept pretty quiet and his wife Frances did not speak at all. In fact I noted that she looked unbelievably depressed. Her face was completely without expression and you could see that there was something wrong in her life or with her herself. Not too long after she took an overdose and died. I remember Reggie as looking like the hardest looking guy I had ever seen. I remembered the Teddy Boys from Gloucester and how some of them had reputations as being real hard guys and nobody would even dare to look at them, but Reggie Kray could put them all in his pocket.

It soon became clear to us that Ronnie Kray had certain things in mind for The Tornados. He continually praised us for our good looks, told us how much better we were than all those other celebrities congregated on the other side of the lounge that were nothing more than snobs, and then mentioned that he was interested in managing the group and had various contacts in the U.S.A. with whom he could arrange a tour of America for us. In fact he requested a phone to be brought to our table and called an American contact that was currently visiting the UK and was staying in London to do some business deals with the Krays. Ronnie raved to him about what a fantastic group we were, continually talking about our good looks. He eventually hung up the phone and assured us that he would be sending us to the States.

The drinks kept coming and the Krays were knocking back the gin one after another. At one point Reggie started to ridicule Ronnie because he had pledged to buy a painting by the famous artist Andrew Vicari, which was a work of art the artist had painted especially in support of the Aberfan disaster. Vicari was actually born in South Wales in 1938 and attended the Swansea College of Art. Ronnie had won the bidding to buy it for 1000 pounds which was a hell of a lot of money back then. The painting had been auctioned during the interval. At one point Dave and Roger decided that they had to go to the men's room and left the table. Ronnie Kray also got up after them and followed them to the toilet. The rest of us just remained there and chatted. When Dave and Roger returned Dave was visibly pale and told me in a whisper that Ronnie had offered him 5 pounds to have a piss with him and that Ronnie kept saying how much he liked Roger's blond hair. Back at the table Ronnie was making an obvious move on Roger who kept complaining that he had a cold and didn't feel too well. Ronnie was whispering to Roger and was showing him this big diamond ring that he was wearing. Later that night Roger told us that Ronnie had said that the ring was worth 5 grand and he offered it to Roger if he would spend the night with him. Ronnie had also told Roger that he preferred boys to girls which offended Roger. When Ronnie asked Roger if he had gone off of him because of what he had said

Roger replied "No" and requested that Ronnie should not talk about those things any more.

This whole scenario was absolutely uncomfortable for us as we feared the Krays because of their reputation as portrayed to us by Dave, and who would have ever dreamed that one of them was gay? This only added to our predicament. After my episodes with Joe I was at least relieved that Ronnie had not made a pass at me. I was off the hook this time.

However it seemed that Ronnie was adopting a certain closeness to Dave as Dave was a Londoner and the rest of us were basically "Up from the country." Just before we left, Ronnie invited Dave to come and meet him in the East End after the Coventry show ended. Dave said that he would but we all knew that Dave was petrified. It was time for us to leave so we all said goodnight. I can't remember if we all shook hands but we left knowing that the Krays, particularly Ronnie had a definite interest in the future of The Tornados.

The general feeling that we got from talking to some members of the cast who were present at the hotel that night, was that the Krays were there to make themselves look good in the public eye. Something to counteract and in some ways to detract attention from all the crimes that they were alleged to have committed. I was only in the company of the Krays for a couple of hours and was awed by their presence but not having heard of them before that night, I could not form any opinion as to their sincerity regarding the disaster benefit. However having read biographies on the Krays and seeing continual references to their generosity, particularly Ronnie's which was sometimes apt to be reckless, and remembering that Reggie had berated his brother for buying the painting at the benefit for 1000 pounds, today I would say that their patronage of the Aberfan Disaster Benefit was sincere. I believe that regardless of where their wealth was gained, be it legally or illegally they were basically willing to share some of it with people or causes that they believed deserved it and needed a helping hand.

We did find out later that the case of wine which had been put backstage to be used by the performers was provided by the Kray Brothers. We also found out later that the famous actor George Raft

(1895-1980) had been scheduled to attend the benefit. Sure enough his name was on the list of acts and celebrities that were to be appearing on the show. He was denied entry into the United Kingdom because of his associations with the underworld. He also managed a high class gambling club in England. It seems highly likely that Raft's involvement with the Aberfan benefit probably came through the Krays. At this time they were courting their counterparts and fellow businessmen from across the pond attempting to set up deals and do business with them. Remember Ronnie had called up a good friend of his who was visiting from the States to impress The Tornados that he could send us to America for a tour.

The following morning we went around to the local bank to cash a cheque that we had been given to cover our petrol expenses but it had been made out to The Tornados and as we had no bank account under that name and couldn't actually prove who we were they would not honour the check. Together we did not have enough money to buy the petrol to return to Coventry. As we returned to the hotel not quite knowing what to do we bumped into Peter Murray the renowned DJ who had been on the benefit show. He asked us how we were doing and we proceeded to tell him our tale of woe. He said that he would put this right for us and would accompany us to the bank and vouch for us. He even said that if they wouldn't cash the cheque he would provide the petrol money for us. When we walked up to the teller Peter Murray was recognized immediately and proceeded to explain our predicament and how we had performed for the Aberfan Benefit. That was about all it took and Pete Murray even endorsed the check for us and we were given the cash. So, many thanks to the famous DJ we were able to get back to Coventry.

It was good to be back in Coventry and to see Jackie Grant again. We had been out a couple of times and she invited me to stay with her and her friend Glennis over in her caravan. She offered to make a steak dinner for us all. After dinner we talked about things and the conversation got around to Joe Meek and his séances with Geoff Goddard and their alleged contact with Buddy Holly. Jackie and Glennis were thrilled at the thought of holding a séance and I was into it too so we decided to get a glass and arrange the letters of the alphabet and see what would happen. After the usual "Is there anybody there?" stuff, and a few more tries, nothing seemed to be happening, so thinking of Joe I suggested that we should try to get in touch with Buddy Holly. After a few attempts the glass began to move and when we asked if Buddy was there it spelled out Yes. Just like Joe had done with Geoff Goddard I decided to ask for help with songs or lyrics. When we asked for a good song title it spelled out "Just A Longing For You Near Me." We also got a reference to a middle of a verse of something but we couldn't make it out. Then all at once the glass began to move quite fast and spelled out "Look for loving in Pamela", which I presumed to be another song title or line. Pretty soon the energy seemed to fade and we lost Buddy and nothing much happened after that. I tried to get in touch with my late Uncle Bill but that was fruitless so we decided to end the séance and have a cup of tea. I guess that I really should have knocked three times on the sideboard just for Joe but unfortunately I forgot. I started reading what we had written on the piece of paper while the kettle was on the boil and referred to the line "Look for loving in Pamela." "Oh that's me" smiled Jackie. "Jackie Grant is my stage name and my real name is Pamela, Pamela Eastwood."

I was surprised and quite tickled to find this out and it felt a bit strange knowing that someone that I had known for a couple of weeks as Jackie was really Pamela. I was happy with both names. Jackie Grant was "flashy" showbiz" and Pamela Eastwood was intriguing and mysterious. Glennis and Jackie swore that they had not pushed the glass during the séance and they were as surprised as I was. One thing I know for sure is I didn't push the glass. That night after we had gone to bed a tremendous rain storm erupted. The rain came down in torrents accompanied by very strong gusts of wind that literally rocked the caravan. It went on for hours and hours with out any let-up and none of us could sleep. Everything seemed extremely weird and you could imagine if you opened the curtains, and looked out into the storm you would see the face of the devil howling at you. I guess that somehow we had angered the spirits with our séance. As I tossed and turned that night I couldn't help thinking there was something about Jackie that I didn't know about, maybe something that was said in the séance, but I had no clue what it could be.

On the show I would still stand and watch her from the wings, as she danced in that sexy Jungle outfit. She would often see me and smile. She started turning up in the wings during our set and we exchanged smiles. When we sang "Let It Be Me" I was hoping that she would think that I was singing it for her. Everything was cool and I was happy and excited with this new person in my life.

One evening as we were walking back to our dressing rooms after the wedding scene I saw Jackie on the public phone which was in the hallway backstage. Roger turned to me and said that she was talking to Uncle Wiggly (not his real name). Uncle Wiggly was a famous ventriloquist who had been on the London Palladium and had done a lot of TV and was actually quite a celebrity. According to Roger he and Jackie had worked together on many shows and although he was married Jackie was apparently his girlfriend and he called her most nights. It seems that everybody knew except me. I felt sick inside and the happy world that I was floating in had now become a world of sadness and gloom. I guess somebody must have wanted me to know and had told Roger to put me wise. I had a gut feeling that it might have been Glennis or even Jackie herself. I guess that this was the unknown thing that I couldn't figure out on the night of the séance and the wild storm.

To make matters worse a few days later one of the dancers held a party at her house as she and her family lived locally. We all attended and Jackie and I went with Pete and Ann in the van as usual. When we arrived, Jackie, who had been acting a bit quiet and strange, told me that she wanted to "circulate" and for the rest of the evening stayed away from me. I watched her with her glass in her hand as she held conversations with the guests and in particular Roger. Towards the end of the party Roger came and told me that Jackie wasn't feeling well and had asked him to drive her home. What could I say? I had no car and couldn't drive anyway. They left together without Jackie saying good night to me I felt pretty rotten. I presumed that it was over and that was that.

I kept pretty quiet for the next couple of days and kept my distance. There were no smiles from the wings.

Anyhow we did get a good laugh when Davie Watts the mischief maker took off his top hat during the wedding sequence to reveal a sock and his underwear on his head which he had carefully placed in his hat. When he bowed his head they slid off and landed in the middle of the stage where they sat until one of the male dancers was able to kick them off into the wings. The girls were all hysterical and we could hardly sing for laughing. It caused a hubbub back stage as the dancers all gathered around laughing and with Bert Weedon and Stan Stennett wanting to find out what all the excitement was about. Even Adele Leigh who was usually secluded in her dressing room poked her head out from behind her door to see what was up. When we were questioned about the occurrence by the theatre manager, Dave maintained that he had forgotten that he had left the items in his hat. We all knew that he did it on purpose. We saw him put them there. Dave always liked to cause a stir and make things happen just like he had done on the Blackpool show, but this was a high class show and these kinds of pranks were definitely not the norm. At one point Jackie approached me asking what had happened on stage as she had not seen what had happened. I took this as a gesture on her part to make contact with me again as I had not spoken to her or ac-knowledged her for the past two days after the party. We met later by chance in the bar and I told her that I had heard about Uncle Wiggly. She said that she was sorry about the party and went on to tell me about her relationship with Uncle Wiggly who she had been seeing since she was sixteen. She told me that her mother was angry with her because she was seeing a married man. She said that she was kind of mixed up with things right now but we could be friends. I accepted that and felt a little happier but knowing that I was up against the famous Uncle Wiggly I realized that there was some hard work ahead to win her over.

On a Saturday afternoon between the shows we got together with Bert Weedon and Stan Stennett back stage for a jam session or as we called it, a blow. It was good fun playing along with such a virtuoso as Bert Weedon and Stan Stennett was a very competent player too. Stan had his own plane and actually took Dave and Pete up for a joy ride one weekend. After the session as we were standing around talking Bert Weedon asked us if we wouldn't mind telling him how much we were getting paid from George Cooper. (Bert worked for the same organization). We told him that we were getting 50 pounds a week which was 250 pounds for the band. Bert said that Cooper had told him that he was paying The Tornados 500 pounds and as we were five in the band and Bert was one he said that he could only get 250 pounds for Bert. Bert assured us that he usually made 500 pounds a week on these shows. Bert reckoned that Cooper was probably getting one thousand pounds a week for The Tornados and Bert Weedon and by paying both parties a total of 500 pounds a week they were probably putting 500 pounds in their pocket instead of their usual 10% which would have been 100 pounds. Bert confronted Harry Dawson on this and was told that the company had been losing money and they had to make it up some way. As The Tornados we never questioned Cooper about this and that was the end of it All we knew was in all likelihood we had probably been cheated by the Cooper Organization once again.

We were into the last couple of weeks of the show and Dave Watts was getting itchy. Since the sock in the hat prank nothing much had happened on the show and it was basically a day in day out routine. This changed rapidly when the great mischief maker Davie Watts decided that he would conduct an experiment with a tin of smoke powder that he had bought at a joke shop for use in our cabaret act. Dave said "Let's try some of this stuff and see how it works." Pete took a look at the directions and read, that for a large amount of white smoke ignite a small amount of powder in a small tray or bottle cap. Pete said that we had nothing to put it in so Dave went ahead and set fire to the whole tin in our small dressing room. In no time at all the room was filled with the thickest white smoke you could imagine. It was like a white fog that was so thick that you couldn't see your hand in front of your face or anybody else in the room. It was lucky that we were ready for the finale as we would not have been able to see to get changed. We couldn't open the dressing room door as we were afraid that the smoke would spread to the outside so we all stood in the dressing room until it was time for the finale and made a speedy exit from the room hoping that nobody would notice anything.

During the finale the whole cast would be on-stage and we were positioned at the back of the stage on a staircase with straw boaters and joined in the singing of "Bye Bye Blackbird." About half way through the song, we began to notice that white smoke was billowing out among the musicians in the orchestra pit, and also from beneath some of the chairs in the first few rows of the audience. As the curtains closed for the end of the show the cast on-stage were all chattering with excitement thinking that the theatre could be on fire. We were saying "Oh shit Davie has really done it this time." We obviously knew what it was and later we found out that the smoke had been sucked out through the ventilation system from the vents in our dressing room. When we arrived backstage and opened the dressing room door, some smoke still remained but most of it had gone out through the vents. We all faked our surprise saying that somebody must have left a lit cigarette near an open tin of smoke powder and that had caused the powder to ignite. Once again The Tornados were at the root of the trouble. The next day when we arrived at the theatre we were told to report to the manager's office. We knew what was up and we sauntered into the office and stood together in a row in front of the manager's desk. He started to question us as to what had happened the previous evening and didn't appear to accept our explanation of what had happened with the smoke powder. After the sock in the hat we were suspected of deliberately setting fire to the powder, and rightfully so. We got a royal dressing down and were warned that this was our last chance and if anything further happened we would be fired from the show.

Jackie and I seemed to be getting a little closer together but the thought of Uncle Wiggly was always present and I noticed that Jackie was still talking to him by phone. I tended to try not to think too much about that and hoped it would go away. Just before the final week of the show we had a Sunday off as The Cooper Organization did not have us booked anywhere. Pete asked if Jackie and I would like to go to Gloucester with him as he was taking Ann down to the farm for the weekend. Jackie said that she would like to go so we arranged to stay with my parents. We left right after the show on Saturday night and arrived at Clegram Road in the early hours of

Sunday morning. I let us in as I always carried a key. My parents were sound asleep upstairs and Jackie and I fulfilled our passions on the living room carpet. It was at that time the most beautiful thing that could have happened and it did really look like I was winning the battle against Uncle Wiggly. We spent that Sunday with my parents and returned to Coventry that evening. Pete was going to stay with Ann over at her place that night so I took Jackie with me over to Peter's place where we snuck in and spent the night together. Jackie and I were hitting it off real well, and so were Pete and Ann.

The final week of the Birthday show had arrived and we were scheduled to do the last show on December 3rd which was the eve of my 21st birthday. On the Friday evening there occurred the third event which had it happened a few weeks earlier would have been the last nail in our coffin and we would have probably been fired from the show. In the finale we as The Tornados were supposed to stand on a staircase that was built on a rolling scaffold. John and Dave stood at the top above a few of the dancing girls and Pete Roger and I stood a little lower on the stairs. The rest of the cast was gathered in front of us with Mike and Bernie at centre stage. On this particular night and as the show was drawing to a close John and Dave were up in the bar having a few drinks. We all took our places on the stairs waiting for the curtain to rise and Dave and John were missing. They had totally forgotten about the finale. The curtain rose and we went into the final song. As it ended and Mike and Bernie were doing their goodnight bit to everybody, a loud clambering noise was heard behind us. Mike and Bernie and the whole cast turned around to see what the commotion was about and witnessed John and Dave appearing over the scaffold as they had climbed up from behind, cocked their legs over the rail and took their places at the top. The audience was in stitches and this comical event stole the show from Mike and Bernie which pissed them off. Thank God there was only one show after that.

The following day being the final show and the eve of my 21st birthday, it brought about a special feeling in the air for me. When I arrived I found an array of birthday cards waiting for me, some from family and friends and some from the dancing girls. The show went just the way it had gone, for the most part, for the past eight weeks, very smoothly and with no problems. The only difference was that we were doing everything for the last time and that tomorrow it would all be over and we would be entering a new phase in our careers as professional musicians, leaving to perform in some other city, in some other club or dance hall. I watched Jackie dance in the Jungle routine for the final time, smiling but knowing that tomorrow I would be going in one direction and that she would be going in another. Just when things were getting real good we would be saying good bye.

When the final curtain came down there was a kind of quietness in the air as all the artists left the stage. It was like everybody knew it was the last show and it was over. For the most part many of the artists hung around and had a few drinks in the bar as an extended way of saying good bye. Jackie and I met there after the show and so did Pete and Ann. At one point Jackie asked me to come upstairs with her to the dancer's dressing room. We took our drinks with us and sat in the room together in front of the mirrors. It was quiet and peaceful in the room away from the usual back stage noise. She told me that she had a present for me and pointed to at a picture she had of Uncle Wiggly taped to her mirror. There he was together with his dummy. She stood up and peeled the photo off the mirror and tore it up in front of me. She told me that it was over between her and Uncle Wiggly. I guessed that I had won the battle with the ventriloquist man and Jackie was mine. She told me that she would be going home to her folks in Barnsley and would soon after be leaving for rehearsals to dance pantomime in Bradford for the holiday season. I told her I was going home too and would stay in Gloucester and then soon after leave for London to make new recordings with Joe Meek. I told her that we were hoping to try to record our first single with a vocal "A" side and it was going to be exciting.

Jackie gave me her mother's home phone number as she would be staying there. I had no number to give her as we had no phone at my parents' house.

We all met again in the bar as Roger and Dave were leaving for London. They were answering the siren call of the Diamond Twins. John Davies was anxious to get going as he wanted to see his girlfriend Debbie as soon as possible, so we had part of the band saying goodbye to their girls and the other part looking forward to saying hello to their girls.

Ann and Jackie were teary eyed and Pete and I kept a stiff upper lip. Jackie said that her brother would come the next day to tow her caravan back to Barnsley. Pete, John and I decided that we would drive back to Gloucester that night and were about ready to leave. We left with hugs, kisses and good byes and "I'll miss you. I'll call you."

I took the back seat in the Commer van and with Pete at the wheel and John as co-pilot we drove off into the night. I was able to stretch out on the bench seat but with everything on my mind I was unable to relax. I stared up out of the window at the dark shapes of the trees as they sped by. It was going to be a long drive and a long night. We had the radio set on Radio Luxembourg which would sometimes fade in and out and just about dawn as we were driving over the Cotswold Hills it started to come in clear. It was Bob Dylan fading in with "Mr. Tambourine Man." I sat up, yawned, rubbed my eyes and with a very peaceful feeling I looked out of the window as the sun began to rise.

I wrote two songs that season and both were about Jackie and me. I was to record "Signs Of You" with Joe in the coming weeks. That recording has yet to be found in the "Tea Chests." The other song was "The Ventriloquist Man" which Joe didn't get to hear. I featured it on my "Joe Meek" tribute CD *Lost Songs of the Sixties.* Both of these songs were personal to me and greatly influenced by my infatuation with Bob Dylan.

1966 Birthday Show

PROGRAMME CONTINUED FROM PAGE 11

THE DANCING GIRLS

Susan Clements, Delia Escombe, Anne Fergus, Christine Goonen, Jackie Grant, Linda Grant, Deidre Holton, Anne Kewley, Pauline Lough, Isabel Metcalf, Elaine Michele, Teresa Minto, Glennis Quinn.

THE COVENTRY THEATRE ORCHESTRA

W. E. Pethers (Musical Director), E. Briars (Leader, Violin and Guitar), J. K. Gwynfo (Harps, Violin), K. Cheever (Violin), N. Simon (Cello), J. Vale (Bass), C. Howard (Alto Sax and Clarinet), G. Lamont (Alto Sax, Clarinet and Oboe), K. Whiting (Baritone Sax and Flute), C. Daniel (Tenor Sax and Clarinet), L. Pegrum (1st Trumpet and District Conductor), D. Spencer (2nd Trumpet), R. Kerr (3rd Trumpet), C. Sandeman (1st Trombone), S. Wright (2nd Trombone), F. L. Collins (Pianist and Arranger), V. Parkinson (Percussionist).

Musical arrangements by RONNIE HANMER and W. E. PETHERS

Scenery constructed and painted by NEWCO PRODUCTIONS LTD.
Costumes executed by ALEC SHANKS STAGE COSTUMES LTD.
and JAY MANN
Draperies by KEN CREASY
Shoes by GAMBA and FREED.   Wigs by WIG CREATIONS LTD.
Wardrobe care by DAZ.   Nylon stockings by KAYSER BONDOR.
Special fluorescent and stage paint supplied by ASTLEY PAINTS LTD., Coventry.

Company and Stage Manager		For			EDWIN THORNLEY
Assistant Stage Manager		Newco Productions Ltd.			ALLEN GODDARD
Wardrobe Supervisor					EVELYN BARNES
Senior Artist					EDWIN P. GRANT
Resident Stage Manager		For			C. BOSWORTH
Chief Electrician		Coventry Theatre			BERT BOYLE
Property Master					F. PULLOM

THE TORNADOS CHAPTER FOUR

Joe calls us back to the studio for more recordings.

Joe changes his attitude towards Dave's Hammond organ and our pleas to do a vocal "A" side.

The Tornados perceive a different demeanor from Joe and he suggests that the band record "No More You And Me" a vocal that he has come up with.

A memorable final recording session with Joe where Joe gets unwelcome visitors and screams at them to leave. Who were these visitors? More contact with Ronnie Kray.

A horrible Christmas away from home.

Roger and Dave relate the details of the last "No More You And Me" session with Joe where Richie Blackmore plays guitar and the Diamond Twins do backing vocals.

Doubling with The Searchers and playing cards with Wee Willie Harris.

Robb spends a little time at home in Gloucester. Then more time off with a visit to Jackie Grant in Bradford.

Robb hears the devastating news of Joe's death on the radio.

The Tornados attend Joe's funeral in Newent.

George Cooper offers The Tornados the Great Yarmouth Summer Season with Freddie and The Dreamers. Under pressure Tornados sign with Cooper to back the Yarmouth show.

More gigs and Robb and Jackie break up.

More time at home and a miserable failed attempt by Robb to get Jackie back, but he will get a song out of it.

Photo of Joe in his lounge - courtesy and copyright of David Peters

It was very nice to be home with my Mum and Dad on my 21st birth-day. They had bought me a watch which they had inscribed to me on the back. Although It was a very happy day I was feeling sad as I was missing Jackie and a bit later in the afternoon I decided to walk up to the end of the street to the phone box to give her a call. She had gotten back home safely and asked me how I was doing. I told her I was fine but that I missed her a lot. She said "I miss you too Luv."

Joe wanted us back in the studio right away so Pete, John and I made our way back to London. Pete was lucky because Ann was re-hearsing for a show in London and they would get to see each other. We dropped John off at a tube station and he went over to stay with his cousin Graham (Grime) Wilkes, and all I could do was hang out with Pete and Ann until we got a hotel to stay at. We stayed at the Mc-Donald hotel where we had stayed at sometime before. It was a semi decent place, but now had become rather run down and decrepit. It made things worse for me as unlike Pete who had Ann with him I was alone in a depressing run down room wishing I could be with Jackie.

We all met up at the studio the following day and gathered together with Joe. Pete had mentioned to me that Joe had sounded down and depressed in the last phone conversation that they had together, and it was clear to see that although Joe was pleasant and complemented us on our good performance at Coventry, underneath, there was something that was keeping him preoccupied. Time has shown that at that time he was financially strapped and was also under all kinds of stress coming from all different directions. As he had mentioned to us in a past letter he was hoping that the "Telstar" case would be over in his favour soon, so he must have been walking on a tight rope not knowing if he would fall off and land in the safety net of the "Telstar" royalties, or that there would be no safety net and he would fall into oblivion.

He was definitely different. That feeling that you had around Joe of not knowing if he would explode or freak out at any time, had seemed to have disappeared and although he was noticeably depressed he seemed more relaxed and did not take a domineering attitude as we talked. As usual we started to implore Joe to let us do a vocal A side for the next single and his reply was that we had "Lawrence Of Arabia" in the can. We continued to plead our case with Joe and to our surprise he suddenly said "You can do whatever you want to do", and that if we wanted to do a vocal he had a great song he wanted us to hear. We went from ecstasy to despair as we dreaded what kind of song it was that Joe wanted to play us. Fortunately we were to be pleasantly surprised for when he played the demo to us we liked the song very much and we thought that the arrangement that we could do for it would put it in with the current trends in music. We had been inspired by The Small Faces at Blackpool and hoped to approach the number with that style of music in mind. Joe suggested that we bring up the gear and rehearse the song in the studio Dave turned to Joe and asked if we could bring up his Hammond for the session and surprise number two, Joe agreed to let us bring it up. This was not the Joe Meek that we were used to. It was hard to believe that he was letting us do whatever we wanted to. We all went down to the Commer and started to bring the equipment upstairs. When it came to the Hammond it was a ceremonious affair. We weren't just lugging an organ upstairs we were lugging it up to Joe Meek's studio, finally accomplishing something that we had been hoping to do for quite sometime. Getting the Hammond up the first flight of stairs was reasonably easy as it was lashed to a sled and the stairs were just a straight flight. However the second staircase was another thing as the steps were very steep and the flight twisted around almost like a spiral staircase. We almost had to hold the organ up vertically to get it up the stairs but after a heavy groaning session we got it up to the control room and pushed it into the studio. Dave was ecstatic and very excited to start the rehearsal. When I was down home in Gloucester I had come across the little 8 watt Selmer amp that had been my first amplifier. When I got my Vox AC30 I lent the Selmer to some friends and when they returned it the speaker was blown out as they had played bass through it. The good part about it was it had that natural bluesy distorted sound which I liked and as I thought it would be good to use for recording I had brought it with me. Joe seemed interested and asked me why I was using the little amp so I explained that I liked the distorted sound. Joe put a mic in the back of the amp and stuffed a blanket in on top of it. The amp made a few little pops and sputters here and there but Joe wasn't worried about that and just gave it a polite tap on the top and the noises stopped. Once we were all set up Joe left us to learn the number and went downstairs to talk to Patrick Pink. It took us very little time to get the number down. It was called "No More You And Me" and was quite a simple song but we thought that it had something special. It began to take shape and with the use of the Hammond and the little distorted amp we developed a different, if not new sound for the band. It was a great feeling that we all shared and we believed that at last we had turned the corner with Joe and were beginning to head in the right direction. There was an air of excitement in the studio and when Joe appeared in the doorway with a smile on his face announcing that it was beginning to sound good we all felt happy and relaxed.

We continued to run through the number and Joe adjusted the

sounds in the control room and from time to time would come into the studio and fiddle with the amps and microphones. At one point he was messing with some of the wires that were trailed through the doorway and round the corner into the control room when there was a pop and a bright flash. He quickly remedied the problem with a little electrical tape and all was well again. He couldn't help but tease Dave about the Hammond saying that we had dragged it all the way upstairs for nothing as the Lowry sounded just as good. The smile on Joe's face as he said it gave it away that he didn't really mean it and probably was pleased by the sound of it.

After running through the backing a few more times Joe's head popped around the corner and he said that he thought that we were ready to put it down. Midway through the second take Patrick Pink appeared nervously at the studio door and when the take was over he whispered something to Joe who throwing his hands into the air said to Patrick "Oh tell 'em to fuck off" and sent him back downstairs. Joe stood at the top of the stairs and hearing that conversation was still going on he charged down the stairs shouting "Fuck off! Fuck off" and everything went quiet and shortly we saw Joe reappear again at the top of the stairs He was a little red in the face but was able to force a nervous smile saying "Well that's got rid of them." It is quite possible that Joe's unwelcome visitor was Ronnie Kray as in later years Patrick Pink had stated that Joe had ordered him to tell Ronnie to fuck off. There is also a possibility that it may have been Violet Shenton who had come upstairs to ask for her rent money. If I had to choose I would say that it was Ronnie Kray as only a few days earlier Dave Watts had met with Ronnie at a pub called The Grave in Whitechapel in the East End. Dave related to us that he had received a phone call from Ronnie and had made arrangements to meet at the pub. When Dave arrived in the afternoon the place was empty except for the bar tender and Dave was feeling nervous and was not sure what to do. So clutching the envelope which contained the publicity shots which Ronnie had requested he decided to wait. He took a seat at one of the tables and sat there hoping and praying that he would not end up in a real grave! Soon after, the doors opened and two burly looking characters appeared. They approached Dave and asked him what he was doing there. Dave answered saying that he was Dave Watts from The Tornados and that he had an appointment to meet Ronnie Kray. One of the men left and his partner walked over to the door and locked it. This made Dave even more nervous. The guy returned to the table and thanked Dave for coming and asked him how much it had cost him to come over to the meeting and Dave answered saying that he had paid 2 shillings and nine pence for his train fare, and was surprised when Ronnie's henchman pulled out a five pound note and handed it to Dave saying "I think this will take care of the train fare for you." Dave began to feel a little better as he had five pounds in his pocket. A fiver in the 1960s was worth a hell of a lot more than a fiver is today. After about twenty or thirty minutes Ronnie Kray arrived with two gang members and sat down with Dave and reaffirmed that he was definitely interested in taking over the band. Ronnie explained that he had a contact in the States who owed him a big favour and that they would set up a tour for The Tornados all over the country. Ronnie looked at the photos that Dave had brought and was pleased and continually made references to the appearance of the band and "What nice looking boys we were." Once again Dave mentioned that we were managed by Joe Meek and that our agents were the George Cooper Agency. Ronnie reassured Dave that he would take care of George Cooper and Joe Meek.

We eventually got the backing track down to Joe's satisfaction and called it a day. There was a different atmosphere in the air as we put away our guitars. Joe seemed to be quite relaxed, his voice had a very gentle timbre to it and as he was talking he seemed to be figuring out something in his head. Sometimes he would look away and his eyes seemed like they were looking into infinity; not just focusing on some nearby object. It really seemed that he was accepting us as friends and there was a certain kind of closeness between us which was probably enhanced by The Tornados themselves. I say this because we were now looking at Joe in a different light. At last we had won our way with him in having him record what we considered to be a more modern type of music which could give us a chance at breaking into the Rock mainstream. Joe had dug up this song from somewhere and we liked it and it looked like everything was beginning to fall into place. We talked about the new song and Dave indicated that he would like to join me on the vocals, as he had done previously on the lost track called "I Wonder Why?" which we had recorded before leaving for Coventry. Joe turned to us with a look of excitement in his eyes and a shy grin of pleasure on his face and said "It's gonna be a double A side" "Theme From Lawrence Of Arabia" with "No More You And Me." Our hearts dropped on hearing this. Was Joe really going to do this and make "Lawrence" technically the A side with "No More You And Me" the B side which was good enough to be the A? He could see that we were upset and when we started to speak in favour of the vocal he said "OK, OK, the vocal will be the A side that's what I had in mind anyway." We made arrangements to meet the following day to put on the vocals and as we were all filing out of the studio Joe stopped us at the door at the top of the stairs and said "I'm going to ask Richie Blackmore to play on your record." We showed up at around 10am. Before we started on the vocals for "No More You And Me", Joe asked what else we had in the way of new songs. As I was the only person in the band who was writing, I offered a song that I had recently written in the few days that we had off after the Coventry show ended. Pete and I were not writing together at that time as we were both pursuing our relationships with our girlfriends. We didn't spend so much time together as we did in The Saxons, and Pete and I never wrote another song together after but I continued to write songs alone. The song I offered was called "Signs Of You" and came out of my relationship with Jackie Grant. The song tells the tale of the guy whose girlfriend has left him and he is haunted by the things he is seeing that remind him of her. It was also inspired by the Bob Dylan album *Blonde on Blonde.* It seems that somehow I knew inside that Jackie would leave me one day. It started to come to me after Jackie had ignored me at the Party and I finished it in Gloucester. To my knowledge it has not been found among the Tea Chest Tapes. It was the very last recording that we did with Joe. I did actually re-record it when I was in the Churchills as a B side. I gave the writer's credit to Romano and Trebich who were the lead guitarist and drummer in the band so they would get some share of any royalties that would be earned.

With "No More You And Me" the vocals went down quite well as I remember and we had them completed in good time. Dave and I sang together which was a change as Pete and I had always sang together before. One of the differences with this session compared to previous sessions with Joe, was that there was no banging on the stairs, dragging bells over a glockenspiel, or jamming a screwdriver into an echo chamber: this time it was a more or less straight recording which made it seem that Joe could have been getting away from the gimmicks that he was used to using and hopefully would produce a more up to date style of recording and music. I believe that I did do the vocals on "Signs Of You", I don't remember if they were that good, only finding the recording amongst the Tea Chests will provide that answer.

I can't really remember what we all talked about after that session. I don't think that Joe said that much only mentioning again that he would use Richie Blackmore and that Dave and Roger should bring Sandy and Sonia, (The Diamond Twins) to the studio after Christmas so that they could put vocal backing on "No More You And Me." We took the gear down to the van as we would be leaving the following day for Sunderland where the Cooper Organization had us booked to play over the Christmas Holidays. Joe said goodnight and we left walking down the stairs and out through the bottom door into the cold evening air of Holloway Road. I lit up a cigarette and climbed into the van. We drove off down the road and I sat there looking out of the window not knowing that this was the last time that I would ever see Joe Meek.

At the beginning of January 1967 Dave Watts began to keep a day by day account in his diary of the events that took place with The Tornados for the whole of that year. Little did we know at that time how important those notes would be forty years down the road. I would like to give a huge thank you to my dear old mate Davie Watts for his cooperation in allowing me access to those invaluable pages of his diary. Over the past forty years memories can get a little cloudy but with Dave's great help we have been able to get a clearer picture of the way it was.

All in all it was a lousy Christmas for us that year 1966. Dave Watts said it was the worse Christmas that he had ever had in his life. We were booked to play in Sunderland at a casino club for the week before Christmas. We opened up on the 18th of December after driving up and booking into some horrible accommodation. It was a decrepit bed and breakfast place. The beds were awful and the breakfast was ghastly and completely inedible. We decided to skip the breakfast for the rest of our stay. The performances in the club were very depressing as there was basically no audience each night. Just a few people trickled in here and there. I guess that we couldn't really have expected anything more than this as people were getting ready for Christmas and the business at the casino was slow. They probably needed to get a band for the week at a cheap rate and The Cooper Agency supplied them with The Tornados. On Christmas Eve which was on a Saturday the casino was completely devoid of any audience and we basically played for ourselves. Pete and Dave went to collect our pay and returned with Dave saying "Well we actually got paid boys." We all felt grateful as we were all dreading that there would be no money to pay the band as the club had been empty all that week. We had made arrangements for an early wake up call at the bed and breakfast for six in the morning as we had to travel to Widnes on Christmas day to appear at the Regency Club. There was a small speaker in the room with a volume control and was connected to somewhere downstairs in the bowels of that horrible place. At precisely six in the morning we woke up to the sound of bells, followed by the radio announcement, "This is the BBC on Sunday the 25th of December 1966, we wish all our listeners a very Merry Christmas." Roger Holder poked his head out from the grimy sheets and moaned, "Oh go to fucking hell."

We couldn't wait to get out of that miserable dump and soon got on the road. As it was Christmas Day morning there was absolutely nowhere open to get any breakfast so with rumbling stomachs we started our journey over the Pennine chain of mountains and sometime around noon apparently in the middle of nowhere we spotted a Chinese restaurant with a sign advertising "Christmas Dinners." I had never eaten a Christmas dinner in a Chinese restaurant in my life. Christmas Dinner was always eaten at home, but we were far away from home and with pangs of hunger in our stomachs we decided to take a chance. If somebody told me I would be celebrating Christmas in a Chinese restaurant in the middle of nowhere on top of a mountain in 1966 I would have said they were crazy. The food turned out to be not bad, not like home of course, but at least it helped to fill a small part of that big hole that was created by the first Christmas that I had ever spent away from home. To add even more sadness to this bleak holiday I had found out a week earlier that Jackie was to be working in Gloucester, of all places, over the holidays and would be staying with my parents while she was appearing at the Gloucester Regal Theatre. I cursed the Cooper Organization for booking us into dead end clubs over the Christmas when I could have spent the holidays at home with my folks and my girlfriend.

Widnes turned out to be just about the same as Sunderland was; a week of miserable, depressing shows in a next to empty club. Christmas night was really bad. The club was almost totally empty and after the show Roger and Pete got invited to a party somewhere and John, Dave and I feeling left out of all the celebrations moped off back to the Hotel in the early hours of Boxing Day morning. It was an old, Gothic, creepy kind of place where you could imagine Vincent Price lurking in the shadows. We climbed up the big wooden staircase in the dim light and bid each other sad goodnight's and went off to our separate rooms. I climbed up onto the high bed with its huge four posts and lifted up the heavy blankets and crawled into bed. Looking around the room I noticed the old landscape paintings on the walls and the huge wardrobe from out of which at any moment I expected some kind of bloodthirsty vampire to emerge. I laid there thinking about Jackie and feeling a bit envious of Pete. He was really the only one of us who was happy. His girl Ann lived in Birkenhead and he stayed over with her for the week; while the rest of us were away from family and friends Pete at least had his girlfriend. I imagined my Mum and Dad sleeping soundly down in Gloucester. It had probably been the usual Christmas with my folks going around next door to celebrate with the Reeces and other friends and neighbours. For sure my Dad had played the piano all night and had probably sunk quite a few pints and so had everybody else. They would all sit around and sing the old songs till about midnight and as the evening wore on they would all get jolly and their noses would turn red just like the characters on an old Christmas card. The only time that the music would stop was when the plates of turkey sandwiches and pickled onions were passed around.

And here I was holed up in some bleak hotel in Widnes, in some spooky bedroom on Christmas night while everybody except John, Dave and I were out partying. I couldn't sleep so after a while I opened the drawer on the big wooden night stand and pulled out a bible that had been placed there by some religious institution. It was black with red edged pages and it looked appealing to me. Flipping through the pages I began reading. I finally put the book down around 4am switched off the light, turned over on to my side and fell asleep. At the end of the week I couldn't resist tucking that bible into my suitcase. It followed me around for many years through different groups and countries. I eventually lost it somewhere and have no idea where.

We were all glad to get out of Widnes and with New Year's Eve over the miserable holiday season came to an end leaving us all to look forward to our second year as professional musicians playing cabaret shows doing one night stands, a summer season and recording with Joe Meek. Back down in Gloucester once more I made my pilgrimage to the phone box to talk to Jackie and was lucky to catch her at home. She explained that she had sometime off before she had to leave for Bradford where she would be working at the Alhambra Theatre in the pantomime which would be running there. As The Tornados next gig was to be at the Cabaret Club in Burnley which was not too far from Barnsley she invited me to stay with her folks for the weekend and she would drive me to the club as we opened up on the Monday night. I accepted her offer gladly and at the end of the week bright and early on Saturday morning I took the train to Barnsley. On the way I thought about what it would be like to see Jackie again. I had not seen her for about a month since the end of the Coventry show. I noted how different it was to carry on a relationship as a full time musician compared to when I was semi- pro. I could see my girlfriend whenever I wanted as I was never away from home but now as I was dating a girl who was a professional dancer and we were both in show business travelling regularly, it became clear to me that this would be a much different relationship. I started to think about what would happen if some day I wanted to get married and raise a family. How would I be able to do that if my fiancé was an entertainer just like Jackie and we were constantly on the move both in different cities at different times and even possibly different countries? The thought was pretty scary so I decided to leave it in the back of my mind and not dwell on it any more.

The train rolled into the station to the sound of the loud speaker system announcing "Barnsley, this is Barnsley." I stepped down to the platform and with suitcase in hand walked towards the exit. As I made my way outside, there she was walking towards me and with her top coat open showing her short skirt and her blonde hair blowing in that cold January wind Jackie Grant looked terrific. After the much welcomed hugs and kisses we got in her car and drove to her parents' home. It was almost like starting over again and we talked about the past month in which we had been apart.

Mr. and Mrs. Eastwood were nice folks and they made me feel welcome. They had pretty strong Yorkshire accents and it took a little getting used to in the beginning to understand everything they said but that was fine. I never really noticed that accent that much when Jackie spoke but it did come out a little more now that she was at home with her folks. During the conversations Jackie's Mom and Dad addressed her as Pam and it was kind of awkward for me as "Pam" had always been "Jackie" as far as I was concerned but I started using "Pam" when with her parents and "Jackie" when we were alone.

On Sunday I found out what real Yorkshire pudding was like. It was excellent and was served as a starter with a good helping of gravy. It was also served with the main course together with the roast beef and potatoes. Dinner was followed by cups of dark brown tea which Jackie's dad sipped as he sat in his armchair beside the coal fire. I believe that he was or had been a coal miner and he looked like a man who had worked hard all his life.

That night the temperature dropped down and the weather forecast predicted ice and snow. Mrs. Eastwood suggested that Jackie should not drive me to Burnley as we had planned due to the bad road conditions, but Jackie insisted that she would take me. We arrived safely in Burnley Monday afternoon and met the rest of the band at the Cabaret club.

As we set up the gear Dave and Roger told us how they had been up at the studio with Joe with the Diamond Twins, and that Sonia and Sandra had put vocal backing on "No More You And Me" Joe really liked the Twins and they did some back ups on another of Joe's recordings. Joe told Sonia and Sandra that he would like them to make a record at R.G.M. so they should start to look for material. We were eager to find out what Ritchie Blackmore was like. Roger said he thought Ritchie was a decent bloke but was most impressed with the fuzz box that he used. Ritchie listened to the track as Joe set up the mics for the girls and with a few suggestions from Joe came up with a nice line. Ritchie completed his part in about an hour. The Twins put on their back ups together with Ritchie and may have possibly double tracked them after Ritchie left. At the end of the session Dave asked Joe if he would play them the recording we had done of the "Theme from Lawrence Of Arabia." Joe consented but Roger said that he thought that Joe had sped up the recording and that it didn't sound as good as before. Versions found in the Tea Chest Tapes show no sign of being sped up. That session was a milestone in the short time that we worked with Joe because at last we thought that there was something new coming out of R.G.M. A more modern and maybe a little more serious music. We looked forward to its release knowing that we could play it on stage with confidence as we felt that "No More You And Me" was up to date. I don't believe that we ever played it live.

As Roger Dave and the Twins left the studio Joe assured everybody that the vocal would still be the A side and "Lawrence", the B side. As they said goodbye to Joe and took the stairs out into the street, this would be the last time they would walk down those stairs and the last time they would see Joe Meek.

That week in Burnley we were doubling with The Searchers which meant that we would play two shows each night. We opened up at the Cabaret Club Burnley at 8pm and closed the show in Brierfield at the 77 club at 11.30pm. The Searchers played the opposite, opening at Brierfield and closing at Burnley. We enquired at the Cabaret club regarding suitable accommodation and were informed of a good place close to the club for 5 guineas per week which included breakfast, an evening meal and the added luxury of central heating. There was also a communal kitchen where guests could prepare tea and snacks and a sitting room to relax in. After we had finished setting up and achieved a good sound balance we made our way over to the digs. Jackie and I left in her car and on the way over we arranged that as Jackie would be staying the night with me that we would have to masquerade as a married couple. Jackie wore no rings so I gave her my amethyst ring which I wore on my little finger which she turned around on her ring finger to make it appear as a wedding ring. I swivelled my onyx ring around in the same way. When we arrived at the digs we were introduced to the proprietor, a very nice lady. Jackie explained that she was a member of the famous Tiller Girls dancers and that we had been recently married and as we were both on the road we were taking the opportunity to spend a night together. The landlady felt sorry for us and immediately began to mother Jackie offering a cup of tea and showed us to our room.

We went down very well at the Cabaret Club but the 77 Club did not have a very good attendance. It was rather awkward to play at the 77 as due to the travelling time between the clubs we had to use The Searchers' gear and as they had no keyboard player Dave had to play the house organ there which was a big old Hammond similar to a B3. When we made it to the club there was no time to experiment with sounds on the keyboard and although Dave was not happy with the situation he made the best of it. This was the first time that Jackie had seen us play a nightclub gig as on the Coventry show we only had a three song set. When we finished our set she remarked on how much she had enjoyed the music which pleased me and I was also very happy that we were together. We all drove back to the Cabaret club in the Commer van and then took our separate cars back to the digs. Dave decided that he would drive the Commer and upon arrival at the digs decided to make a cup of tea before going to bed. When the rest of us returned we couldn't find Dave anywhere. He was not in his room and the van was parked outside and we began to get worried. Suddenly Dave appeared through the front door in fits of laughter as he had made a mistake and entered the house next door. Hearing some noise downstairs the house owners came down in their pyjamas and asked Dave what the hell he was doing in their house and were ready to call the police. At that point Dave realized that he was in the wrong place, politely apologized and made a hasty exit. Those were the days when, unlike today people left their doors unlocked at night. The following day Jackie and I went down to breakfast at around 11am. We had spent a great night together but as the weather was getting worse she decided that she should leave for home. There was no snow but the wet roads had turned to ice. I warned her to drive carefully and sadly kissed her goodbye.

Frank Allen, The Searchers bass player was staying at our digs together with their drummer. I don't remember the drummer's name but I do remember that he was a coal man in London before he played pro. We all hung around together in the afternoon and played a few games of cards and swapped stories, experiences and generally talked about the business. Frank Allen was a seasoned pro with a confident personality He was very funny and all in all a likeable character. He had previously played with The Rebel Rousers, Cliff Bennett's band and had replaced Tony Jackson. Chris Curtis had also left The Searchers by this time. Mike Pender and John McNally both lived in that area so they were staying at home and we didn't get to meet them.

Frank Allen told us that the legendary Wee Willie Harris was also staying at our digs and a little later that afternoon he entered the sitting room. We expected to see him clothed in his Teddy Boy outfit together with his bright pink afro hairstyle, but all in all, his late fifties image was not present and he had the appearance of a regular guy with short greying hair. He did however have a terrific personality. He entertained us with card tricks, magic shows and funny jokes which had us pissing in our pants with laughter. Just before tea time I decided to call Jackie to make sure that she had arrived home safely. When I got through I found out that she had skidded off the icy road on the way home and crashed into a shop front. Luckily she was OK and there was little damage but as she was a bit shook up her brother had met her to drive her home. Needless to say Jackie's mother was quite angry as she had warned her not to drive me to Burnley.

On that Monday we had played a few card games with The Searchers and Wee Willie Harris but as the week wore on the card games started as soon as we woke up and lasted until we left for the gig. John Davies and I were not card players or gamblers so we decided to watch while the rest of The Tornados matched their wits against The Searchers and Wee Willie. It was interesting to see how the game would go back and forth with winners and losers continually changing places and with The Searchers drummer continually threatening to bet ten quid on his hand, things sometimes got a little scary. The shows were going quite well at the clubs and at the end of the week we got three encores at the end of our set which left us feeling in good spirits. At the end of the week we had a Sunday night gig at the Princess and Domino clubs in Manchester after which we all made our way home. The New Year seemed to be starting off with a lack of gigs and we would not be working for another 12 days. When Pete dropped me off at Clegram Road I decided to unload my Marshall amp and guitar in the hope that I might write something new during the time off.

It was always cold in January in Gloucester and sometimes that cold rain would fall in the evening. It was always nice to be home for a while especially when it was cold; and instead of sleeping in some grubby hotel or bed and breakfast in some depressing place up north, I found myself enjoying the luxury of home cooked food, and sleeping in my once familiar bed in the back bedroom, with so many layers of blankets on it that once I got into bed it was almost impossible to move. It was nice to sit in my father's chair and to warm my feet in front of the fire place, sip on a cup of tea and toast crumpets in front of the fire.

All this comfort of being back home helped me come up with a song. I imagined my sister Georgina and I sitting together with our mum in the glow of the fire in the evening. We were looking at the old photo album and my mother was turning the pages, informing my sister and me who the various relatives were. The rain was tapping on the window and the wind was howling in the chimney. I called it the "Sunday Evening Song." It ended up with my mum brushing a tear from her cheek when we were putting the book away. This song would wind up almost two years later sung in Hebrew on an album of children songs by then top Israeli singer Arik Einstein.

My sister's boyfriend Ray would often take me out for a drink and we'd ride on his motorcycle. I took a ride up the town and said hello to some of my friends at the department store. I had spoken to Jackie and she told me that she would soon be leaving for rehearsals in Bradford and she gave me the phone number and address of the Alhambra. I wanted to send her something as a surprise and Ray said he could get me a nice teddy bear so I decided to send it to her. Ray drove my sister and me out to the country to see some poodle puppies at a breeder. They had only one left and the breeder said he was the pick of the litter and was saving him for last. Georgina fell in love with the puppy immediately. The breeder said she would take eleven pounds for "Sweep" so I bought him for my sister.

By the end of the twelve days off I was getting itchy to be playing again. We all met at Drayton Manor Park for the Friday night gig and drove to Barton upon Humber to play the Saturday night at the Army Drill Hall. Dave said that he hadn't received any contracts from The Cooper Organization except for one that had just come for a gig at the Starlight Rooms in the Kingsway Casinos in Southport. This sounded quite impressive to us but it would not be until February 9th which meant that we would be off for another eleven days. I called Jackie and was able to reach her at the Alhambra and hearing that I had sometime off she said I could come and stay with her if I wanted. I decided to go by train Saturday night and Jackie would meet me at the Station in the morning.

It was a long dark night on that train journey. Those night trains were always slow as they had to schedule the times for the mail pick ups. We had to change at Leeds and had to wait for a few hours for the connection to Bradford. It was weird to be the only person in the waiting room in the dead of night with nothing to do but huddle over the coal fire that was burning in the fireplace. Each time a train pulled in I would walk out onto the platform hoping that it would be the train for Bradford. I asked a few railway men who were standing around and one of them said that he was the driver who would be taking the train to Bradford and it would be due in about an hour.

After what was the longest hour the Bradford train pulled in and I climbed on board and entered what I thought to be an empty compartment. I opened the sliding door and put my suitcase up on the rack and in the dim light I saw an old lady who looked like she was about to stretch out on the seat and fall asleep. She sat up as I entered and seemed a little unhappy that somebody was invading her little space. I decided that I would stay and as we sat down on opposite sides of the compartment we struck up a conversation. After a while she said she was going to sleep and I said that I would do the same. I have never been able to sleep in trains or planes so I basically laid there while she snored away. At one point I must have dozed off and was woken by a sound. I opened my eyes to see in the dim light the old lady standing up and releasing a fusillade of farts one after the other in a way that I can only call a "Real Razzmatazz." Dave Watts had a certain expertise which enabled him to fart at will. Once in a hotel room he claimed that he could do 300 farts one after the other. He in fact did that and we counted them. I laid there trying to hold back my laughter as I imagined Dave Watts and the old lady embroiled in a farting contest. At one point in the night she got up and left the compartment as we pulled into a station and got off the train. I laid back and tried to get some sleep but it didn't come. My mind was far too active with the sound of the Saturday gig still ringing in my ears and the excitement of seeing Jackie again.

It wasn't until the sun started to come up and it's early morning rays penetrated that musty compartment through the condensation on the window that I really thought that I could actually fall asleep. I was almost disappointed when the train pulled into Bradford Station as I was in that state when you feel that you are so tired that you could just drift off to the most peaceful sleep that you ever had but you had to get up. I straightened up my clothes, ran my fingers through my hair and dragged my suitcase down from the rack. It was a crisp cold morning as I walked along the platform looking toward the exit to see if Jackie was waiting there for me. I didn't see her anywhere as I handed in my ticket stub at the gate. I hoped that I would see her car parked by the curbside but it wasn't there. I walked back and forth a bit not knowing what to do wondering if something had happened. Once the noise of the train pulling away was over there seemed to fall a very still silence and apart from a pigeon that was cooing somewhere it was totally quiet. I sat down on one of the benches and waited for sometime. It was early Sunday morning and it seemed like all of Bradford was still asleep, when I finally heard the noise of a vehicle approaching from some distance. And there she came around the corner driving a bit faster than she should have and pulling up by the curb she rolled down the window "Throw your case in the back, sorry I'm late luv, the alarm didn't go off."

Jackie drove me around the city centre and showed me the Alhambra where she was working at and then we went on to where her caravan was parked in an empty lot next to a transport café of sorts. It was a convenient spot as it was not too far from the theatre and we were able to use the facilities at the café. We spent the rest of the afternoon making up for lost time and talked about what we both had been doing since we last saw each other. She told me that they were still rehearsing the pantomime for another week and the opening night would be on the coming Saturday which was 4th February. I could go with her to hang out at the theatre for the week and Johnny Webster was there as he and another male dancer were working on that show. I had worked with Johnny and his brother Jimmie Webster on the Birthday Show in Coventry.

We arrived around 10am on Monday morning at the theatre where Jackie proceeded to introduce me to everyone. The director was a very nice guy and told me that I could watch the rehearsals or be back stage as I wished so I felt at home and comfortable. I spent most of the time that week hanging around in the male dancers' dressing room with Johnny and the other dancer, but from time to time I strolled around back stage to watch the rehearsals. At lunch time we would all meet at an Italian restaurant down the street and eat spaghetti together with the director who was a real pleasant guy who always made sure that I could get in on the conversation. The rehearsals were going along as planned and by the time that Friday came around for some reason I told Jackie that I might just stay at the caravan for the day instead of going to the theatre. I didn't want to wear my welcome out there and anyway Jackie had got me a ticket to the opening night show on Saturday so it would be good to take a break so that I could enjoy the show more. Around 12 noon I was beginning to feel sorry that I didn't go down to the Alhambra. I had nothing to do, no guitar to play and was totally bored. I took a walk outside in that rather bleak looking empty lot and strolled over to the café for a cup of tea. Later back in the caravan I remembered that Jackie had told me that she had a portable radio and looking above the bed on the shelf I spotted it nestled in the corner. Luckily the batteries were in good shape and the BBC came in fine. After the 1pm news was over I laid out on the bed and snoozed for a while, drifting in and out of sleep Just as the 2pm news was beginning I began to stir and turned on my side to hear the announcer reporting that the independent record producer Joe Meek had been found shot dead in his London studio. He went on to say that Joe Meek was the composer of "Telstar" which was a multi million seller recorded by The Tornados, and that was that.

I immediately jumped up from the bed and then sat right down again. Did I hear that right? Yes Joe Meek, shot! I sat there hearing the news bulletin repeat itself over and over again in my head it was almost like a mantra which stopped me from thinking of anything else. I didn't think of the guys in the band or where they were at the time or what we were going to do without our manager and record producer and how it might affect our future in the music business; all I could think of was that Joe was dead and that somehow he had been shot. Due to the lack of information given on the news I presumed that somebody had gone by the studio and shot him.

I had a feeling of helplessness as there was no way that I could talk to anybody about this. I had no phone or for that matter anybody's phone numbers. I knew that Pete was in Liverpool with Ann but I had no idea how to contact him. On the 3pm news it was reported that Joe Meek had in fact shot himself with a shotgun after apparently shooting his Landlady Mrs. Violet Shenton. This was absolutely unthinkable that Joe had shot and killed Mrs. Shenton and then shot himself, but it was true. All I did was sit there in total silence, just like the time when Joe had gone berserk and told us all to fuck off back to Gloucester. Eventually when Jackie finally returned home I could at least talk to somebody about it. It wasn't the same as being able to talk to the guys in the band but it was the next best thing. Although Jackie knew little of Joe and could not feel it as I did it was still good to be able to talk to somebody.

The following day, Joe's death and everything that was affected by it really hit home, and I decided to return to Gloucester on Sunday morning by train and hope to contact Pete Holder at the farm if he had returned from Liverpool. Jackie and I had spent a great week together but I had to leave, regrettably, and after going to see the opening night Pantomime show which did take my mind off things a bit, on Sunday morning Jackie drove me to the station and we said our goodbyes It seemed we were always saying goodbyes not knowing when we would see each other again. I had lots of time to think on that train ride back to Gloucester and for quite sometime I sat alone in a compartment. At one stop a large group of what I thought to be soccer or rugby fans joined me in my compartment. They were a noisy bunch of hooligans who proceeded to tear the place apart. They pulled all the light bulbs out of the sockets and threw them at each other while I sat there trying to look cool and unaffected by the mayhem they were creating. It was a great relief when they all finally got off the train. I was grateful that I didn't get the shit beat out of me and was happy just to shake the bits of broken light bulbs from my hair. Passing through Stroud I got up and stood in the passageway and pulled down the window and stuck my head out to breathe the fresh air. From time to time when the wind changed direction I got a face full of smoke from the engine and everything seemed very strange because I was coming home to the area where Joe Meek came from knowing that he was gone, and thinking how things were with his family in Newent. I knew that they had to be completely devastated. Joe Meek was gone and would never throw a temper tantrum, create another "Telstar", kick another organ or sneak a kiss from an unsuspecting boy in the studio, ever again.

Back home in Gloucester, my folks had heard about the tragedy. We sat and talked about it but there was very little that I could really say except that I knew Mrs. Shenton was Joe's landlady and that we had seen her briefly on a couple of occasions when we were at the studio. I called the farm and Mrs. Holder told me that Pete was not there but she had heard from him and that he was on his way home. She also said that everyone was in a state of shock in Newent and that they were all wondering what could have happened. In the early part of the week it was announced in the *Gloucester Citizen* that the funeral for Joe Meek was to be held at St Mary's church in Newent at 11am on Friday 10th February just one short week to the day of the mysterious murder-suicide. I finally got to speak to Pete who said that he had been at the Royal Court Theatre in Liverpool staying with Ann his girlfriend as she was working on the pantomime *Tom Thumb* starring who else but Jimmy Clitheroe. At sometime in the evening somebody came up to Pete and said that they were playing "Telstar" on the radio and talking about Joe Meek. It was then that Pete heard the terrible news and just like me was in a state of having nobody to contact and that I was the first member of the band he had spoken to. As we talked there was really very little that we could say. We didn't even talk about how or why and it just seemed that we were in a numb state of shock. The main thing at that time was that we could not understand why Joe had shot Mrs. Shenton. On the few occasions that we had met her when she was visiting Joe at the studio she was always all smiles and very pleasant in her demeanour. There have been many stories of how she was constantly complaining about the noise but in all the times we were recording there I do not remember that she came to complain.

On Thursday 9th February the day before the funeral we were booked to play at the Starlight room at the Kingsway Casino in Southport. We decided that we would have to drive home directly after the gig and that Pete, John and I would stay at the farm so we would all be available to attend the funeral. When Pete came to pick me up Thursday morning we decided to get some Valentine cards as February 14th was coming up shortly and send them to Jackie and Ann as a surprise. I thought that I would send Jackie's card to her mother's address and decided that I would put Uncle Wiggley's initials on the card. He was the Ventriloquist that I mentioned earlier in the story and that was not his real name. I did this because somehow I didn't really trust Jackie and thought that she may have still been seeing him occasionally. By doing this I was testing her to find out if she would mention the card to me. This would prove to be a stupid mistake on my behalf that I would pay for in the future.

Pete had brought Joe Cavanaugh with him. Joe was a farm hand who worked for Mr. and Mrs. Holder and took care of the milking. He wanted to come along for the ride and act as our road manager and set up the gear for us as he had done this for us on several occasions when we were The Saxons. As it turned out he did nothing but complain the whole time about all the work he had to do to the point that Pete wished that he had not brought him along. When we arrived at John Davies' place we discovered that John had only just heard about Joe's death as he had not listened to the radio or read a newspaper in the past few days. Just like us John was in a bewildered state not understanding why this whole thing had happened.

We met up with Dave and Roger in Southport. This was the first time we had all been together since the tragedy and we were all basically in the same state of disbelief and completely baffled by the mystery of the whole thing. Dave said that he was with his brother at Biggin Hill working on a car outside in the driveway and had heard the news on the radio late that afternoon when he had gone into the house to get something from the kitchen. At first he thought that it may have been a hoax of some sort but did find out that it was the truth and just like us Dave could not figure out why it had happened. In fact in his diary for Friday February 3rd 1967 Dave had written "Joe Meek...Dead" followed by a question mark, which seemed to ask was it really true and why did it happen. Roger said that he had been staying with Sandra (Diamond Twins) at her parents' home in Maidstone in Kent. They had tried to call Joe that fateful morning to see if he had any news of a release date for "No More You And Me" but got no answer. They decided to go into town to do some shopping and upon their arrival back home they were met at the front door by Sandy's father who informed them that he had heard on the radio that Joe Meek had been shot dead at the studio. Roger and Sandy were in complete shock and disbelief but when the news came through again on the radio the sad truth became clear to them. It seems that I was the first member of The New Tornados to hear of Joe's death as I sat there alone in Jackie's caravan on that cold bleak morning in Bradford.

We sat around in the dressing room as we waited to play our set, all of us feeling that we were in the "Twilight Zone." Surprisingly enough we didn't talk about how we were going to make records from now on or who would manage us; all we knew was that Joe was gone and our minds were totally numb from the shock and mystery of the whole tragedy. The only thing that we could ask was "Why?" We did talk about "No More You And Me" and in that conversation we realized that our dream to have the first ever "A" side vocal single to be put out by The Tornados was now totally shattered and completely unreachable. Just when it seemed that Joe was coming around to our way of thinking and everything was looking good, it was all over, and could never be again. There would be no second chance this time, Joe was gone and couldn't give any more second chances.

We decided that we would all return to the farm after the gig so that we would be ready to attend the funeral that morning. John, Pete and I drove back in the van whilst Dave and Roger drove by car and after only a few short hours of sleep we woke up on Friday morning and sat around the long dining table while Mrs. Holder made breakfast for us. We wondered what the approaching funeral would be like and still talked about Joe's death with the family. We all got ready and drove down to the church at around 10.45am and we waited in the churchyard for the family to arrive. Dave and Roger drove into Gloucester as Sonia and Sandra were arriving on the train from London. When they arrived Sonia and Sandra were wearing matching trouser suits and they looked very attractive as always. When the funeral party arrived Joe's casket was rolled into the church followed by the Meek family. Mrs. Meek was supported on each side by Joe's brothers Eric and Arthur who were accompanied by Joe's sister Pam. It was difficult for Mrs. Meek to walk at the best of times as she was partially crippled and even with her two sons as support, this would be the hardest walk that she would ever have to make. The total devastation and heartbreak could be seen on her face and also on the family's faces. This modest hard working country family had lost their beloved Joe who had moved to London to seek his fortune and fame and from very simple sources had produced some huge hits including the world famous "Telstar." There was also a certain air of sadness at that time. It was because it was bad enough that Joe had committed suicide but even worse because he had also murdered Mrs. Shenton. Under these circumstances it would be very difficult to sing the praises for one of the most important forerunners in the history of modern recording and mourn his loss because all of that was over-shadowed by his crime of murdering his landlady. As far as a eulogy went I really don't remember the vicar saying that much. It must have been an awkward situation as most people in Newent, although saddened by the loss of the greatest phenomenon to ever come out of their small town, felt that Joe Meek had brought disgrace upon them as he had murdered Mrs. Shenton. The scene at the grave site was very sad and upsetting as poor Mrs. Meek finally said goodbye to her beloved Joe. Eric and Arthur although they tried to remain stoic were obviously under great pressure to contain their grief, whilst their sister Pamela openly wept as she threw a handful of soil into the grave. She was tragically killed by a drunk driver in 1975 and Mrs. Meek (Biddy) passed away four years later. As The Tornados, the grief and disbelief was apparent on our faces as we all stared at each other not knowing what to say to anybody. Earlier that morning as we sat at the farm we thought that we would see an outpouring of Joe's artists and business associates attending the funeral but nobody showed up. Apart from The Tornados and the Diamond Twins the only other people that could have been from show business were two older guys dressed in cowboy hats and wearing bootlace ties. Nobody seemed to know who they were except that they may have come from the Forest Of Dean. We didn't speak to them but we did exchange polite smiles with them. It is possible that they may have been from a band called The Foresters who recorded with Joe back in the early days of his recording career.

We were indeed surprised that there were none of Joe's other artists present at the funeral. We expected to see The Honeycombs, members of previous Tornados, Heinz, Geoff Goddard, or people from the Cooper Organization, but not a single soul was there. Obviously there had been a falling out with Joe and many of his artists which could have been a reason for some of them not to attend, but knowing that the methods of communication were not then as they are today, that could account for the absence of other artists. In those days you just couldn't bring up a website and read about Joe Meek's upcoming funeral arrangements on your computer. As The Tornados we were basically local, and due to the Holder family's close ties to Joe Meek's family we knew all the details concerning the funeral arrangements. We were lucky to be able to say our last goodbye to Joe Meek, who had taken us from our humble beginnings as The Whirlwinds and Saxons from his home town of Newent and by using us to create The New Tornados introduced us to the world of professional show business. In the lives of all his other artists, few friends and associates Joe Meek disappeared just as quickly as he had appeared and was now gone forever.

The New Tornados were now alone without the figurehead of Joe Meek to guide and provide for them. At this point we would have to fend for ourselves and make our own decisions, something that we never had to worry about before as Joe had made all our decisions for us. We never questioned anything and if Joe said that The Cooper Organization had us playing on the "Moon" we would have gone along with it. Now that the cushion called Joe Meek had been removed we were dealing directly with our agents and representing ourselves.

Just before the funeral, the Cooper Organization began their approach to get The Tornados to commit to be the backing group and appear on the Great Yarmouth summer season show which starred Freddie and The Dreamers. Dave Watts' records show that the gigs had been few and far between ever since we finished the Coventry show in December, and what gigs we did have had been mostly depressing, low paying venues. We were working a little more than once a month. We met at their offices where George Cooper and Harry Dawson showed their disbelief in Joe's murder suicide and hoped that we could shed some light on the mystery; but even though we were probably among the closest people to Joe we still had no idea how or why the whole thing happened.

When the subject of the Summer Season came up they wanted us to back the show and do our own act as we had done in Blackpool but the money they were offering was about the same as we had made in

Blackpool and we thought that we were worth more than that. We brought up the lack of work and decent venues and said that we couldn't make a decision. Harry Dawson hinted that they had not been getting good reports on our cabaret shows and had they been better then we would have been working more. We left agreeing that we would let them know our decision. As there was no work available in the next few weeks everyone left for their respective homes.

That weekend I decided to give Jackie a call at the Alhambra. She told me that she had received a Valentine's card from Uncle Wiggly. Her mother had seen it and had called him about it but he had sworn that he had not sent it and that there was nothing between him and Jackie any more. It was then that I should have kept silent and been happy to know that Jackie had told me about the card, but like the poor honest fool that I was I confessed to having sent it myself. Jackie was pissed off about the whole thing, and rightfully so and ended up asking me why I did it. "Just to know if you would tell me" I said. "Well you know now don't you?" she hissed and that was the end of the conversation. I walked sadly back down the street knowing that I had probably lost the girl that I had stolen from the ventriloquist man and all because of my own paranoia and stupidity. I called her after a few days and was received with the same if not colder reception than before and as our conversations drifted apart I knew that our relationship had come to an end.

As there was no work to keep me occupied all I could do was hang around the house feeling totally sorry for myself. It didn't take long for my parents to figure out that there was something wrong. Eventually my dad asked me how things were with Jackie and I told him that it looked like it was over. He was sorry to hear the news and said that he had liked Jackie very much as she reminded him of a girl he knew when he lived in Portsmouth as a teenager. During the war she was killed by a direct hit on the air raid shelter she was in, and her body was never found. Just a few scraps of her clothing and some of her blonde hair was all that remained.

The next two and a half weeks dragged by very slowly and I was looking forward to getting on the road again. I was able at least to start writing a new song which turned out to be called "St. Valentines

Day Anniversary Dream" which was written around the sad situation that I had brought upon myself. Optimistically, I hoped that it would all turn out to be a bad dream in which everything turned out fine in the end and I was reunited with my love. If only it would have turned out to be like that.

It was a relief to be back on the road again and on Sunday March 5th we drove to Sunderland where the Jimmy Dunn agency had arranged a few gigs for us for that week. After the first gig on Monday night we had two days off and basically just hung around the digs with nothing much to do. We called the agency for details of the Thursday night gig only to find out that it was cancelled and in order to deal with the boredom that had set in we ended up in a cinema on Thursday night watching the film *It's A Mad, Mad, Mad, Mad World.* Friday we appeared at the Ivy League club and Saturday morning we showed up at the Dunn Agency to collect our pay for the gigs and get details of that evening's venue. A letter had arrived addressed to Dave Watts and The Tornados from the Cooper Organization. This being a rather unusual occurrence, Dave hurriedly opened up the envelope to find a letter from Harry Dawson. Harry said that he was amazed and disgusted with the attitude of the band with regard to the Great Yarmouth summer season and pointed out that they had represented The Tornados since their first hit "Telstar" in 1963 and had handled every Tornados group since then. They told us that they had an existing contract stating that they had sole rights to represent The Tornados and enough correspondence with Joe Meek to prove the close tie up with them and The Tornados. Harry's final paragraph in the letter stated that we most likely did not know, that if they wanted to, the Cooper Organization could stop us from using The Tornados name and they themselves could form another group of The Tornados, all this being in accordance with contractual agreements with the late Joe Meek. Whether or not this was in fact true most likely will never be known, but the Cooper Organization was basically saying that at that time they had the rights to the name of The Tornados. As we didn't relish the idea of calling their bluff on this Dave and Pete appeared at Evelyn House on 14th March and signed the contract for the summer season at Great Yarmouth. It is unclear whether Dawson offered us more money as we had requested on our prior meeting with them but he did say that he was working on a certain deal that would be a benefit to us while we were in Great Yarmouth. Had Joe been alive at this time this scenario would never have taken place. There would have been no question whether or not we would play the summer season, but we cannot rule out whether as The Tornados we might have asked Joe to push Dawson to pay us more money. After all Joe was on our side and would probably have taken our side on the matter. Now with Joe being dead the Cooper Organization did not have to arrange any commissions for him which was a savings on their behalf.

Harry Dawson called Dave Watts towards the end of March with news that he had got us free digs for the summer season. We would be staying at a resort called the Ponderosa and would be given a two bedroom cabin to stay in complete with kitchen and bathroom. In exchange for this we had to do a thirty minute spot Sunday lunchtimes, in the clubhouse for the guests. It did look like Harry Dawson had made some effort to try to help us out after all and thirty minutes a week was not much to pay for free digs.

The last week of March found us playing some of the most unusual and out of the way venues that the Cooper Organization could come up with. After playing at the X L bowling alley in Middlesbrough where we spent the night at the Studley Hotel we spent the next day driving twelve hours to the next gig which was in Falmouth way down in the county of Cornwall. We arrived in the small town at around ten o'clock at night only to find out that there was nowhere to stay. We drove around the tiny place searching for accommodation thinking that we would probably have to spend the night sleeping in the van. Suddenly in a small side street we spotted a sign in the window of a residence which read "Bed and Breakfast Vacancy." It was well after ten pm at the time and when it looked like there would be no reply to our knocking we heard the sound of footsteps from inside. The front door was opened by the proprietor and his wife receiving us with looks of trepidation so we quickly explained that we were entertainers and would be appearing at the night club the following day. They were sorry to say that they didn't have enough room for all of us. After some discussion they said that we could stay if we liked but the accommodation would be rather cramped. As we had no choice in the matter we ended up sleeping three in a bed and paid one pound and ten shillings each for the stay. The following day, much to our surprise the venue turned out to be pretty good and we played for a decent audience.

We had a relatively short drive the next day to the Hartland Heritage coastal area in Devon where we were scheduled to perform. We were surprised to find that the gig was to be held in a hall situated in the small village of Hartland. We arrived in the afternoon at the rather ramshackle place where we found an elderly custodian there. He was the only living being that we could see as the whole village was completely deserted and looked like some place that you might see in a horror film. We set up the gear and talked to each other and laughed about this strange place. We could not imagine what kind of audience, if any, we would have that evening. We asked the old custodian if there was a hotel anywhere in the village. He shook his head and in his thick Devonshire accent said that the only place we could stay at was at the Manor which was located down the street. We pulled up outside of the old very creepy looking place and noticed above the door carved in stone above some old crest, the date 1066. We knocked at the door using the big old fashioned knocker and the door was opened by an old man who looked something like a retired colonel from the army. We entered the gloomy looking foyer, signed the guest registry and paid for our rooms. Everyone that worked in that mysterious creepy place was old. The lady who showed us to our rooms had to have been well into her eighties and kept giving us these strange looks. At any moment we expected her to say that nobody ever stays in this place after dark due to the moans of the ghosts and the rattling of the chains. The walls were lined with old ancestral paintings and the heads of various animal trophies stared at us as we walked along the dim hallways to the sound of creaking floorboards. Our rooms were just as eerie. It was like stepping back in time. The bed was very high and creaky and the sheets felt damp and smelled musty. There was a night stand with a large pitcher of water and a wash bowl on it. We were all beginning to have second thoughts about this scary place but as there was nowhere else to stay we decided to stick it out and spend an hour or so resting in our rooms. Late in the afternoon we heard the sound of thunder and a rainstorm blew in off the coast. Dave Watts knocked on my door and invited me to his room where he pointed at the rain that was leaking in from the roof onto his bed. "Here Robbie this bloody place must have been built in 1066 and they've never had the bleeding roof repaired." he joked. John Davies joined us saying that he had decided to take a snooze but couldn't sleep because of all the weird sounds he was hearing. We met in Pete's room together with Roger who was totally freaked out by this "Haunted" house and we all decided that we would not stay there the night and that it would be best to leave after the gig, drive through the night, and return to our homes.

As it turned out 400 tickets were sold at seven shillings and six-pence each for the venue and it turned out to be an enjoyable gig. We couldn't figure out where the people had come from and how they knew about the show as we had seen no signs posted that advertised the dance. We could only presume that they must have come from Bude or Bideford which were the closest towns to the village. After the show we drove off through the village past the creepy old manor imagining the ghostly sounds of creaking and groaning that were probably taking place inside in the dead of night. As Roger was going to meet Sandy at a venue where the Diamond Twins were working Dave decided that he would come with the rest of us to Gloucester and then get a train to London. Pete dropped us off at Clegram Road at 5am that morning and my dad drove Dave up to the station on his way into work.

Arriving home in Bromley at 11.30am Dave was greeted by his mum who told him that somebody named Ronnie Kray had just called to speak to him and wasn't that the man that the police had been questioning about some murders? Dave called Ronnie and made arrangements to meet him that afternoon at the Blind Beggar pub in the East End. Dave does not remember exactly what happened at that meeting but thinks that being as Joe Meek was now out of the picture that Ronnie's interest in managing The Tornados was becoming greater.

Back home in Gloucester I was again faced with another three weeks of nothing to do as there was no work on the horizon until around the end of the month. I was reduced to moping around my parents' house grieving for my lost love, Jackie Grant. One weekend my dad and I were talking and knowing how much he would love to play on a Hammond organ I called out to Aylesmore to speak to Pete but found out that he had left to visit Ann. Mrs. Holder said that Pete had unloaded the band's equipment and it was in the barn over at the Welsh House where we used to rehearse. My dad and I drove over and got the key to the barn where we set up the organ and we had a blow together. My dad was in seventh heaven as he had always wanted to play an organ but at that time had never been able to afford one. I plugged in my guitar and we played a few of my dad's favourite songs together. At one point he told me that he had only ever written one song in his life which was for one of his old girlfriends and he played it for me. It was a romantic waltz with words like "My love for you will last forever like the waves flow to the shore". Talking about old girlfriends our conversation came around to Jackie. We had a heart to heart talk about the failed romance and my dad mentioned that he would be working in Bradford the following week and asked me if I would like him to go over to Barnsley to see Jackie. I thought that it might be a last chance for me to regain my love and we decided that he would pay her a visit.

While my father was away in Bradford for the first week in April I spent most of the evenings at home talking with my mother and raiding my dad's supply of home made wines. The days really seemed to drag and all I really could do was to keep waiting until my father returned hoping that he would bring some good news for me. Upon his return he did bring good news. He had been over to see Jackie and luckily she was at home with her parents as the pantomime in Bradford had come to an end. He told me with a hint of happiness in his voice that Jackie said that I could go up to visit her if I wished and to give her a call. For the first time in many weeks I started to feel a little happier as it looked like I might be renewing my relationship with Jackie. That evening standing in the call box I pressed button A when I heard Jackie's voice answer the phone. The coldness seemed to have gone from her voice and after the usual chit-chat we arranged that I would come up to Barnsley by train the following Friday.

The reception I received from Jackie was what I might call cool when we met at the station. There were no hugs or kisses, just polite conversation. I could definitely feel that things were not the way they used to be, but I hoped that given time things would work themselves out. At her home things were not the same either. She basically ignored me for most of the time and I had to make conversation with her mother and felt out of place and uncomfortable. That evening Jackie went off to bed early leaving me alone with her mother downstairs. I felt awkward and miserable so as I was unable to talk to Jackie about us, I decided that I would see what I could find out from her mum. I could obviously see that everything was not working out the way I had hoped. During the conversation with her mum I asked what was the matter with Jackie and I was told that she just didn't feel the same way about me any more after I had shown my distrust in her and sent her the card from Uncle Wiggly. I explained to Mrs. Eastwood that I was very, very sorry that I had made such a stupid mistake and I wished that I could undo everything that I had done. She thought that it was a bit late for that and I went off to bed wondering what the hell I was doing there and began to feel worse than if I was at home moping around.

I spent that night unable to sleep, tossing and turning feeling that I was being punished for what I had done and by the time morning came I resolved to leave. As Jackie and I sat together in the kitchen that Saturday morning I told her that there was no point in my staying any longer and asked her to drive me to the station. She stretched out her hand and touched me softly and said, "Oh don't go, my cousin will come over tonight and take us to a cabaret club to see a show."

At that point I thought that well maybe things were going to be alright after all and a glimmer of hope appeared. We spent the rest of the afternoon watching the Rugby match on the TV and didn't get into much conversation. That evening her cousin showed up and drove us to the club. Jackie decided that she would sit in the front seat with him and I was left alone sitting in the back seat feeling really bad and completely left out of the conversations that they were having. She spent the whole time talking to him and completely ignored me. As the night wore on I began to feel really bad and was now sure that the only reason that she had asked me to stay was to prolong my punishment.

The next morning I told Jackie that there was a train leaving for Gloucester at noon and asked her to drop me off at the station. I told her that I couldn't figure out why she had said that I could visit her only to be treated in this way and her reply was that she couldn't stop me from coming to visit her if I wanted to. What I thought was to be a healing and forgiving time turned out to be no more than a way for her to hurt me for the unintentional stupid mistake that I had made. As we said goodbye at the station I had a feeling of sadness but at the same time a feeling of relief that I knew that it was finally over. In a way I felt glad that I had made the decision to leave and as the train pulled out of the station I decided that I would put her out of my mind, start to enjoy myself and get on with my life.

A few years later when I played in Jericho Jones (A continuation of the Churchills) I wrote a song called "There Is Always A Train" on our album *Junkies Monkeys, and Donkeys*

I can find a train in the afternoon,
No need to explain, I'll be leaving soon,
Take me away; I'll be leaving soon,
Take me away, in the afternoon,
You could take my place if you wanted to,
I can hide my face it's not hard to do,
Take me away; it's not hard to do,
Take me away, if you wanted to.
Who, in his little mind likes leaving you behind?
I can find a train on the evening line,
No need to explain, 'cause I need the time,
Take me away, 'cause I need the time
Take me away on the evening line

The last week in April found us in Northampton, from where we went for a week's engagement at the Top Hat club in Spennymoor. The Top Hat was a night club which featured a casino. There was a resident band there with the now famous organist Brian Sharp playing keyboards. The house band played all night and we came on at 1am in the morning and did our forty minute set. There was not enough room on the small stage area for both of the Hammond organs so we decided to leave Dave's in the van. This meant that in order to make a smooth take over between the house band and us, Dave would gradually slide over the seat taking over the keyboard from Brian and would finish the number off and be ready to launch into "Telstar" as the club manager introduced The Tornados. They were a nice bunch of guys in the house band and we struck up a friendly relationship with them. John Davies liked their drummer as he looked like jazz drummer Phil Seaman. Early one morning as we were leaving the club after downing several pints of Newcastle brown ale, John, the house drummer and I fell into a photo booth all posing as Phil Seaman, each with a cigarette hanging from his mouth.

We stayed at a guest house called the Knicky Knack, which was a big old house with a lounge downstairs. It was within walking distance from the club. We had decided that it was time to work on some new numbers for our act so we were lucky to be able to get access to the club in the afternoon to do some rehearsals. After one of the rehearsals John Davies and I decided to take a stroll and walk back to the guest house. We were about halfway there when I suddenly felt a very sharp pain in my backside right at the top of my leg. It was so intense and felt like getting stung by a hundred bees at the same time causing me to literally jump up and down with pain. John was totally befuddled by my outburst and jumping up and down, that he burst out laughing thinking that I was just fooling around and acting stupid like we often did just like *Monty Python*. When he saw the look of pain on my face he realized that I was actually hurt and became concerned. "What happened to you Robbie?" he asked. "I think I've been shot" I replied while rubbing the stinging spot with my hand. Looking around on the ground we soon found an air rifle slug and concluded that I had actually been shot in the butt by somebody with an air gun.

On our way to the Knicky Knack we suddenly saw a young kid appear from out of the bushes with an air rifle. He didn't seem that concerned as we walked up to him and asked him what he was doing and why he had shot me in my ass. He said that it wasn't him and that all the kids in that area had air rifles and they were all out shooting. I kind of thought that he could be telling the truth so we didn't press him any further. Back at the digs we met up with Dave Watts and after we had taken a look at the wound Dave said that he would drive us down to the police station to make a report.

The three of us walked into the police station and I approached the desk behind which stood a sergeant and two constables. I told them that I wanted to report that there were some sharpshooters down the road in Spennymoor. They looked at us in a puzzled way and asked me what I meant by "Sharpshooters" I went on to tell them that somebody had shot me in the ass with an air rifle and smiles appeared on their stern faces. John and Dave were trying hard not to laugh but they couldn't help breaking out into wide grins along with the officers. In fact everyone present was either smiling or tittering except for me. Well I suppose it was funny in some ways and eventually I managed to force a slight grin.

The officers said they wanted to see the wound and motioned that we should all adjourn to a side room where I pulled down my trousers and everybody went "Ooooh" as they gazed upon the red disc at the top of my leg which resembled the Japanese flag all red and inflamed and far too close to my testicles to even think about. We told them that we were The Tornados and that we were appearing at the Top Hat club and staying at the Knicky Knack guest house but even that didn't seem to influence them they just wrote out a report and had me sign it and we left the station with the constables still smiling at each other.

THE TORNADOS CHAPTER FIVE

More cabaret gigs, The Tornados go horse riding and fun with some groupies.

The fakir in the van and the strange story of Robb's ring.

Down on the farm The Tornados begin working on the music for the Great Yarmouth Show, and go drinking with Tom Holder.

Dave and Robb get scared to death while holding a séance to contact the spirit of Joe Meek.

Drug use and remembering being searched for drugs outside of Joe's studio. The rehearsals begin with bickering between some cast members.

The end of a gruelling week of rehearsals ends with a party and The Tornados get high acclaim for their work and performance.

Robb has an unusual fortune telling episode with a gypsy.

The Morecambe and Wise cricket match.

Dave has an erotic experience with Ruby Murray.

Ruby has a narrow escape and the hilarious story of the filming of the Joe Baker TV show.

Escapades on the Norfolk Broads where Dave speeds up a rental boat causing havoc on the river.

Big surprise for The Tornados as the Holder brothers announce their intended departure from the band at the end of the season.

The Tornados search for a new bass player and a group van and find both.

The Yarmouth show closes and back in London The Tornados land a new job as Billy Fury's backing band.

Robb meets Jackie Grant again and for the last time.

The Tornados on stage at The Windmill Theatre in Great Yarmouth in Norfolk during the summer season show of 1967.

(L-R) Pete Holder playing Gibson 335 right handed (Pete plays left handed)/Dave Watts, organist (Playing rhythm guitar)/Roger Holder, bass guitarist (Playing Drums)/John Davies, Drummer (Playing Bass guitar)/Robb Huxley, vocalist, Guitarist (Playing Keyboard)/plus the Fox Miller Boys and Girls.

With the week's work finished at Spennymoor we left for Sunderland to appear for the first week in May at the Parama Club. As was usual, we regularly found digs through the clubs we played at and found a good place where the New Vaudeville Band was staying. We shared the bill with a fire eating magician who looked like Ali Baba without his forty thieves. His magic tricks were the kind that you might find in a child's teach yourself magic set and we soon figured them out, but his fire eating display was impressive as he blew streams of spirits into an open flame. From where we stood upstairs looking down to watch the show, we could feel the heat from the burst of flames that shot into the air. We spoke to him in the dressing room after his performance and asked him about his fire eating which we told him that we enjoyed immensely. He said that it was really quite easy to do but you had to make sure that you turned your head to the side at the end of the burst of fire in order to cut off the stream of spirits from the flames. By doing that you would avoid getting burned.

While at the Top Hat at Spennymoor we saw that The Symbols band were following us the next week. They were good friends of Dave Watts and Dave had actually played with some of the band members at one time. As we had the Tuesday off at Sunderland we decided to visit the Top Hat and have a blow with the house band and watch the Symbols play their set. They were staying at the Knicky Knack guest house and we went by to see them and had a jam with their guitarist Sean. That night we got up and played a few numbers with the house band and had a real good time downing a few pints. The Symbols played their set doing a collection of Beach Boys style numbers which they did very well. They were a good vocal group. After the show we hung out with them at the casino chatting, drinking and losing more money than we intended at the roulette table. The Symbols were to go horse riding the following day and Dave and I decided that we would go along with them. We all met at a stable near Spennymoor and were asked if we had ridden before. We all said yes but our reply was not what I might call exactly truthful. I had only been on a horse once before myself and that was at the Holders' farm. All I had basically done was to sit on the pony as he walked round the farmyard. I doubt very much if Dave had ridden before and as for The Symbols the rate at which they were falling off their mounts more or less answered that question. There were two girls who escorted us on the ride and at one point they said that we were going to canter up the hill that we were approaching. I was terrified but managed to hold on tight as in front of me I saw the Symbols come flying off their horses in all directions. At the top of the hill there was a large open field where we were invited to ride around at our pleasure. I saw Dave get his horse up to a pretty fast gallop and was careering across the field whooping and hollering like the Lone Ranger. As he passed by me in a fuzzy blur he started shouting "I can't stop this bloody horse." It was hilarious to see him race up to a hedgerow where his horse stopped abruptly causing Dave to fly off over the horse's head into the air, where he disappeared behind the hedge. We all had a good laugh at that to see Dave reappear picking his way back through the prickly hedge and much the worse for wear he painfully remounted his steed. Gone were the shouts of "Hi Ho Silver!" and our escorts seeing that they thought that we had had enough began to lead us back down the hill to the stables. I for one was proud and surprised that I together with Sean from The Symbols were the only two riders who had not fallen off. As we arrived back at the stables I noticed that I had quite a headache from bouncing up and down and my legs were sore from holding on so tightly.

La Reserve at Sutton Coldfield was our next weeks work and actually turned out to be a good paying gig. We were paid 225 pounds for the week which meant that after paying the Cooper Agency their 10% we made roughly 40 pounds each for that week. This was about four times as much as a factory worker made and over eight times as much as I was making at the department store. I don't remember too much about the gig itself but I do remember that we stayed at a guest house that was frequented mostly by entertainers. So we usually got to meet other musicians and show biz people who were appearing in the area. It was like a home away from home atmosphere with all of us artists sitting around a long table eating, drinking and entertaining each other with tales of the "Road", comparing venues and agencies and general show business chit chat.

Our accommodation was conveniently located away from the guest house at the rear of the building in what was probably once a garage which was converted to a two bedroom unit with a bathroom. Pete and Roger took the room with the two beds while Dave, John and I shared a room with three beds. At the end of the week on Friday night around two in the morning, we had all just got to bed when we heard a gentle tap at our door. Dave switched on the light and went to see who it was. There in the doorway stood two chicks and they asked if we were The Tornados; and Dave standing in his skimpy underwear told them that yes indeed we were The Tornados of "Telstar" Fame. They boldly entered the room and out of the blue the cute cuddly little blonde one strutted up to my bed saying "Oh I like you" and stripped down to her underwear and jumped in bed with me. I barely had time enough to find out that her name was Anna Marie. Meanwhile the second chick had done the same thing and jumped in bed with John Davies, leaving poor Dave the guy who had opened the door, looking completely astounded with the realisation that Robbie and John were suddenly in bed with a couple of chicks while he was standing there with the door handle still in his hand.

John and I began to reap the benefit of our good fortune but when the lights went off, Dave, like the mischievous schoolboy that he was, started to disrupt the proceedings with his unique sense of humour. Just when he thought that John and I were getting down to business he'd say "Sorry lads I got to get a drink of water" and he'd put the lights on and take his time at the sink. At one point I felt a rustling sound coming from the foot of the bed together with a bright light shining up through the bed clothes. There he was the world famous gynaecologist Dr. David Watts performing a little overtime with a flash light that he carried in his suitcase. It was only after, when the two girls agreed to show Dave their tits and let him have a quick feel that the lights went off and things stayed quiet

Around 9am the next morning when we were all still in bed another gentle knock came at the door. As we began to stir the gentle tap was repeated and followed by "Breakfast." Anna Marie sat bolt upright saying "Oh no it's my mother." "Your mother" we all said in disbelief. "She works here, that's how we knew you were staying here."

In a twinkling of an eye the two girls leapt out of bed picked up their clothes and jumped inside of a big old fashioned wardrobe that was in the room and was basically empty. I pulled on my trousers and walked over to open the door. And there she stood in the doorway holding the breakfast tray, the same lady who had brought our breakfast each morning and her looks could not deny that she was in fact the mother of Anna Marie. She stood in the room holding the tray no more that a few inches from where her daughter was hiding in the wardrobe.

When she had left and the girls emerged from the wardrobe we all breathed a sigh of relief and began to laugh about it all. We shared our breakfast with the girls before they said that they had to leave. As they were leaving Anna Marie pulled out a small note book and a pencil from her handbag, and looking my way she made a short notation and waved goodbye. A little later on I pondered whether she had written down my name and the date to refer to just in case she might get pregnant or maybe she was just keeping a log of all the artists in show biz that she had spent the night with.

Mid May once again found us doing a double, up in Blackburn. We shuttled between the Starlight Club and the Cabaret Club. It was a typical week's cabaret work as we appeared alongside of magicians, fire eaters and dancing girls. One entertainer who looked something like an Italian gypsy featured sword swallowing and ate champagne glasses and light bulbs. We consented to let him ride in the group van with us between the venues. He entertained us with all kinds of magic tricks during the journey and took a liking to an amethyst ring that I wore on my little finger. He outstretched his arm towards me, opened his hand and asked me to place the ring in his palm, which I did and while closing his hand around the ring told me that I would never see the ring again. Then without moving his hand in any way he re-opened his palm and the ring was gone. I was totally amazed and a bit worried to say the least, thinking that I would never see the ring again. Then he smiled, closed his hand again and reopened it immediately and there was my ring back again. "Just kidding" he joked and dropped it back in my palm. "Remember this" he said "You have lost this ring before but you will only lose it three times." We all begged him to do it again or at least show us how it was done but he just laughed. "It's a secret" he said.

As it happens he was right. I had already lost that ring twice. One time when we were rehearsing at the Welsh House in Newent I went outside and picked up a stone to throw across the field. Upon doing this the ring flew off my finger and landed somewhere in the field in the grass which was about two feet high at the time. It was pointless to look for it so I gave it up for lost. Several months later Mick Holder was mowing the grass in that same field and as he was finishing up he saw something glistening in the late afternoon sunlight. It was my ring and he returned it to me. Sometime after that when we were on the road and had left a bed and breakfast place I suddenly saw that the ring was missing from my finger. I was sitting in the back of Roger's Ford Anglia and asked if we could return to the guest house as I had probably dropped it somewhere in the bedroom. I asked the receptionist if anyone had seen it in my room. She said that nobody had found it but she gave me the key so I could look for it myself. It was nowhere to be found. I spent a miserable day driving to our next gig mourning the loss of my ring. Late that afternoon as I was getting out of the car at the club I looked down and there it was close to the floor mat in the back of the car. It finally disappeared the following year when I was in Israel and I never saw it again.

Then he pulled out a couple of photos and in the dim light of the back of the van he passed them around to us. They showed him accompanied by two scantily dressed girls who looked like they could have come from the Amazon. They had pushed three feet long skewers through the side of his body, through his arms and tongue. "I don't do this in my act at the clubs" he said, "They won't allow me to, they say it would be too intense for the audience". We were inclined to agree with him. We asked him how come he didn't bleed when this was done to him, whereupon he went into a lengthy explanation talking about mind over matter and meditation but none of us really understood much of what he was talking about.

When the Burnley week was over we all went our separate ways. Pete and I left for Gloucester, Roger went to meet Sandra of the Diamonds, John disappeared like he usually did and nobody would hear from him until he would suddenly turn up, and Dave caught a train to London. Harry Dawson had left a message for Dave to call him. Now that Harry knew we would be backing the Great Yarmouth show he had changed his tune about the band. Now all of a sudden he was very pleased with all the great reports that he was receiving about The Tornados from the venues that we had appeared at. We had not changed and were still playing our same act but somehow now we were great once more in the eyes of the Cooper Organization. Dawson instructed Dave to go to Hampstead to pick up the musical scores for the show. These scores were for piano, organ, lead guitar, rhythm guitar, bass and drums. Dave held on to the keyboard parts and mailed the rest down to Aylesmore farm where I was staying with Pete. All the artists' music was included along with the dance routines and so on. The music parts were a little more difficult than the ones for Blackpool the previous year so Dave got some help from The Diamond Twins' pianist, Les Baguley, who was currently lodging at Dave's parents home.

On May 24th Dave caught the train to Gloucester and then hired a taxi to Newent and that's as far as the driver could take him, so with his music bag under his arm Dave trudged the extra few miles out to the farm. Roger had already arrived and together with Pete and me we had gotten a look at the music before Dave showed up. We had worked out some of it but we knew that it would fall together better once we got together with Dave. We were scheduled to rehearse from the 24th till the 26th of May at the Welsh House barn. Pete and I had set up the gear ready for the rehearsals and we started in the afternoon but to our disappointment John Davies failed to show. There was no reply at his parents' home so we had no other choice except to proceed without him. The following day the rehearsals were coming along fine but John had still not showed up and we were beginning to get worried. Finally that night as we sat around the dining table the phone rang and it was John saying that he had been away on holiday with his parents and he would be over the next day. This was typical John. He would never let us know of things like this and would invariably show up late. We were all relieved to hear the news and were able to relax now.

After supper Roger and Pete's dad, Tom Holder, stood up and said "Come on you buggers, I'll take you all out for a drink". We all piled into his car and he drove us over to the Feathers Hotel in Ledbury. The Feathers was a three storied inn with an attractive Elizabethan black and white exterior. As The Saxons we had played there on occasions. Tom Holder was in his element as he walked into the bar accompanied by his two sons Roger and Pete along with Dave and me in tow. He wouldn't let any of us buy a drink all evening and proceeded to introduce us all to his farmer friends as The Tornados who had been Joe Meek's top group. He gave them all the details on the band and told them that we were spending a few days at the farm before leaving to appear in a summer show in Great Yarmouth. Tom was well known in the area and was pretty good with his fists, one night knocking out a drunk who was causing some trouble, and then driving him home afterwards. As the night wore on we all got quite merry with Tom approaching us one by one with a grin from ear to ear offering us five pounds to fuck the milkmaid who worked at the farm. He followed his offer with that remarkable wheezy laugh that he had. By the time closing time came around we staggered out of the Feathers and Tom drove us back to the farm via those narrow winding country roads while that cool, night time country air laced with the aroma of wild flowers and hops, soothed us as we sped past the hedgerows that lined the side of the road.

After everyone else went to bed, Dave and I decided to stay up and chat for a while. That whole area was steeped in superstition and mystery with ghost stories galore. I was telling Dave of some of these that I had heard around the Holders' dining table on dark winter nights when Dave suddenly suggested that we should conduct a séance due to the area being rife with all the stories of robbery and murder. We set up the table with a glass surrounded by the alphabet which we had written out on squares of paper torn out of a writing pad in Dave's music case. It seemed to get very quiet as we began with the séance and a deathly hush seemed to fall upon us. We were conscious of every little sound that would occur as we placed our fingers on the glass with Dave starting to ask" Is anybody there?" The atmosphere began to get quite eerie and coldness seemed to penetrate the air. "If there's anybody there give us a sign" Dave asked, putting on a voice with a mysterious tone attached. A creaking sound suddenly emanated from nearby causing Dave to freeze and with his eyes coming out like organ stops he said" Bloody 'ell Robbie, did you hear that?" We tried to get in touch with one of Dave's relatives who had passed away and apart from the occasional little sounds and the rustling of the trees outside the letters failed to spell out anything of any consequence. Dave, being the impatient guy that he was and wanting to get some results suggested that we should try to get in touch with Joe Meek. As the remains of Joe were lying in the cemetery in Newent only a mile or so away from where we sat at the farm we thought that it was a pretty good idea. Even though we did not get much of a response from the glass we pressed on. With nothing much happening Dave asked "What really happened up at the studio Joe?" The question was answered by a long mournful moan that appeared to come from outside causing Dave to jump up from his seat at the table and with a terrified look on his face he stammered" Fuckin' 'ell Robbie, let's get out of here". I jumped up too knocking over the glass and as some of the cut out letters fluttered off the table onto the floor we both bolted up the stairs to the bedrooms leaving the light on and seeking the protection of our beds where we could disappear under the covers.

The following morning Mrs. Holder who got up early to prepare breakfast, finding the lights still on and the remains of our séance on the kitchen floor and table, asked what we buggers had been up to last night. Dave and I apologized for the mess and related the events of the night before and the strange, haunting, mournful moan we had heard when we had presumed that we had contacted the ghost of Joe Meek. We in turn asked if anybody else, for that matter had heard it. Nobody else had and Mrs. Holder concluded that it was probably her husband Tom snoring while sleeping off the effects of the several whiskeys that he had downed at the Feathers. Dave and I knew for sure though that this had not been a snoring sound but definitely a moan scary enough to make your blood run cold.

Roger drove over to Cheltenham to pick up John and we began to rehearse the numbers later that morning. John refused to look at the drum parts stating that he didn't need that crap and he just played along with us as we ran through the tunes. We rehearsed till late that night and we were pretty tired at the end of the evening but quite pleased how everything had worked out. A year had passed since we did our first Summer Season in Blackpool. Gone was any trepidation on behalf of the Cooper Agency with no rumours of a stand in band if The Tornados failed to hit the mark with their musical ability. We were taking it all in our stride and becoming confident and seasoned professionals.

Saturday morning Roger drove Dave to Gloucester station where Dave departed for London and left for a holiday in Spain together with his parents and Sonia. I decided that I would hang out at the farm with Pete to practice our guitar parts a little more and before long Roger left to meet up with Sandy.

Just about a week later as Pete and I relaxed at the farm a news bulletin appeared on the TV stating that the Israelis had attacked Egypt and the famous Six Day War had just begun. Israel was vastly outnumbered and with the exception of the sea to the west, was surrounded by Arab countries that were bent on the total destruction of the State of Israel. As Pete and I watched the footage of Israeli jets totally annihilating their hostile neighbours' air force as it sat on the ground, we thought about the occasions that we had played charity shows for the Jewish Federation where the aim was to raise money for weapons and tanks to protect Israel. We felt in some way that we were part of this whole thing with Pete even saying "Good for them" and I agreed with him. Our only disappointment was that we most likely would not be going on the tour of Israel that the Cooper Agency had been working on for us. We were tentatively scheduled to embark on that tour sometime after the end of the Yarmouth Season, but it didn't happen. However if somebody had predicted that six or seven months down the road that I would actually be walking along those narrow streets in the old city of Jerusalem I would very much have doubted that.

On Sunday June 11th we all arrived at The Windmill Theatre in Great Yarmouth. Dave had left London around 6am picking up John at Victoria Station. Dave was able to use his dad's yellow Zephyr for the time we would be in Yarmouth. Pete and I showed up in the van and Roger showed up in a newly acquired MG 1100. We all met at The Windmill Theatre. It was an old looking structure with actual revolving windmill vanes. At night they were illuminated by hundreds of light bulbs. The most striking thing was that our faces had been painted on cut out boards and along with the rest of the cast they had been attached to the exterior of the building and now adorned the front of the theatre We had not expected this and we were quite tickled to see our faces up in lights. We stood outside in the street looking up as passers by stared at us and recognized who we were. This became embarrassing so we quickly entered the front of the theatre and made our way through the auditorium towards the stage.

We gazed down into the orchestra pit which was to be our musical home for the next three months. This year's group of the Fox Miller dancers was already on stage limbering up and we noticed that they were a completely different batch to the Blackpool group. We made our way around to the back of the stage where we were approached by a guy who was smoking a pipe which he withdrew from his mouth and introduced himself as John Redgrave. He was to be stage manager and was related to the famous showbiz family of Lynn, Vanessa and Michael Redgrave. He instructed us to bring in our gear and set it up in the orchestra pit. As we were doing this John Redgrave introduced us to Fred Perry, the director who had devised and produced the show. Perry had an impressive career and at that time at the age of twenty seven had worked with many top of the line artists such as Bob Dylan, Shirley Bassey, Val Doonican, Peter Paul and Mary and so on. We spent that Sunday afternoon rehearsing the dance routines with the Fox Millers. Everything went very smoothly with Fred Perry commenting to us that he was very pleased with the way things had started out. It looked like this show was going to be a lot more professional unlike the Blackpool show a year before.

That evening there was a big get together party with the whole cast which was held at St. Nick's. St. Nick's was originally an old vicarage set on its own grounds. It had been converted into a guest house of sorts with a bar/clubhouse. Several chalets had been built surrounding the main building. Many of the artists were staying there, with five of the girl dancers sharing the spacious apartment over the bar. We all got acquainted and what a party it was. Once more I was surrounded by show business stars that up until that time I had only seen on TV. The drinks were flowing fast and free and we all circulated among the artists introducing ourselves and participating in the usual show business banter that was always part of those occasions. The Dreamers, Freddie's backing group seemed like a nice bunch of guys whereas Freddie himself acted rather aloof. Pete Birrell, Dreamers bass player confided in me that The Dreamers had not played on any of the singles that had been released so far but they were scheduled to record a new album with Freddie where they would actually play the backing tracks. He said that their whole comedy routine was developed to basically cover up their inadequacies as musicians. Derek Quinn guitarist was a quiet rather mysterious individual, hiding behind his dark glasses that he wore. Roy Crewsdon, guitarist was a nice kind of guy who had a glass eye which made it seem that he was looking in another direction when he was talking to you.

Drummer Bernie Dwyer was a kind of character that, who we found out at subsequent parties, would get drunk and start to shout and rant and rave in a way that you could never quite figure out if he was being serious or not.

Dev Shawn was a comedian who was basically at the bottom of the bill who claimed that he was the highest paid entertainer on the show and was making more money than anybody else. We didn't question this and didn't give any credence to his statement.

Ruby Murray was a very sweet and completely unaffected person. She would always make you feel very comfortable as she spoke to you with that remarkable husky Irish accent that she had. The huskiness in her voice stemmed back to her childhood when she underwent an operation on her throat. The sound of her singing voice did not suffer from this operation and is clearly demonstrated by the success of her career; with five singles in the top twenty all in the same week!

Ruby was married to Bernie Burgess who was once a member of the Jones Boys vocal group and was now her personal manager. Bernie went on to manage Sonia and Sandra the Diamond Twins for a short time.

There was no mistaking Tony Dalli. He was a big and tall, rather loud Italian guy who really stood out in a crowd. He kind of reminded me of Mario Lanza. He spent the evening circulating with a drink in his hand at all times. His talking voice really penetrated the air and rose above the surrounding conversations. He had originally emigrated from Italy and had worked as a coal miner and a foundry worker before turning professional.

Joe Baker was the top comedian on the bill. He conducted himself in a very professional manner being reasonably friendly but knowing when to turn on that aloof or distant attitude that certain artists in show business portray. Ruby Murray was always the same no matter what, always polite and smiling. Joe however could sometimes be quite amusing and funny but at other times he could make cutting remarks and act quite scathingly. At that time he had a very successful TV series called *My Man Joe* and throughout the season he was filming parts of the new series, his fifth for ATV. He also lived on his 35 foot yacht which was moored in Great Yarmouth.

Joe Baker in his dressing room at The Windmill Theatre, Great Yarmouth

By the early hours of Monday morning the whole cast including The Tornados were stoned out of their minds on alcohol. Dave Watts in particular was totally blitzed. We all made it back to the Ponderosa to the chalet where we would spend the next few months together. There were two bedrooms with double beds and a couch. Pete and Roger took one room, John and Dave the other and I crashed on the couch.

Monday morning came fast and furious as we had a 9am call for rehearsals and were all in our respective stages of recovery from the Sunday night party. Dave was the worst of all of us. At the theatre you could almost see auras of hangovers surrounding the cast. When Dev Shawn heard that Dave was suffering badly from the night before, he promptly pulled out a little packet from his pocket and handed Dave two "Purple Hearts" saying "Take a couple of these Dave, you'll be as right as rain."

Sure enough Dave did very shortly become "Right as rain" and was transformed from a hungover, lifeless shadow of his former self, into a confident musical director, taking charge of the situation at hand, with no signs of the aftermath of the previous night's drinking session to be seen.

This was the first time that I had ever witnessed any use of drugs in "my world" of show business. I had of course seen alcohol use but that was accepted. It is quite well known and confirmed by many of Joe Meek's artists that he would regularly pop pills under cover of the control room when he thought that nobody was watching. Pete Holder in fact definitely remembers seeing Joe turn his head to one side and pop something into his mouth. The police definitely had Joe's premises under surveillance during the time when we were recording "Is That A Ship I Hear" and the situation with Dev Shawn and the "Purple Hearts" brought to my mind the time when we were outside the studio in Holloway Road and were hanging about on the pavement as we could not get any answer when we knocked on the door at the top of the stairs. This of course was rather unusual as Joe had never refused to open the door at any other previous time. All at once we were approached by what we were soon to discover were two undercover police officers. When they asked us what we were doing there we replied that we were waiting to do a recording session. As a part of the enquiry one officer in a strong Scottish accent asked us if we had any "Purple Hearts." We looked at them in amazement asking why they would ask us such a question. The Scot said that we looked like the kind of people who would be using those kinds of drugs and began to ask John Davies what was in the top pocket of his jacket. John being the devil may care character that he was, told them that his pen was full of heroin. They pulled it out of his pocket and began to inspect it and when finding nothing asked John what else he had in there.

"All I've got is some Monopoly money" he told them and pulled out a 5 and a 10 pound note and it "was" Monopoly money. We all looked at each other and together with the cops tried not to laugh.

They must have thought that John was some kind of a nut who was walking around with Monopoly money in his pocket. Very soon after that they decided to get into their car and leave without asking anyone else any questions. I remember feeling quite mad that they said that we looked like drug users. Nobody in The New Tornados was taking any drugs. All we did was have a few drinks here and there. After this incident we climbed the stairs again and this time our knocks were answered by Joe who opened the door. Could it have been that Joe had not opened the door previously as he knew that the drug squad was casing the studio and thought that we were the cops knocking at his door? He could have been watching the whole thing from an upstairs window and seeing the cops pull away he knew that it would be safe to open the door. I don't remember if we told Joe about the incident and don't recall him mentioning anything either.

That Monday we began to settle into that usual routine of rehearsing with the artists. There were certain parts of the show which featured spots involving the artists working together in comical situations. We rehearsed these spots and with direction from Fred Perry things got done at a reasonable pace without too many problems. The worst thing that happened that day was when Dave was playing the piano that was in the orchestra pit. He played it for the sequence in which Ruby and Freddie were walking in a park and the Fox Miller dancers were riding bicycles around the stage. Suddenly in the middle of the dance routine with Freddie and Ruby as Dave tinkled on that old upright piano the whole front of the piano collapsed creating a loud discordant bang which scared everybody to death. Pete Rog and I faced each other grinning with that "Watts is up to his tricks again" looks on our faces. Dave spent a minute or two putting the front of the piano back together but when the same thing happened again in the next run through it was decided that we should leave the front off.

During the short lunch break John disappeared like he usually would and then suddenly reappeared from under the stage behind his drum kit. He called to me and Dave to take a look under the stage with him. "Take a look at this Robbie" John whispered as we entered the small opening from behind John's drums. The light was very dim under the stage but in the darkness with the help of the light that was shining through the opening my eyes gradually made out rows and rows of what appeared to be Victorian looking bird cages each one inhabited by some kind of stuffed bird species. There were all kinds of colourful parrots and hawks and eagles. It was quite an eerie scene to see all those stuffed birds, sitting in silence imprisoned in their ornate cages. We later found out that Jack Jay who was the owner of The Windmill Theatre was the father of Peter Jay the drummer of Peter Jay and The Jaywalkers. The bird collection belonged to Jack and was probably a part of a one time exhibit that he had featured somewhere.

The Windmill Theatre Great Yarmouth

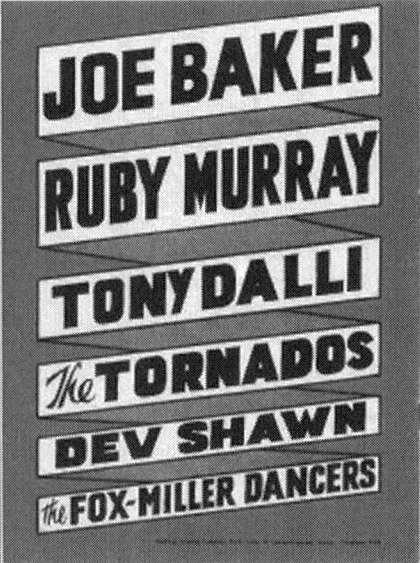

(L-R) Janet and Mandy (Fox Miller Girls) at Great Yarmouth.
note Freddie's photo in the background.

The next morning Toni Dalli was already complaining to Fred Perry that he had expected to be backed by a full orchestra, not a rock band. He was teaming up with Joe Baker to get support for his complaint. Joe Baker agreed with Tony and so began our rehearsals with them. From that point there started a competition between Joe Baker and Toni Dalli to see which one of them could waste the most time with the band continually going over and over their music and finding all kinds of little insignificant parts to get right. When Tony finished his set Joe did his and then Tony would jump back in again to redo something followed by Joe again asking me to shout "Drei, Vier" in German and have Dave play the German National Anthem on the

Hammond. At one point during a break Joe Baker summoned us into his dressing room. He complained to us that he thought that we were spending too much time with Tony Dalli's material and after all he was a bigger draw that Dalli and should be entitled to a greater share of the rehearsal time. It dragged on till late that night and even Fred Perry was getting annoyed with Dalli and Baker. He sympathized with us saying that everything was fine and did not direct his annoyance to The Tornados. We were all glad to get back to our humble Chalet at the Ponderosa and get some sleep. It had been an exhausting day.

Ruby Murray's rehearsal was the easiest and most enjoyable. It was just a case of running through her numbers which were really quite simple tunes. She in her own special, polite way, graciously demonstrated to us how she would like to hear the numbers sound, and we in turn did our best to carry out her requests. The rest of the week went quite well with no major problems. Thursday was a long hard day for us. We started at 9am and finally got finished at midnight. We went through a dress rehearsal at 8pm which went very smoothly. The only noticeable mistake occurred when the wrong music was put on during the bicycle scene. Instead of the correct music someone had put on "God Save The Queen" which had us all in fits. That whole 15 hour day we spent sitting with our instruments in the orchestra pit, except for a 10 minute break we had to grab a cup of tea.

Friday was the opening night show which started at 8pm but we were all still there again at 9am for rehearsals. That night the show went over very well with no problems. Our set was well received and "The Theme From Lawrence Of Arabia" was always a dramatic set closer. The only set back was that Dave had to play our set on a Vox organ which could not compare with the Hammond. We obviously had to come up out of the pit to play our set on stage so we used The Dreamers gear. They had these brand new Vox amps which were transistorized and sounded quite tinny.

Everybody met over at Jack Jay's house after the show and once again the drinks were flowing freely. The Tornados received many compliments and we were congratulated on a fantastic job. We were told that we had such a big sound for a small group of musicians.

From time to time artists from some of the other shows in town dropped in for a drink. We saw some familiar faces from Coventry and Blackpool.

The next morning which was Saturday found us once again feeling the effects of the night before; but we were still all there at 9am for band call. Fred Perry announced to the cast that the show had over run by at least an hour which meant that certain acts would have to be shortened to cut the length of the show. The comedians were given a strict amount of time for their acts, and The Dreamers shortened their act a little by cutting down some of the verbal comedy in their set. By the end of the afternoon the show was shortened to the desired time. We were happy that we were not asked to shorten our set. I think that Fred Perry liked us as a group as he had mentioned that we were a good contrasting act. We didn't feature any comedy in our act while at The Windmill as we thought it would be inappropriate. The new, shortened Saturday night show went over well but we were tired out from the intensive week of rehearsals. We all looked forward to a rest, but that did not come until after we had to break down the gear and load it into the van, ready for the gig at the Ponderosa at noon on Sunday.

The Ponderosa was basically a camp-site with log cabins instead of caravans or trailers. A husband and wife team ran the site. They were a young couple and usually dressed in western outfits and could have probably passed for Billy The Kid and Annie Oakley. They had a singing and comedy act that they performed as a warm up for The Tornados. We played about a forty minute set on Sunday lunchtimes and this we did in exchange for our accommodation. We played in the clubhouse for the guests that were staying at the Ponderosa. The lunchtime show was quite enjoyable the only downside was that we had to move the gear every weekend.

With the first week under our belt we settled in to the day in day out routine of backing the show. In many ways the Great Yarmouth summer season was different to the Blackpool show of 1966. Joe Meek was no longer around and there were no letters arriving from him and no talk within the band of getting a new single put out. In fact our prospects of doing any recordings in the future were non-existent.

We just expected that at the end of the season we would continue with our cabaret shows and one night stands. Dev Shawn was sharing our dressing room with us and overhearing our conversations about how we should expand our act came up with some good vocal numbers and song combinations which he offered us. He was at one time part of an Irish vocal trio and was actually a pretty good singer. We thought that his ideas were good but when he found out that we were starting to rehearse some of the creations that he had offered us he turned around and told us that we could not use them. This left us wondering why he had offered them to us in the beginning only to deny us use of them when he discovered our interest in using his ideas.

Although a few members of the cast seemed rather aloof, on the whole it was a closer, friendlier atmosphere than we had experienced at Blackpool. Ruby Murray always kept a good supply of alcohol in her dressing room and invited us in regularly for drinks during the intermissions. We had a lot of fun swapping jokes with The Dreamers while hanging out with them in their dressing rooms. I actually bought a knee length black frock coat from Derek Quinn. It had a velvet collar and he wanted six pounds for it which I gladly paid. I loved it and kept it for a long time. I took it to Israel with me and wore it on our travels all over Europe when I played in the Churchills. It finally disappeared when my future father in law gathered up all my old belongings which I had left behind and sold them to a vendor at the flea market in Jaffa.

We got real friendly with the dancers and as most of them were staying over at St. Nick's we visited them regularly and hung out with them at their place. On Thursday nights, after the show we would all go to the midnight movies together and watch Vincent Price in various horror movies. One of the male dancers by the name of Wayne was a big Bob Dylan fan just as I was and on sunny afternoons you could see us sitting together outside at St. Nick's singing Dylan songs with me on guitar and Wayne playing the harmonica backed by the "rat a tat tat" of Dev Shawn's typewriter as he sat nearby working on material for his comedy routine.

A few weeks into the show Roger and Pete said that they would be moving out of the chalet at the Ponderosa due to the cramped conditions and would be moving over to St. Nick's as the rent was reasonable and there was a spare unit available there. This left Dave, John and I together, but I was still unable to get off the couch that I slept on as Sonia and Debbie regularly stayed with Dave and John. I finally got my own bedroom when John and Debbie got their own chalet as Debbie had got out of college and would be staying for the rest of the season. One day some wandering gypsies came around the chalets at the Ponderosa offering to tell our fortunes. Right away one old lady gypsy told me that I was an entertainer in music which impressed me. She also said that there would be some changes coming up for me and that I would not be living in England for much longer. When she looked at my hand after I had "crossed her palm with silver" and given her a shilling she told me that I had a broken life line which scared me a little. She didn't explain its meaning and I didn't know what to make of it. After the gypsies had left and I was contemplating my fortune telling experience I noticed that my Gibson 335 was propped up against the couch as I had been working on a song that morning and knowing that they had seen it through the open door I realized how they had been able to predict that I was a musician. I then disregarded all that they had told me and presumed that I had been hoodwinked by some clever clairvoyant. However upon reflection the gypsy was correct about the changes that would surely come up before the end of the season and at that time I did not know that in the coming month of December that I would leave for Israel with The Tornados which would bring about a big change in my life and that I would in fact not be living in England again for a few years.

As we were to be staying in Great Yarmouth for a few months John and I decided that we would take driving lessons and get our licenses. I had always felt at a disadvantage at not being able to drive particularly with regard to my past relationship with Jackie Grant. I always had to depend on her for transport. John and I took a few lessons per week and would be able to take our tests by the end of the season. When Debbie came down to stay with John she also decided to take driving lessons too and on several occasions we took lessons together all riding in the same car with the instructor.

There was much more of a social life with the cast at Yarmouth with frequent parties. Freddie threw a party at his place one Saturday night. He did not live at St Nick's as he stayed at a nice rented house. It was a wild party with plenty of booze. At one point we heard some shouting going on and once again it was Bernie Dwyer The Dreamers drummer ranting and raving when he got drunk. I thought that he was just acting belligerent for fun just like John Davies and I used to do at times and decided to play along with him by shouting back at him. I kept waiting for him to stop and break out in laughter but it seemed that he was getting very serious and as I was getting warning looks from Pete Birrell I decided it would be wise to back off. The party lasted all night long and we ended up leaving on Sunday morning with just about enough time to get to the Ponderosa to play our lunchtime show. It was a rough performance as we had not slept all night and were still feeling the affects of the drinks.

One night there was a big scare over at St Nick's. Some of the dancing girls were screaming that a gorilla had been seen roaming around the grounds. Most of the cast were woken up by the disturbance. Ruby Murray was standing in her doorway in her underwear, Dev Shawn together with his wife who was six months pregnant were peering out from their window and Tony Dalli came running out in his "Y" fronts carrying a shotgun. Tony ran around the grounds and upon seeing the gorilla disappear behind a tree he took aim and fired. With all the commotion going on somebody had called the police who, when they arrived found that the gorilla was none other than Wayne the dancer who was dressed up in a gorilla suit and was roaming around the grounds hoping to scare the girl dancers. He was painfully picking out shot gun pellets from his backside!

With Pete and Roger now staying over at St. Nicks I found myself spending a lot of time on my own. John was with Debbie in their chalet and Sonia would visit Dave regularly so I began to use my time to write new songs. Pete was still seeing Ann whenever she was within driving distance. As she was appearing at Bournemouth with Tommy Cooper and Des O'Connor Pete was lucky to get to see her when he volunteered to drive Freddie down there in Freddie's Alpha Romeo. The Dreamers' road manager was away and unable to

provide the service. Also on the bill in Bournemouth were The Rockin'
Berries. They had a few hits in the early sixties and also featured comedy and impressions in their act. Backstage, Pete was treated to an im-
promptu session of impressions by singer Geoff Turton of the Berries
who did an excellent Tommy Cooper impression. However Pete's attachment to Ann didn't last much longer as they had a falling out at
the London Palladium not long after the Yarmouth season and he
never saw her again.

*(L-R) Pete Holder, Dave Watts, Robb Huxley, John Davies (Just be-
hind Robb) and Roger Holder at our Sunday lunchtime gig at the
Ponderosa.*

We decided that on a Sunday night we would hold a party down
on the beach together with the dancers. Dave and I drove out to the
Norfolk Broads and collected a bunch of logs and branches and that
night we lit a huge bonfire at the beach. We swam in the sea in the
dark and noticed bright phosphorescence in the water. It was beautiful to see the little points of light swirling around in the dark water. I
had gotten friendly with a young girl who was related to one of the
dancers and we walked down the beach together and lay on the sand.
That night I stayed with her at St. Nick's and we slept in one of the
spare bedrooms in the dancers' apartments. Early the next morning

we were woken up by the girl's cousin who warned us that the brother had arrived to take her back home. It was decided that I would stay in the bedroom so that he would not discover that his young sister had spent the night with one of The Tornados. Only when somebody was able to coax him outside was I able to make my entrance by suddenly appearing in the room. I realized how lucky I was after they had left when I found out that the girl was really quite young and that I would have caught hell from her brother if he had found out that we had spent the night together.

A

View of St. Nick's

Eric Morecambe and Ernie Wise who were appearing in Great Yarmouth for the season announced that they were organizing a cricket match to be held at the local sports arena. It would be a charity affair on a Sunday afternoon. Eric's team would play against Ernie's team. The team members were to be made up of all the show biz folks in town that wished to be involved. More than enough artists showed up to make the two teams so we all hung around and from time to time we were invited to go in and bowl a few overs or be a batsman.

Most of the cricketers who showed up were dressed in the traditional white flannels and shirts. Being the rebel that I was I decided that I would be different and wear an all black outfit. I wore the black jacket that I had recently bought from Derek Quinn with black trousers. They announced me as Robbie Gayle of The Tornados as I walked out onto the pitch. As I neared the centre of the field all heads were turned in my direction with Eric and Ernie exchanging puzzled looks and asking "Is he one of ours?" I was definitely the black sheep in the fold that day. I guess they didn't appreciate my sense of humour or the *Monty Python* style of statement that I was hoping to make. They let me bowl six balls and were relieved to get me off the field.

After the show one night, Ruby Murray's manager/husband, Bernie Burgess asked Dave if he would come over to their place at St Nick's as he wanted two of Ruby's songs transposed to other keys. As soon as Dave found out that Bernie was willing to pay five pounds a song Dave eagerly agreed and they made arrangements to meet the following day. Dave came back with ten pounds in his pocket and a report on how it was over at Ruby's. He related to us how Ruby had opened the door and stood there dressed in a "see through" negligee wearing very little underneath it. Dave wondered what he was in for and as she ushered him into the living room he caught sight of Bernie who was seated on the sofa. Dave tried to act cool but inside he was wondering what this strange scenario was all about. Here he was in Ruby Murray's place to do some musical work and she was walking around almost naked with her husband relaxing calmly without even batting an eyelid.

According to Dave he was there for close to two hours while she continued to display her feminine attributes which could clearly be seen through the fabric of her negligee. He said that at times it was hard to concentrate especially when she leaned forward over the table to examine the music that he was writing out. He apparently made a few screw ups here and there but managed to get it finished somehow.

We also got a similar report from Roger who said that Ruby had invited him over for a drink after the show on a few occasions and Ruby was usually in her underwear. Just as in Dave's situation Bernie was there too. We also noted that Roger was a regular in Ruby's dressing room between shows where they would share some sherry together. Ruby escaped injury one night during her act. She was about half way through "Goodbye Jimmy Goodbye" when one of the large white pillars that were part of her backdrop began to sway and looked like it wouldn't take much to make it topple over. As usual she would throw a glance at us down in the orchestra pit from time to time. She could see the concerned looks on our faces as we tried to visually warn her about the precarious pillar but she could only look back at us in bewilderment. When the pillar finally came down it was headed straight for Ruby. Roger was quick enough to shout out "Ruby!" and point to her left. As she turned round to look she stepped to the side and the pillar missed her by inches and there was an audible sigh of relief that came from the audience as they too, along with The Tornados, were witnesses to Ruby's close call with misfortune. Ruby was able to keep going and finished her set with the pillar still lying across the stage. I couldn't help thinking that I might have heard a little voice coming from somewhere up above whispering "Now be a good girl Ruby and put your knickers on."

One night Joe Baker honoured us with an appearance in our dressing room. He wished us a good evening, looked at Pete and shook his head, looked at Roger and nodded, then at John and me shaking his head and then at Dave and nodded. We were mystified at this and wondered what it was all about. Joe went on to tell us that he was currently filming segments for his next TV series, *Baker's Half Dozen* and needed two guys to act as German soldiers. He had chosen Roger and Dave and offered them the parts. Dave and Roger accepted and were even more pleased to hear that they would be paid. I intended to go along to watch the filming but had a driving lesson that day. Dave said it was a blast, when he and Roger returned after the day's filming. They had been dressed up in German army uniforms along with Joe Baker who looked like Rommel himself. They also used an old, Gestapo style convertible automobile with which at one point they had to create a fake accident to appear as if they had crashed into a tree. They all had to push it into the tree and then the bonnet was raised and a smoking device was ignited under it for added effect. Later on Dave and Roger were instructed to hide behind a hedgerow and on command they should spring up from behind the hedge and race across the field holding their rifles and screaming loudly. They crouched in their hiding place and on the word "Go" they did as they were told and began screaming their way across the field as fast as they could. All of a sudden and quite unexpectedly, the figure of an old man with a walking stick emerged from the trees and they almost ran into him. He looked a bit like an old country yokel who could very well have been a veteran from the First World War. Roger and Dave, thinking that he was part of the scene charged at him, screaming loudly. The old man threw his hands up causing his stick to fly into the air. He let out a yell and turned and ran off as fast as his arthritic legs could carry him. He scrambled his way through the hedgerow and as he disappeared he was heard shouting "We're being invaded." When they stopped running they looked toward Joe Baker, who was standing next to the director and the film crew. They were all falling about in fits of laughter. Roger and Dave thought that they must have really done a good job but they thought that the guy who played the old man deserved all the credit for his splendid performance. When the laughing finally died down and Joe had gained his composure he explained that the old guy had nothing to do with the scene and must have just stumbled onto the set by accident. somebody picked up his discarded walking stick and they went off searching for him but they never saw him again. It was a very comical mystery and was never solved. Nobody knew where the old man came from or where he went. All that remained was the walking stick.

For the next part of the filming Dave and Roger were to run across the field while a Spitfire fighter plane flew in low over them. The production team had spent a lot of time laying out electrical lines with small explosive devices attached that when activated would make it appear that the spitfire was strafing the two German soldiers as they were running. When the scene was put into action the Spitfire flew in over Dave and Roger as they ran and the devices were activated causing Dave to jump up in the air as he heard the reports of the explosive devices. Seeing a funny side to it Dave burst out laughing as he ran. This really pissed off Joe Baker who yelling at Dave shouted, "You're not supposed to laugh when somebody is trying to shoot you. We didn't come here to waste our time and film." With that the crew had to laboriously begin to set out the electrical lines again, reset the scene and synchronize the arrival of the Spitfire once more.

Later that morning Joe Baker seemed to be getting agitated with the developments of the filming and began to berate the crew and the director to the point that everybody was getting totally pissed off with him. In the following scene that they were filming Baker was to have jumped by parachute and landed in a tree where his chute got caught up. The crew went to great pains to get him up into a tall tree and fasten him into the harness. Throughout this procedure Baker continued to bitch and complain to the director. When Joe Baker was at last firmly secured about 15 feet off the ground the producer called a lunch break and walked off with the crew with Roger and Dave included and left him hanging there for over an hour. When they returned, Baker who was still hanging up in the tree, screamed and cursed everybody until his face turned purple. When they finally let him down he stormed off in a rage and that was the end of the day's filming.

About half way through the season I was beginning to feel the effects of the way things had changed. The Holder brothers and I had always been close, as we were together since The Whirlwinds. Pete and I for the most part always used to stay together and I thought it just a little unusual at the time that they would have decided to stay together over at St Nick's. John and Debbie were together and Dave saw Sonia regularly which created a lot of time for me on my own. I had no car and had not yet taken my driving test, so I had to rely on Dave for transport as he had his dad's car. I was never the kind of guy that was into having a lot of different chicks. I preferred to have a relationship with just one girl like I had with Jackie Grant. Still feeling the loss of Jackie I decided to try to heal that loss by having a few casual affairs. I started to try to hang out with the girl dancers over at their place at St Nick's. Mandy was good fun. She was arty, and liked to write poetry and was accompanied by her collie dog whose name was Penny. We had a lot of fun with séances, writing poetry and generally acted like a couple of little kids, but after we spent the night together everything changed and Mandy said that it had spoilt everything, because we had lost that child like friendship that we had shared. I guess that she was right.

The Fox Miller girls in their flat above the bar at St. Nick's.
(L-R) Marion, Ann, Carol. Linda, Penny (Mandy's dog) and Mandy.

The countryside outside of Great Yarmouth is comprised of an area known as the Broads which is a network of rivers and small lakes. It was then, as it is now a very popular tourist attraction with boat rentals available. Dave and I decided that it would be good fun to take some of the dancers with us and rent a boat. We invited Mandy, Carol,

Ann and Wayne to join us. We found a small boathouse on one of the many rivers and rented a boat for the afternoon. It was really just like a big tub and after we had all jumped in we chugged very slowly away from the dock. With Dave at the wheel we gradually disappeared around the bend of the river, at a snail's pace. It seemed that it was taking us forever to get anywhere, until Dave said "This is no bloody good Robbie, let's pull over." Dave turned off the engine and opened up the cover and after a brief scan of the engine he said "There's a bloody governor on the engine." Using a pair of pliers that we found in a small tool box Dave relieved the engine of its governor and restarted the engine. As we pulled away you could feel the difference and even though there were six of us on board Dave soon got her up to full speed. The girls loved it as they laughed out loud with their hair blown about by the wind. Soon we were creating a huge wake behind the boat which caused large waves to break over the riverbanks. All at once up ahead we saw that we were bearing down on some approaching boats that were chugging merrily along under the control of their "Governors".

Dave shut off the engine in an attempt to slow us down but we were still going too fast, and as we sailed by, our wake caused the other boats to get tossed so violently up and down that the passengers were hanging on for dear life.

Although what we did was irresponsible we couldn't stop from laughing and Dave was literally pissing himself. We then proceeded at a more careful speed until it looked clear ahead and Dave got us, once again up to full speed.

This time we were swamping the fishermen on the banks. They glared and shook their fists at us as they watched their rods and keep nets getting tossed around by our wake. We pulled over shortly after wreaking havoc with all those poor people who had just wanted to go "mucking about on the river."

We enjoyed the sun for a while and then decided that we should start to head back as we had to work that night. Once again it was full throttle all the way back. Luckily we didn't encounter any other boats on the way and it looked like the fishermen had gotten disgusted and had gone home or to the pub.

(L-R) Ann, Dave Watts, Mandy and Carol on the infamous "Broads boat trip"

We had no idea how far we were from the boathouse and kept at a good clip until we came careering around a bend and there was the boathouse right up ahead. Dave cut the engine but it was too late. We completely overshot the boathouse and were forced to try to turn around in the turbulent wake that followed us.

The boat rental owners came out on the dock and watched us as we approached and tied up. We all jumped out like mischievous school kids with the girls laughing and Dave, Wayne and I trying to look innocent.

They didn't say anything to us but we could tell that they were pissed off. They must have known that we had tinkered with the engine and had probably heard complaints from the other boaters that we had swamped them.

They didn't smile back when we piled into Dave's car and bid them goodbye. They were just glad to get rid of us.

So the Pirate captain Davey Watts who had terrorized the Norfolk Broads and had broken all previous speed records, drove off in a cloud of dust with his motley crew in the direction of Great Yarmouth and The Windmill Theatre.

(L-R) Robb Huxley, Dave Watts and Wayne of the Fox Millers (Broads boat trip)

Marion, Ann and Mandy posing by Joe Baker's Jag. Outside at St. Nick's.

Outside at St. Nick's.
(L-R) Ann, Carol, Ruby Murray's daughter, Fred (a visitor) Mandy and Marion.

The parties continued to come and go and we got to meet quite a few celebrities from the other shows in town. I became friendly with the guys from Val Doonican's backing band and used to watch them rehearse over at St. Nick's in the clubroom. Roger and Pete bought a small boat so I didn't see that much of them and it did seem like we were drifting apart as I only saw them when we were working. Tony Dalli had a Jaguar that he wanted to sell and Pete Holder at one time was interested in buying it, particularly as the license plate was PH 67 but the price was too high. The show went on in the sameway, there were no major changes, nobody left the show and nobody got fired. Freddie got pissed off at John Davies one time though, as John had deliberately played the park dance sequence too fast so that Freddie and his dancing partner could barely keep up. In the intermission Freddie told John that he was going to have him fired, but that didn't happen, although I think that John heard a few words from the stage manager John Redgrave. My driving test finally came around and I failed it. When the examiner asked me to pull in and park at the nearest place and I parked in a no parking zone that sealed my fate. I was told that I had failed, but with a few more lessons I should be OK on the second test. I later found out from my instructor that the next available test would be about a week before the end of the season, so it looked like I would be able to get it all finished up before we had to leave.

At one of the parties I hooked up with one of the dancers and after a few drinks we joined the guests who were dancing, and we wound up dancing together all through the night. We were hip to hip and pelvis to pelvis gyrating simulated sex till the early hours. From time to time we would sit down to take a breather, and in part of our conversation she wondered if I knew that Pete and Roger were rehearsing with another band or singer over at St. Nick's? We were both quite tipsy at the time and I didn't really pay much attention to her babbling and really didn't give it much thought but it did come right into my head the following morning when I woke up with Ann the dancer over at St Nick's. Later in the day I asked her what it was that she had told me about Pete and Roger last night at the party. She said that she had heard them singing and playing with other musicians here at the resort in the clubhouse. I still didn't know what to make of it; maybe they were just jamming with people? Dave and John picked me up from the resort for the show that night and as soon as I got into the car Dave told me that Pete and Roger were leaving the band at the end of the season. They were forming a vocal trio together with the lead singer of Billy Fury's backing group The Gamblers. He also said that they would be called The Holder Brothers and they would be appearing on a big show at The Aquarium Ballroom in Great Yarmouth towards the end of the season. "It's true Robbie" John confirmed as he twisted around to look at me from the front seat "They really are leaving, Roger told the whole story to Dave this afternoon." Now I figured it all out and understood what it was that Ann was trying to tell me.

I felt a little strange that night when we were all gathered in our dressing room, getting into our suits. Roger was explaining that they would be managed by John Redgrave with Larry Parnes being involved and they were joining up with Tony Tait the lead singer of The

Gamblers to form a band in the same style as The Walker Brothers. That night in the orchestra pit and on stage I looked across at Roger and Pete with the knowledge that it would only be a few short weeks and we would be going separate ways. We had been together for close to four years from our beginning as Robb Gayle and The Whirlwinds, to our involvement with Joe Meek, followed by The Saxons and then finally to The New Tornados, as full time professional musicians and Joe Meek's most trusted and loyal group. We had all been touched by the trauma and mystery of Joe Meek's murder/suicide. We had driven through many dark nights and slept in many decrepit hovels together. We had faced each other across many different stages, from tiny village halls in Gloucestershire to cabaret clubs, working men's clubs, theatres and TV shows but now that was over. Pete and Roger were going on to do their thing together and John, Dave and I were going on to something unknown but one thing we did know was that we would have to get together the next day to plot a course of action.

Dave poured us out a cup of tea as we sat around the table in our chalet at the Ponderosa and we began to weigh up the situation. With the Holder brothers out of the picture we would end up without a bass player, or a lead player; no transport, possibly no P. A. system and what would the Cooper Agency's reaction be to all this. It was a scary situation but we just pressed on with what we knew had to be done. We put an ad in the *Melody Maker*. "Name Group currently appearing in Great Yarmouth is looking for pro bass player." We left the phone number and address of The Windmill together with the time to call. We started searching the newspaper looking for a van for sale.

That night at The Windmill during the intermission I found myself alone with Roger and Pete in the dressing room. Roger said that he and Pete felt bad and were sorry that they could not include me in their plans but they did offer me a way to keep the P. A. system for The Tornados. As we had owned the system since The Saxons I was entitled to a share in it. We figured out that their share would be about 45 pounds so if I could pay them off, the voice system would be mine. After discussing this with John and Dave I gave the Holders the money and John and Dave clubbed together and paid for the microphones. We needed to make a few repairs to the PA system as some of the plugs were faulty and got some help from The Dreamers' roadie who recommended a place in Yarmouth that did good repair work.

Tony Dalli approached Dave to ask him if he would play the organ for him, for "I'll Walk With God" at a charity concert after the show that coming Friday. It was to be held at the Olympia Theatre in Great Yarmouth and many stars were to be on the bill. The main artists were The Eric Delaney Big Band, Morecambe and Wise, Joe Henderson, Mike and Bernie Winters, Rolf Harris, Joe Baker, Susan Maugham and of course Tony Dalli. Dave admitted that the day before the show he was literally shitting himself, with his stomach in knots feeling quite concerned about being alone there at the show and backing Tony Dalli without his fellow Tornados; also knowing that there were to be many excellent musicians on the show added to Dave's plight. As it turned out he had nothing to worry about as the whole show was a great success with Dave getting numerous compliments on his playing from many artists on the show. The only downside was that Dave had to lug his organ and amplification down there and back.

Tornados on stage at Great Yarmouth

The season was beginning to wind down. The show was scheduled to close on September 9th so there was about three weeks left and we still had no new bass player or van. The Holder brothers were rehearsing regularly with Tony Tait over at St Nick's. They were getting ready for their opening show which was only a week away. Each night at the show everything The Tornados did in the way of appearing at The Windmill became matter of fact and just like clocking in and out at a regular job. Pete and Roger would be pursuing their musical careers and presumably going on to bigger and better things leaving the remainder of The Tornados still barely floating in a pool of total uncertainty. There seemed to be an air of sadness brought about by these changing events. At that time Dave, John and I had no idea that the next few weeks would be bombarded by a series of unexpected events that would turn our luck around and catapult us into a new world of entertainment. As these events began to unfold my thoughts kept returning to the words that the gypsy had told me at the Ponderosa several weeks earlier.

We did however get one good laugh in before the end of the season. As the curtains opened for the ballet sequence in which Freddie Garrity would dance with "Prima Ballerina" Linda Goffin of the Fox Miller Dancers, the microphone and stand got caught up and was dragged off to the side of the stage and left suspended in the air as it was tangled up in the curtains. Freddie was unaware of this until it came to the part when he was to approach the front of the stage and pick up the microphone to sing his song. It seemed that nobody back stage was aware that the mic had suddenly changed its location so when Freddie directed anxious glances toward the wings John Redgrave realizing what had happened, rushed to let the curtains down enough so that Freddie could reach up to grab the microphone. We all had a good giggle down in the orchestra pit and Dave looked across at me with a grin on his face and whispered "Serves him right that cocky little bastard."

When we were just about giving up hearing from any bass players, we received a call from a guy who said that he used to play bass for Johnny Hallyday, his name was Pete Hollis and we invited him down to The Windmill for an audition. As it turned out he had his own gear but he didn't have a group van. He showed up at The Windmill on September 25th and we went through some of our numbers and he seemed to be working out OK, and because there were no other applicants from the *Melody Maker* ad and we were running out of time we took him on. We decided that he would stay in Yarmouth with us over at the Ponderosa and rehearse in the afternoons at The Windmill. He was about our age and looked like he could have been French, as he had a dark complexion and black wavy hair combed back. The very fact that, as he said, he played for Johnny Hallyday, made him appear even more French looking. He was actually a Londoner and quite respectable. He told us that his father was a dentist and they lived in a decent part of town. We introduced Pete Hollis to Roger and Pete and Roger was kind enough to let Hollis use his bass amp for the rehearsals. We put in a couple of good days of rehearsals with Pete Hollis and by Saturday afternoon we had The Tornados repertoire down pat. This was helped along by the use of some manuscript paper I had bought on which Dave had written out all the music for our set. We also worked on a set for the Diamond Twins as they were to appear at the Oasis Club the following Monday. Sonia had asked Dave if we could back the twins for this one nighter as they had played that venue before and were not happy with the backing group there.

After our Sunday gig at the Ponderosa, Pete and Roger rushed off for last minute rehearsals for their first appearance with Tony Tait as The Holder Brothers. John Redgrave, now their manager, had got them a spot on the rock show that was to be held at the Aquarium Theatre. Redgrave was able to pull this off as he knew Larry Parnes who was the promoter of the show. The Move who were part of the big star line up had been fired for playing too loud so this had opened up an opportunity for him to get the Holders on the show. Billy Fury was topping the bill which included artists such as Amen Corner and The Nashville Teens. The Holder brothers were to be backed by Billy Fury's band that Tony Tait had once been a part of. Dave, Pete Hollis and I went down to the Aquarium that night to see the show. We turned up at the box office and told the cashier that we were The Tornados from The Windmill Theatre and we got free admission. We made our way upstairs to watch the show from the balcony. When the curtains opened for the Holder's set we saw the three of them dressed in white suits that were made for them by Dougie Millings. Their appearance as the curtains opened was accompanied by screams from girls in the audience. We looked down from the balcony and saw that the screamers were none other than the Fox Miller Girls who had consented to show up to scream for the boys. They performed three numbers which were embellished by a series of three hundred lighting combinations that were carried out by John Redgrave. All in all it was a good set but for me it felt very strange to see my long time band mates performing with another singer in another group. It gave me an empty feeling inside and in some ways created a feeling of sadness for me. Although it was not the kind of line up that I would have wanted to have been involved in, I still felt that I should have been up there with them in some way. I walked away from the theatre after the show with Dave and Pete Hollis realizing that it was in fact over between the Holder Brothers and me.

Monday afternoon when we arrived at The Windmill we were told by John Redgrave that the show would be closing a week early on September 2nd. We never found out why but we knew that now, more than ever that we had to work on getting a van quickly. This also meant that I would have to stay down in Yarmouth for an extra few days to take my driving test. The show at the Oasis that night where we backed up the Diamond Twins, went smoothly considering that it was our first engagement with our new bass player. Pete Hollis turned out to be pretty good and Roger actually was kind enough to lend Pete his stage suit to wear for the gig. Roger actually ended up selling the suit to Pete at the end of the season.

Things took a change for the better when Dave spotted a van for sale in the local newspaper. It was a Bedford and they were asking fifty pounds for it. The van was to be found at an address in London so we got up at 6am and drove to the location. We spotted the Bedford parked on the side of the road. It was blue and looked like it had seen better days. There was a kangaroo emblem on the back door along with an Australian flag and I couldn't help feeling that somebody had probably driven it all the way from Sydney to London. We walked up to the front door of the house only to find that there was nobody home. We were totally pissed off knowing that we had driven all that way for nothing. Pete Hollis came up with a good idea which was that Dave and I should return to Yarmouth and that he would go home and come back the next day to try to buy the van and if successful he would drive down to Yarmouth. We agreed and dropped him off in the West End with Dave giving him a blank cheque to pay for the van. As we drove off I turned to Dave and said "Bloody 'ell Dave what if he cashes the cheque and we never see him again?" Dave looked at me and said "I never thought about that Robbie, but wait a minute we still have his bass guitar and that's worth a lot more than the van so he'll be back." Dave was right, Pete did come back and he drove up to the Ponderosa on Saturday afternoon just as we were getting ready to leave for our final show at The Windmill. We decided that we would travel down to the theatre in our newly acquired van. The Bedford coughed and sputtered all the way there and it looked as if we would need to have it worked on at sometime, but for now we were doing fine we had a sound system, a van and a new bass player.

Whole cast on stage at Great Yarmouth for the finale

That night we played our final show at The Windmill. It was a regular show. There were no practical jokes or attempts by the stage crew to sabotage anybody's act; in fact it was the complete opposite of the fiasco that had occurred on the final show in Blackpool a year before. This would be the last show that I would ever play with Pete and Rog.

I would not see them again for seven or so years I don't remember shaking hands saying "Good Luck" or even saying goodbye and thoughts of that have a much bigger impact on me today than they had back then. The show was followed by a big party over at St Nick's with an abundance of alcohol flowing freely. It was a party where a cast of people who had worked together for the past three months were saying goodbye and going on to other shows in all different locations; one nighters, weeks of cabaret TV and Radio. As The Tornados our future was uncertain. Joe Meek was out of the picture, we had not yet told the Cooper Organization of the split in the band, we were working with a new bass player and we had heard no news of any up coming work for the band.

The final week of the show I had been talking to a girl who was working in the booking office at The Windmill I can't remember her name but she had caught my eye and we had become quite friendly. She accepted my invitation and accompanied me to the party. We spent our time at the party chatting mostly about music with me talking about the new jazz albums that I had recently bought. I told her that I would be staying on at the Ponderosa for a few more days as I was to take my driving test. She felt a little sorry for me as I would be all alone for those few days and suggested that we might hang out together. I took her up on her offer and made arrangements to meet her again on Sunday evening.

Sunday turned out to be a nightmare. We had an awful time trying to make the gear fit into the van. The seats in the back needed to be taken out to make enough space but we had no tools to accomplish this so after about four hours of sweating and cursing we finally got it all in having to place some stuff on the passenger seat and a few extra items in Dave's Zephyr. John and Debbie hitched a ride with Pete Hollis who dropped them off in Acton as they had got a place to stay there together. Dave drove the van to his parents' house in Bromley as that Monday we were scheduled to back the Diamond Twins on a TV show in Dover. I of course was unable to make the gig, so just Dave, John and Roger played and were paid fifteen guineas each which was pretty good money. Returning from the show Dave was stopped by the police and was issued a fine for having no road tax on the van.

The cost of the fine ate up the money he was paid for the show so Dave had nothing to show for his labour.

Meanwhile back at the Ponderosa, having no transport I caught the bus down into Yarmouth and met my date at The Windmill. She invited me to her place telling me that her parents were away on holiday and we could listen to some music together. I had brought a couple of albums so we listened to Wes Montgomery and Charlie Byrd and spent a very pleasant evening together. I guess that I could have spent the night there but a little voice in my head said "You better not" so I decided to catch the last bus and returned to the Ponderosa. On Monday she came over and we hung out together all day long. The chalet was quiet now as the band had left the day before and I took advantage of this spending most of the time in the bedroom. When the time came to say goodbye she started to cry asking if we would ever see each other again. I consoled her saying that I would be back again some day and we would get together. I never returned to Great Yarmouth and never got to see her again.

This time, the driving test was a breeze. It looked like the examiner was uninterested in anything that I was doing and spent most of the time looking out of the window at the shop fronts and passers by. On our return to the driver license station I was happy to tell my instructor that I had passed my test and we chatted amiably as he drove me back to the Ponderosa where I spent the evening getting my suitcase packed. Next morning I said goodbye to the managers of the Ponderosa and handed them the key to the Chalet. On the train ride to London I began to wonder how things had been going with Dave and what might be in store for yet another "New" Tornados band. I looked up at my green suitcase that I had thrown up onto the luggage rack. It was no longer shiny and new like it was when I had bought it a year and a half ago in the Bon Marche in Gloucester. Now it bore the scuffs, scratches and battle scars of one night stands, variety and cabaret shows and countless trips up and down the M1. It had been dragged in and out of hotels and guest houses and forced in between amps and drum cases in the back of the group van. I gazed out of the compartment window at the countryside and thought of where that suitcase might be another year down the road. I smiled to myself as I remembered that I had passed my driving test and fantasized about maybe being able to save up enough money to buy a Zephyr 4, or even a 6. It would be nice to have my own car and not have to travel by train everywhere.

On my arrival at the Watts' residence I rang the door bell which was answered by Dave who proceeded to jump up and down, smiling from ear to ear. "Wait till you hear this, Robbie" Dave beamed. I followed Dave into the kitchen where Mrs. Watts had just made a pot of tea, and over a welcome "cuppa" Dave told me the news of the past few days. He thought that there was something fishy going on over at the Cooper Organization as on Tuesday morning he had received a call from Harry Dawson. Harry wanted to make a deal with The Tornados that would involve him being the sole manager of the band. It looked like Dawson might be leaving Cooper and would be setting up his own agency. Dave told Harry that we could not commit to a deal like that as he would have to discuss it with the rest of the band. A few weeks later we found out that Dawson had actually been fired from the Cooper Organization for allegedly cheating George Cooper out of a lot of money. It seems that they not only cheated their acts, but also stole from each other. On top of this, Dave got a call from Larry Parnes the following morning with an offer for The Tornados to back Billy Fury on his cabaret dates and one-nighters. Parnes was closely connected to the Cooper Organization and as he had met us a year ago at the Blackpool Show, which he had promoted along with Cooper, he knew our capabilities and offered us the job.

He had taken us all out to dinner one night in Blackpool and after dinner we wound up at his flat for drinks. He loved to talk about cooking and said how much he enjoyed making spaghetti. The only thing he didn't like was having to stand holding the pasta in the boiling water and waiting for it to soften. He also seemed to be interested in Pete Holder and made some comments about making him a film star. The thing I remember the most about that night was travelling in Parnes' Bentley and having fun operating the power windows. Now a year later he had invited Dave over to his luxurious penthouse on Park Lane where Dave had been that very afternoon. Dave told me that the place was absolutely unbelievable and that he had not seen so much luxury in all his life. Larry offered Dave a drink which he poured from a cocktail bar that was hidden inside the wall. Parnes pushed a button and a huge array of liquor appeared just like magic. Larry went on to tell Dave that he was very interested in The Tornados and could be very helpful to us in our careers. We would have to be ready to back Billy Fury on the coming Sunday at the Batley Variety club which at that time was the biggest cabaret venue in the country. Dave, although realizing that we would only have three days to prepare for Billy's act, went ahead and accepted Parnes' offer, knowing that the band would have no objections. When the conversation came around to The Holder Brothers, Larry Parnes told Dave that he wanted nothing to do with them. This signalled to us that maybe the future did not look so bright for Roger and Pete after all. He may have had no further interest in them as John Redgrave was their manager and this left no room for him to get in on the scene. Throughout his meeting with Dave, Parnes continually sprinkled sexual innuendos into the conversation and only when his intentions became clearer and direct did Dave decide that it was time to leave. Larry Parnes had tried the same thing a year before with Pete Holder in Blackpool. He had invited Pete out for dinner at a ritzy night club in Manchester and sent a chauffeur driven limousine to pick him up. All night long he impressed Pete with his ideas that Pete could be an actor like Terence Stamp and at one point in the evening, much to Pete's embarrassment, he had the emcee announce that there was a celebrity in the house. Pete was introduced as the lead guitarist of The Tornados of "Telstar" fame and with the spotlight directed at him he was made to stand up and take a bow. Later that night back at Parnes' hotel room when Pete refused Larry's sexual advances and offers to spend the night, he was ushered out and driven back home to Blackpool but not in a limo this time. Pete joked about how he was picked up in a limousine and brought back home in a Ford. To make matters worse when Pete arrived home at four in the morning without a key to get in he climbed up a drainpipe and broke the bathroom window to get access as he didn't want to wake us up.

On the sixth of September 1967 The Tornados' world had completely turned around. We had gone from not knowing what we would be doing after the season at Great Yarmouth, to suddenly becoming Billy Fury's backing group with the promise of regular work and maybe some opportunities in the future. That night Dave and I along with Mickey Watts, (Dave's dad) sat in the front room of the house and sampled some of Mickey's alcohol which was mostly made up of liqueurs that he had bought and collected on trips abroad; mainly Spain. It was nice to go to bed that night feeling a little nervous, but very excited about what the coming week would bring.

We were woken up the next morning by Dave's mum as she knocked on the bedroom door "Dave… There's somebody on the phone." It was Pete Hollis calling to tell us that he was on the way over for the rehearsal with Billy. John had not called as yet and knew nothing of the "Billy Fury" deal. We did hear from him about an hour later when he called to see what was happening. John surprisingly seemed to be full of trepidation as Dave told him of the deal. "We can't do it, we'll never pull it off, I don't know if I can do this and I can't make it for the rehearsal". Once again we were plunged into that world of uncertainty and disappointment. But Dave just told John in a matter of fact way "That's alright John, we're going anyway and I think I'll give Mickey Simmons a call, he used to play for the Symbols, he might want the gig."

Pete Hollis, Dave and I arrived at the rehearsal hall and set up our gear. We were warming up and running through a few numbers when Billy walked in. He was alone with no managers or entourage following him. We stopped playing and he walked up to us and smiling he greeted us and shook hands with us. It was a knock-out experience for me as I was a big Billy Fury fan and once again I was enjoying the thrill of being close to and working with a rock star that I had gone to see at the local rock shows that came to town. My sister and I would go together and she would scream "Billy!" and I would sit there just wishing that I could be up on that stage. Be careful what you wish for! Billy was great. He looked great and dressed great and had a very pleasant if slightly shy demeanour.

We told him that our drummer was ill but he would be coming tomorrow which didn't bother him. We actually had no idea at that time if we had a drummer or not but we just hoped for the best. Billy had brought some tapes with him and he used my Gibson 335 to show me some of the chords in the songs. We listened on a tape recorder that he had brought to the 8 or 9 songs he did in his set. I knew most of them and along with Pete Hollis working out the bass and Dave doing his thing on the Hammond the first get together with Billy Fury went well. The vibes were good and it was a big pleasure to work with Billy. He was just a very nice, down to earth, regular kind of guy that had a special aura about him. He was a star, albeit not as big as he once was, but he still had that charisma, that something very special. He was the closest thing that we ever had to Elvis. There was Cliff Richard of course but he was a little too nice. Billy could pull off that mean sexy look together with those Elvis style movements on stage. We watched as he drove off in his Mercedes Benz then turned around to pack up the gear still not knowing who, or if anybody at all would be playing drums for us at the next rehearsal.

Later that night Dave and I listened to Billy's tapes and Dave started to write out the music for the songs. At one point the phone rang and it was John calling to ask how it went with Billy. From what I could understand from the conversation it seemed like John would be coming to the rehearsal and Dave confirmed that after he had hung up the phone. "Yeah Robbie it looks like John will be coming after all. It's just as well, I couldn't get hold of Mickey Simmons, and he's playing away somewhere anyway." Once again we were back on the plus side. We gave Pete Hollis a call to let him know that John would be showing up after all and with a feeling of relief Dave and I continued our work on Billy's numbers. When it got very late I had to go off to bed but Dave stayed up most of the night writing out the parts for us.

The next day it was great to rehearse with the whole band present. We arrived early so that we could run through some of the numbers before Billy arrived. We were about halfway through "I'll Never Find Another You" when Billy arrived. Once again he was alone and as we stopped playing he walked up and with a smile he said "Sounds good boys." We ran through a few numbers with Billy and everything felt real good and relaxed. It was great to work with him as he never attempted to be the big star singer, treating us as humble musicians. He, although older than us, he was twenty seven at the time, was just like a member of the band and one of the lads. I always felt very comfortable with Billy, he didn't have any attitudes. At the end of a good rehearsal as Billy was leaving, he said that he had a 100 watt Marshall PA system that we could use if we wanted and all we had to do was pick it up from him. This was a great thing for us as the Vox column speakers and 50 watt Dynachord PA amp we had, didn't amount to much so now with this most desirable PA within reach things were really looking good. We would be able to use it on our gigs too. It was remarkable that Roger and Pete had bought a Marshall PA for The Holder Brothers and now suddenly we were to have a Marshall too and it wasn't costing us anything. That evening Dave and I unbolted all the seats in the back of the van, took them out and put them down at the end of the back yard where they would rust in peace. Now we were truly ready for the road. There was plenty of room in the back of the Bedford now for all our gear including the PA that we picked up from Billy the next day. On the way back to Bromley we stopped off in the West End to buy a couple of Shure Mics and cables. As we got out of the van and walked towards the music store we saw Ginger Baker and Jack Bruce standing outside. We nodded and they nodded and we walked inside. The rest of the afternoon Dave and I spent testing out the PA. With a celebration curry down at the local Indian or "Brownie" as we called it, the day ended with a good feeling that we had accomplished something.

Sunday would be an exciting and challenging day for us. It would be our first gig with Billy Fury; the first of a set of seven nightly shows at the Batley Variety Club. Dave and I were out of the house by 7am, with Dave driving the "Old Banger" van and me following cautiously behind in Mickey Watts' yellow and black Zephyr, losing my driving virginity by embarking on my first ever solo drive. Dave seemed to be able to get access to his dad's car as needed. We picked up Pete Hollis and his gear and headed up the M1 to rendezvous with John Davies at the Blue Boar Café and then make our way up north. We pulled up outside the café and looked around for John but he was nowhere to be seen. We waited for about a half hour but no sign of him. Dave suggested that Pete and I take off in the van and that he would stay behind and wait for John. He said he could travel faster than us and could make up for the lost time quicker by car. Pete and I thought that was a good idea and took off up the M1. We left not knowing if John would even show up. If he didn't, Dave wouldn't even be able to let us know. We didn't have the luxury of cell phones in those days and for the most part we just went ahead like pioneers into the great unknown jungle of the entertainment world, and hoped for the best.

With the old Bedford coughing and sputtering Pete Hollis and I made our way up the M1 with everything looking as if we would reach our destination in Batley with no hitches. When Pete took a wrong exit from the motorway our luck changed. Unable to find our way back to the M1 we pushed on blindly, stopping here and there on the way to ask directions to Batley from various pedestrians. The best we could get out of them was that we were a long way from there and nobody could really give us any dependable directions. As we proceeded to drive from one small town to another we started to become aware of an ominous knocking sound that was coming from somewhere in the back of the van. It sounded like it was coming from the rear axle. We stopped to take a look at the axle, but with both of us not really knowing what we were looking for we continued on hoping to find a petrol station with a repair shop. It was Sunday afternoon and everywhere was deserted and with the knocking sound becoming louder by the minute we began to worry. By now it was mid afternoon and our prospects of reaching Batley in time looked fairly remote. The knocking sound had increased to a heavy thudding and just when we thought that it was the end for us we suddenly spotted a filling station ahead and pulled up at the pumps. The repair shop was closed but the attendant who turned out to be the owner offered to try to help us out. "You've got the wrong size wheel on the back left hand side. If you would have gone another mile the bloody wheel would have fallen off" was the news he gave us as he crawled out from under the back of the van. He then went on to give us a lengthy explanation of how many pounds per square inch of added pressure had been exerted on the axle due to the wrong size rim and with it being Sunday there was nowhere open to get a replacement so we were basically stuck. Pete and I were at a loss to know what to do. We could not contact Dave and we had no phone number for the club. It looked as if we would be letting Billy Fury down on our first ever engagement with him. When all seemed totally lost the mechanic said "Wait a minute" and walked off disappearing behind the filling station. Pete and I looked at each other hoping that some kind of miracle would happen that could turn our desperate situation around. A few minutes later he appeared carrying a rim which he joyously told us that he had found in a pile of rubbish at the back of the station. Upon investigation he found that it was indeed the right size that we needed. After he had mounted the tire and all was ready we thanked him profusely. We settled up with him and after getting some good directions we set off again and eventually pulled into Batley at around 7pm that evening.

We found the club and drove around to the stage door and saw Dave's car parked there. At least he had made it on time and presumably with John. As Pete and I entered the dressing room Dave exploded "Where the fucking hell have you been" he shouted "We're supposed to go in 30 minutes." There was very little time for explanations so we hurriedly brought the gear inside and set it up on the stage. Billy was hanging around back stage and was visibly concerned but happy that we had made it. An announcement was made in the club that the show would be running half an hour late and we finally got to appear at 8pm. We were to perform our 30 minute set which would be followed by Billy's act. After the stress of the day I was very nervous on stage and totally fucked up the guitar solos in "Telstar" and "Lawrence Of Arabia" much to the displeasure of Dave who glared at me from across the stage. Our first performance as the new set of Tornados was disappointing due mainly to my bad playing. One thing we had not really thought about was my playing of Pete Holder's lead parts. I had always been rhythm guitarist and lead vocalist since Robb Gayle and The Whirlwinds and playing melodies was not a strong point with me. I was more into blues type of improvisation and never was any good at playing Hank Marvin style guitar.

We had more success with Billy's act. There were no specific lead parts for guitar and I was comfortable just to play rhythm guitar as I had always done. We played the set without any problems and got our first ever set with Billy Fury under our belts. Back in the dressing room after the show Dave asked what the fuck I was doing in the guitar solos and said "Well we really missed Pete Holder tonight didn't we boys?" I was embarrassed and felt bad inside. I kind of knew that it wouldn't get any better, and it didn't. Near the end of the week after I had continued to fuck up the solos each night Dave said "Okay Robbie, that's enough I'll play them from now on." I was off the hook and felt relieved that I would no longer have to be faced with that problem, but I was upset and felt that my musicianship was questionable. I dealt with it by telling myself that it was because I was not into that kind of playing and that was not what I wanted to play. Although true, it was still an excuse. I was just unable to play those parts correctly, simple as they may have been.

I didn't realize it at the time but that unfortunate situation would lead to a turning point in my musical career. I would gradually come to experience the reality of working in a band in which I was one of the main songwriters, where we performed only our own original material and were able to preserve that music on three LPs. It would be part of the "psychedelic" era moving towards "psyche-hard rock". Forty years down the road we would be considered a curiosity in musical history. Rare copies of our first album would sell for up to $3000 each and would be called the "Rarest psychedelic record in the world."

The nightclub recommended us a place to stay for the week. It was a cottage that was attached to a large mansion house and was once probably used as a gamekeeper's residence or servants' quarters. It was up on a hillside with thick woods at the back of the property. The only bad point was the gas works down the street. When the wind blew in the right direction the unmistakable smell of coal gas wafted in through the windows. Although old, the accommodation was comfortable so we settled in for the week. We made arrangements to rehearse with Billy the following afternoon at the club. Everything went very well, Billy was pleased and we had got his act down well as a band. Billy was in my opinion the coolest singer that I ever worked with. Even though we did have a great rehearsal we did have a mishap on the show that night. During Billy's act he announced the number and Dave counted it in. Unfortunately Dave had his music sheets in the wrong order and while the rest of us were on the right song, Dave was playing another number in a totally different key. Billy turned round and in a very polite way said "No, no lads that's the wrong number." We got ourselves together and Dave professionally counted it in again and off we went with the right song. Billy never mentioned anything to us about the mistake. He didn't throw any temper tantrums in the dressing room afterwards. We did apologize to him but he said that it was okay and to forget about it. Tuesday night the singing duo Peter and Gordon appeared on the bill for a one nighter. Backstage they acted aloof and didn't speak to us although Gordon Waller may have mumbled "Hi." I don't think that they even acknowledged Billy. Somebody from their company did mention to us that there would be a big party at Peter Asher's place at the end of the week and we were invited and it sounded like fun.

About half way through that week at Batley it occurred to me that we were not that far from Barnsley. That was where my ex girlfriend Jackie Grant lived with her parents; unless she was away working somewhere. Now that I could drive and had access to the van I was able to do things without having to rely on others for my transport. With this new feeling of independence I boldly decided that I would drive over to Barnsley to see if Jackie was home and if she was I would invite her to the show. Don't ask me how I remembered her address or how to get there but I did show up one afternoon and knocked at the door. It was opened by her mum who called out," Ay by gum, it's Rob, Pam" and invited me in. Well at least I knew that Jackie was home and that it had not been a waste of time to drive over there. I followed Mrs. Eastwood into the living room and caught sight of Jackie sitting on the sofa, nervously fixing her hair. It had been almost 6 months since we last saw each other and it seemed like we were strangers. Her mum shuffled off into the kitchen to put the kettle on while we chatted about what we were doing and so forth. I decided to leave after about an hour and on my way out I asked Jackie if she would like to come to the show the following evening. She said that she would and I arranged to pick her up the next day. On the drive back to Batley I felt good and thought that I might have accomplished something. Jackie looked good and I carried a hope some-where inside of me that maybe we could renew our relationship.

That hope was blown away the following evening when I arrived to find Jackie and her mum all dressed up and ready to go. "Me mum said she'd like to come with us, if that's alright." What could I say? Although I knew at that point that there was no hope, I continued to act like a gentleman. I got them some good seats and a couple of drinks and they actually seemed to be enjoying themselves. I looked out into the audience and picked her out when I was singing "Let It Be Me" and remembered when she used to stand in the wings at Coventry in her sexy little jungle suit and watch me and smile from the side of the stage. After the show I brought them backstage and introduced them to Billy and the rest of the band. On the drive back to Barnsley the conversation was upbeat between Jackie, her mum and I. I thought that maybe there was still a chance that her mum might go on in and leave Jackie and me alone for a few minutes when we got to their home. That didn't happen but I did get invited in for a cup of tea with a chance to chat a little more, although not on an intimate level. I mentioned that there was some talk about The Tornados possibly going to France to tour with Billy Fury. Jackie said that she might be going to Paris with a dancing group. "Maybe we'll meet again in France" I said with a smile as I left. "Maybe we will" Jackie answered. I bid them goodbye, got into the Bedford and drove off and never saw her again.

On the way back to Batley while stopped at a red light I accidentally hit the ignition key and cut off the engine. Within half a second I turned the key to restart it creating the loudest backfire I had ever heard. It was late at night but a few pedestrians were still walking home and I saw them all literally jump out of their skins when the van backfired. Later on at the cottage I told the guys what had happened and we all had a good laugh about it. Of course, the next day Dave and Pete couldn't wait to try to recreate the backfire and we decided to take a drive downtown that afternoon. Looking up ahead we saw about a dozen people standing in line at a bus stop. That all too familiar look of mischief appeared on Dave's face as he slowed the Bedford down and when we got adjacent to the queue at the bus stop he quickly turned the ignition on and off. It was a great success, he had reproduced a huge backfire and we all burst into fits of laughter as we saw the whole line of people jump into the air altogether with terrified looks wondering where this huge bang had come from. We spent the next hour driving around Batley and Dewsbury looking for suitable bus queues and heavy pedestrian areas where we could work our backfire mischief. As we hung out at the cottage later that afternoon we began to notice that Pete Hollis had a moody side to him. He would suddenly become very quiet and soon would disappear for a long time in his room He was washing his hair and blow drying it for what seemed like hours. We saw this to become a daily routine with him and Dave would say "Oh oh, Pete's washing his hair again."

Thursday night in our dressing room before the show, Billy walked in and told us that he wanted us to be his permanent backing group which we were happy to hear. He told us that we would also be working again the following week in Warrington. We would be doing two shows a night at two different venues and would be sharing the bill with Freddy Starr and The Delmonts. He also asked me what the song was that I was playing and singing as he walked in. I told him that it was one of my own songs and he asked me to play it for him. It was a song called "The Wedding Of Mr. James And Mrs. Brown." He listened closely and when it came to the end he said "That's a great song man, I really like it and I'd like to record it on my next album." I was thrilled to hear Billy Fury say that he wanted to record one of my songs. That never happened, but I do believe that he would have done a great version of it probably using an orchestral style backing. I shortened the title to "The Wedding" and finally recorded it myself some thirty eight years later and featured it on the Joe Meek tribute album called *Lost Songs of the Sixties*.

Friday night after the show we decided to check out the Peter and Gordon party. When we arrived we found out that it turned out to be some kind of fancy dress party and everybody was in "drag." We definitely stuck out like sore thumbs dressed in our regular everyday "Mod gear." We were definitely out of place and felt uncomfortable and at one point when we were approached by some guy wearing a dress informing us that there was a charge of 30 "bob" per person to go towards the drinks. Dave said "Well that's it then boys", and we planned to make our escape. We were a little embarrassed about just walking out altogether and leaving, so we decided that we should leave discretely one by one as if we were going to the toilet. Dave was first off followed a minute later by John and then by Pete leaving me the last and alone in the room. Just as I was turning to leave, the guy who was collecting the money walked up asking "Are you staying then?" I just walked off and turning my head to him I said "I'm just going to the toilet, I'll be back in a minute" and made my way to the toilet but scooted out of the front door. Dave was at the wheel of the Zephyr with John and Pete and walking briskly out through the front gate I jumped in beside the guys and we drove off into the night laughing about our weird, short trip to the "Peter and Gordon Drag Party".

Somebody at the club told us about a very nice van that was for sale which would be suitable for us. As the old Bedford was getting the worst for wear with its muffler totally blown out due to our repeated "backfire" antics, on Saturday morning we drove over to take a look at it. It was a total piece of crap actually much worse that what we already had so we decided to keep the Bedford for the time being anyway.

Saturday night we were in high spirits. It was the last night of the week at Batley and we were feeling satisfied that we had done a pretty good job backing Billy on our first week with him As we hung out that evening back stage in our dressing room a knock came at the door. It was a reporter from the local newspaper who introduced himself and requested an interview with us and Billy Fury. Billy had not yet arrived so we went ahead with the interview. Placing his "Nikon" down on the table and pulling out his notebook he asked us what it was like to be backing Billy, but most of the interview was centred around our experiences with Joe Meek in particular the murder/suicide. From time to time he would pick up his camera and snap shots of us. When another knock came at the door it was the Mayor of Batley who was attending the show that night and wanted to meet Billy. We chatted with him and the reporter until Billy showed up. They decided that they would move into the dressing room next door to interview Billy and the three of them stood up and left. A minute or two later as we began to get into our stage clothes we noticed that the reporter had left his camera sitting on the table and as Pete Hollis moved to pick it up and return it Dave said" Hold on a minute Pete" and I saw that all too familiar, mischievous twinkle appear in Dave's eyes. Dave said "Keep an eye on the door Robbie" and pulling down his underwear he passed the camera to John saying "Here Johnnie take a real good shot of my arse." Dave got up on the table, raised his legs in the air and spread his cheeks. John sprang into action and assuming the stance of a professional photographer he promptly snapped a great shot of Dave's lower extremity. As Dave hurriedly pulled up his underpants we were once more surprised by another knock at the door and it was the reporter who had returned to retrieve his forgotten camera. Trying hard to contain our laughter we watched as John handed it to him. "We were just about to bring it back to you" said Johnnie and the reporter said "Thanks boys" and left. We all fell about laughing as Pete said "I bet he'll get a bloody big surprise when that film gets developed." We could only imagine the look on his face as he would sift through the photos and come across that beautiful close up of Dave's anus.

Sunday afternoon it was time to "pay the piper" for our irresponsible abuse of the muffler backfires. When we were about half way over the Pennines the complete muffler assembly fell off the van. We stopped and threw it into the back of the van and banged around until we reached Warrington and found the club. The poster outside the club read Billy Fury and The Tornados and Freddy Starr and The Delmonts. We never got to see Freddy Starr, or The Delmonts for that matter as both bands were in transit between the shows. We opened at the Garrick Lea Towers and closed in Warrington. It was always agreed that bands would use each others amps and drums as there was no time to break down the gear between the shows. We found out that there was a huge concert organ at Warrington which Dave was not eager to play so we decided that we would try to take Dave's Hammond organ, his big "coffin" speaker cabinet and 100 Watt amplifier from gig to gig. The first night it was like a nightmare trying to get Dave's gear out of the club and into the van. It became clear that we would be running late due to the delay with the equipment. We rushed into the club with only a few minutes to spare before we were due to appear but as soon as we got Dave's organ set up we discovered that we had forgotten the plug board and with a shortage of electrical outlets we were unable to get Dave's gear plugged in. We did our show with Dave doing his best to play the huge concert organ with its multiple keyboards and vast array of knobs and stops but we got through our set and Billy's set went well too On the way back to the digs after the show Dave said "Well boys there's not enough time to move the Hammond and it was such a muck up tonight I suppose I'll just have to play that bloody big organ and sound just like Sandy McPherson."

Early in the week John Redgrave showed up at the club. He said that he had come to help us with our stage act and presentation. I thought it rather strange that here he was buzzing around The Tornados when I thought he should have been working with The Holder Brothers. I suppose that he was trying to get in with whoever he could to manifest his desire to be a group manager. The week passed without incident with Dave making the best out of the Sandy McPherson organ and with Billy seemingly satisfied with our backing. We did notice however the moodiness of Pete Hollis when we hung out at the digs during the day. He would suddenly get very quiet and his regular hair washing and mega blow dry sessions were a ritual. I noticed how it was beginning to bother John and Dave. They often made comments about him and said that he was a bit on the weird side and not one of the boys. The Joe Baker show together with Dave and Roger's performance was aired on that Friday night when we were at Warrington. We never got to see it as we were working. I was disappointed to say the least as I was looking forward to seeing the show after Dave had told me all about those hilarious events that took place during the filming.

THE TORNADOS CHAPTER SIX

More changes in the line-up and Sonia from the Diamond Twins joins the band.

More gig stories on the road doing Cabaret clubs and one nighters with Billy.

Recording sessions and the band is offered a tour of Israel and accepts.

A last minute set back before we leave for Israel and another line-up change.

A gruelling journey through France and a horrendous Mediterranean crossing.

The Tornados meet Mandy Rice Davies in Tel Aviv.

Robb strikes up a friendship with Stan Solomon of The Churchills.

The Tornados final gig and the band breaks up.

Robb Tel Aviv 1968

We had heard from George Cooper that we had a one–nighter in Manchester right at the end of the month so as we needed more re-hearsals with Pete Hollis in order to fulfil that gig, we decided that we would give the Top Hat club in Spennymoor a call and ask the man-ager whose name happened to be Johnny Ray if we could do some rehearsals during the day at the club. He kindly consented so we decided to spend sometime in Spennymoor to get The Tornados up to scratch. We checked in to the Knicky Knack Guest House once again and found out that our old mates The Symbols were appearing at the Top Hat for the week. They were also staying at the Guest House. We got the rehearsals underway in the afternoons when Johnny Ray was getting the bar set up for the night. One afternoon he asked us if we would like to do a residency gig at the Top Hat for 200 pounds a week. It would be steady work and money. 50 pounds a week each sounded appealing but we decided to turn it down. After all we were The Tornados and The Tornados were not a residency band. We had our gigs with Billy and there were some things coming up so we decided that we would continue as we were. Anyway the thought of continuously having to learn and perform all the top ten hits was unappealing to us, and it would just turn us into a nothing kind of residency band playing everybody else's hits. The future of The Tornados was uncertain but we felt that it would be better to stick with what we had.

After spending a couple of days down in Gloucester I drove the old Bedford to Bromley and met Dave at his parents' house. Dave told me that John had found us a new bass player and not only that, Dave said that he had received a call from George Cooper to say that we were booked to do a radio show with Billy Fury on October the 5th for the BBC programme called *Swingalong*. This was to be in two days time so once again we were under the gun to get ready with our new bass player. We had often expressed to each other how we felt about Pete Hollis and his moody ways and felt that if someone suitable should come along we would make the change. John had mentioned Chris Lethbridge who I remembered from the Saxon days. He played in a band from Cheltenham called the Road Hogs. I can't say that I really knew him but I had seen him play a couple of times so he was not like a complete stranger. John apparently had gone to Cheltenham to look for Chris only to find out that he was playing in a residency down in Torquay. The name of the club they played at was called Pegotty's and they were called Pegotty's People. When John failed to find any phone number for a club called Pegotty's and knowing the urgency of the situation, he decided to call the police station in Torquay. He had been given Chris's address by his sister but there was no phone there. John said that it was urgent that Chris call him as he had news that Chris's uncle was here from Canada and wanted to see him. So the local constable went around delivering the urgent news. When he heard "Police! Open the door" Chris thought for sure that it must be some kind of drug raid and feared the worst. He was very relieved when he heard the news about his uncle from Canada who of course did not exist and thought that John was playing some kind of practical joke on him. Chris called John to curse him out for playing such a dangerous trick on him involving the police. Anyway Chris took up John's offer to join The Tornados.

On Tuesday 3rd of October at 11am John showed up in Bromley with Chris in tow. Chris and I acknowledged that we remembered one another and after the usual chit chat we introduced Chris to Dave. Chris was about 20 years old, had medium length mousey brown hair. He was wearing a grey double breasted RAF overcoat which he proudly told us that he had bought at the Army and Navy surplus store. Under his arm he carried his blond Gibson EBO bass which was Gibson's best selling bass guitar for the 60s and 70s. Without delay we started to work on the six songs that we were to record with Billy. Together we carried Dave's Hammond into the front room and I brought in my Marshall amp which Chris and I played through while John tapped away with his drum sticks on a cardboard box. We were coming along very well with the rehearsal when we heard the phone ring. Mrs. Watts who had just been preparing a pot of tea for us popped her head around the door announcing that Pete Hollis was on the phone. With all our attention directed towards the rehearsal we had totally forgotten all about him and now we were faced with a dilemma. What were we going to tell him and who was going to speak to him? It was quickly decided that the thankless job would be given to me. I picked up the phone and putting on the saddest voice I explained to Pete that the band had broken up and I was getting my stuff together to move back to Gloucester When he asked to speak to Dave I told him that Dave had left the band and was rehearsing with The Symbols and I had no idea where John was. So that was that, I said goodbye and wished him luck and with a high degree of relief I returned to the front room and continued to rehearse.

Chris turned out to be very quick to learn the bass parts for Billy's songs and by the early evening we had them all completed. Chris was really a likeable character with a great dry sense of humour although at times a little on the sarcastic side. His favourite television show was *Captain Pugwash* (a popular kid's programme at the time). During conversation he would regularly inject the line "Back to the Black Pig Tom" which he said with a put on voice in the style of the Captain Pugwash character. The following day we met up with Billy at a rehearsal hall and ran through the numbers. Everything went along very well and Billy was pleased with the sound. Chris fit in very well and played well and by the end of the rehearsal we were all confident that the session for *Swingalong* would turn out successfully.

On the 5th we all met at the Aeolian Hall in New Bond Street and just as we had hoped everything went well. We basically recorded the numbers live just as if we were playing a gig. Billy sang very well and we got most of the songs down in one take. Billy stood behind a screen while we and our amps were all separated so as to get the best sound possible. Apart from the obvious surroundings the session reminded me of recording in Joe Meek's studio. It was almost a year since we had last recorded "No More You And Me" at Holloway Road and that session really brought back memories of all the recording that we had done with Joe since the days of The Whirlwinds. The recording engineers commented on how good it all sounded and commended us on our professional conduct. At the end of the session we were paid thirty pounds which when divided up gave the four of us seven pounds ten shillings each which was roughly what session musicians were paid in those days.

Hoping to find a new direction for The Tornados, Dave and I had discussed the possibility of recruiting Sonia from the Diamond Twins to join The Tornados so that we could put together a cabaret act. We thought that as Billy Fury's gigs were not so numerous that we might be able to fill in the time off between those gigs doing cabaret shows. We considered that Sonia being a very attractive girl with a great voice would add greatly to our appeal on the cabaret scene. There was talk that Sonia's sister Sandra may have been thinking about leaving the duo and getting married to Roger Holder, now with The Holder Brothers, so this would open a door for Sonia to join The Tornados. The Diamond Twins were booked to appear at the Casino Club in Southport for a week so it was decided that the band would drive up and rehearse in the club with Sonia and prepare a set of music for cabaret shows.

Saturday 7th October found John, Dave and I driving to Watford to pick up Chris who was staying there with his girlfriend. The old Bedford was beginning to sound pretty rough and it looked as if we might not make it to Southport so we decided that we would try to make it to Gloucester where we would stay the night at my folks place and ask my dad if we could use his car to make the trip up north. We made it to Gloucester and Sunday morning we drove up to Southport using my dad's car. We were able to find a flat in Southport where we could stay at and we began to rehearse with Sonia in the daytime at the club. The house band was kind enough to let us use their gear to rehearse on. We started with numbers like "I've Got You Under My Skin", "Autumn Leaves", "Yesterday", "To Sir With Love" and a medley that Dave and I had been working on which was to be called "A Musical Tour Of The World." Using a theme song "Faraway Places" we would take the audience to Spain for "Granada" which we already had played with Tony Dalli in Yarmouth, to Brazil for "Coffee In Brazil", to the USA using the song "On Broadway" eventually ending up in good old England with "London By Night".

We were thinking that we might see Roger at some point to find out how things were coming along with The Holder Brothers but he did not make an appearance and by the 11th we found out from Sonia that he had left and had returned to the farm in Newent. In the middle of the week when parking my dad's car I backed it into a lamp post and broke the tail light and dented the rear fender causing the back bumper to become detached. Luckily we were close to a body shop and dropped the car off for repair. Unfortunately we were left without transport for a few days and were forced to hang out at the flat all day running through songs as best we could. A general air of depression began to set in which was caused by our confinement and also by news from Dave that he had called the Cooper Organization only to find out that there was no work on the horizon.

Friday 13th we picked up the car from the repair shop and I paid out 11 pounds for the work they had done. The following morning we drove back down to Gloucester. Chris said that his brother was a mechanic and would take a look at the Bedford and could possibly make the repairs at his home near Cheltenham. The rest of the band caught the train to return to London while I stayed with my parents to await the repairs on the van.

Having picked up the repaired Bedford from Chris' brother I drove to Bromley to find Dave feeling pretty down and depressed. He had spoken to John Redgrave in an attempt to get something going but although Redgrave tried to give encouragement he still really had nothing to offer.

Over the next few weeks we had a lot of rehearsing to do along with Chris and Sonia. We had to get the rest of Billy Fury's repertoire down, finish off the remainder of numbers for The Tornados one night stand shows and get the additional cabaret pieces completed with Sonia. Dave and I decided to pay a visit to Dougie Millings' tailor shop to get measured for a casual suit each. I got a beige two piece made for 30 pounds which looked real sharp. I paid for it by cheque from my bank account. Although there was no money in the account the bank honoured it and sent a letter to my home address in Gloucester. My Dad ended up paying the money to the bank to cover the bounced check to keep me out of trouble.

We did however get a little encouraging news from John Redgrave saying that he was working on getting us an audition with Ronnie King who at that time was a booking agent in London. As the Cooper Organization was coming up with next to nothing in the way of work we decided to pin our hopes on something materializing in that direction. Sonia gave us the news that the Diamond Twins would be leaving at the end of October to perform in Singapore for 3 weeks so we stepped up the rehearsals to make up for the time that she would be away. At last a trickling of work came in from Cooper who had booked us for a gig at the Lyceum in Bradford on October 21st which was to be followed by a week of Cabaret in Jarrow at the Club Franchi. The Lyceum turned out to be a horrible gig where we were told to play two sets starting at midnight with the second set starting at 2.30am. After the first set at around 1 am the lights went out in the club after which we were told that we would not be required to play the second set. According to what we had been told by the Cooper Organization we were booked for one 45 minute set only so we thought that something was up. At the point when we decided to leave the club the lights came on again under rather mysterious circumstances and when Dave went to pick up the money we were told that we had not fulfilled our part of the contract and we ended up only being able to get 4 pounds 10 shillings from the manager. That worked out to be just over a pound each. Being that we had gotten the gear put away in the van and also seeing the threatening looks that we were getting from the bouncers we decided not to pursue the situation any further and got the hell out of there.

Sunday we drove to Jarrow and found some digs. As we were not due to perform at the Club Franchi until Monday night we hung out all day and in the evening Dave and I decided that we would go to watch a movie at the local cinema. John and Chris opting not to come along stayed at the digs. Dave had a set of walkie talkies that he had got from somewhere and taking one along with us he told Chris that he would try to contact them after the show just for fun. When the movie was over and everyone was leaving the cinema Dave and I went to the men's toilets and because two way radios were illegal at that time Dave hid in one of the stalls and began to try to contact the boys at the digs. I waited by the door and saw the puzzled looks on men's faces as they entered the toilet hearing a static crackling coming from inside and the sound of Dave's voice giggling and saying "Hey man I can't hear you." I turned around to see what was going on in the Foyer and saw the presence of several police constables busily searching for something. "Holy Christ" I said to myself, the cops must have somehow picked up on the walkie talkie radio and were searching for the person who was operating the then illegal device.

Trying to look inconspicuous I entered the toilet and walking over to the stall in which Dave was hiding I whispered "Hey Davie the place is crawling with cops." Dave immediately flushed the toilet and quickly hiding the radio in his jacket pocket we both walked out into the foyer past the cops and into the street. "Bloody 'ell that was a close one Robbie" said Dave as we jumped into the Bedford and drove away from the cinema.

When we got back to the digs and related the tale to Chris and John they burst out laughing and admitted that they had called the police to say that there was a bomb in the theatre so that the presence of the police would make Dave and I think that they were looking for us and the two way radio. Dave had to smile but he was pissed off. "You bastards could have got us busted" he complained.

As we were booked to appear for the week at the Club Franchi and it was a cabaret gig Sonia came in on the train on Monday. This was to be our first official gig with Sonia where we were to try out our new cabaret act. We showed up at the venue in the afternoon to get set up and run through a few numbers. We thought that it was strange that there was no mention anywhere at the entrance of the club advertising that The Tornados would be appearing there for the week. We just thought that they had forgotten to post the announcement. We played our set that night to a very small audience but all in all we thought that the act went over reasonably well considering. The house band took over as we left the stage and returned to the dressing room. Presently a knock came at the door. It was one of the bartenders who asked us which one of us was the leader of the group. We all looked at each other and Dave said "I am." He was told that the club manager wanted to see him at once. Dave returned after about five minutes or so and announced that we had been "Paid off". Thinking that Dave was up to one of his pranks again we all fell about laughing and we ignored his words of assertion that we had indeed been paid off and he was not joking. Being paid off in show biz terms basically meant that the club was firing you and that you would just be paid for the night's work and asked to leave. When the grim truth was eventually realized by the rest of The Tornados the dressing room got very quiet. The usual reason for being paid off was because the entertainment had put on a bad or sub-standard show. Dave went on to explain that the manager had told him that many of the audience had walked out and had voiced complaints at the exit. This puzzled us as there was not a large audience to begin with. When we asked the doorman if anyone had left and had complained about the band he answered in the negative. We also asked the house band if we had sounded bad. They had no adverse comments about our act. Dave was told that we could pick up the cheque for the night's show the following day.

All the following day we hung around and waited outside the club for it to open. Needless to say we were all in a state of deep depression. When the club finally opened up in the late afternoon we entered to find posters advertising that Johnny DeLittle would be appearing there that night and for the rest of the week. As Johnny De-Little was the son of Dave Macbeth who was the booking agent for the Club Franchi we smelled a rat and came to the conclusion that we were victims of some kind of a fiddle. Although we felt a little better about the humbling experience we had been subjected to, on the long drive back to Bromley I still had a nagging feeling inside of me that we might not have been up to par after all and maybe it was not a fiddle.

When we finally made it back to Bromley we expected that we would all stay at Dave's place but we got a cold reception from Dave's mum and dad who complained that there would be too many people staying at the house so we continued to drive down to Sonia's folks' home in Maidstone where we were able to stay the night and thus let things cool down a bit in Bromley. The next day when we returned to Bromley Mrs. Watts said that I could stay there for two pounds a week but there was no room for Chris as Les Baguley the Diamond's pianist was staying there too. I would have to sleep on a camp bed that my Dad had given to me on my last trip to Gloucester. He used to use it when he worked away from home at places like the Farnborough Air Show where he and his workmates slept on site in a large tent. He said it might come in useful for me and as it could be rolled up into a small package I could fit it into my suitcase and would always have something to sleep on in any kind of emergency situations.

After the "getting paid off" episode we were still depressed and we were all getting low on money and as Chris had nowhere to go he said he would sleep in Mr. Watts' car outside in the street. This could not have been very comfortable as it was near the end of October and the nights were getting colder. But Chris being the character that he was took it all in stride and didn't complain. Dave called John Redgrave again and after hearing our tale of woe said that he would arrange for us to meet with Ronnie King. In the meantime we continued to rehearse our set and Billy's numbers at the Black Horse pub in Bromley with Chris still roughing it in the car.

Towards the end of the month just before Sonia was due to leave for Singapore we went over to see Ronnie King where we had a meeting with him and along with Sonia we did an audition. For some strange reason we did not play well but King showed a lot of interest in Sonia so we thought that there may still have been a chance for us. Even so a heavy depression was still hanging over the band.

We called Duncan Burns who was Billy Fury's agent who told us there would be some work coming up soon, in particular a gig at the American Embassy in Grosvenor Square. We also spoke to George Cooper to complain about the lack of work. We told him that we were almost out of money and were getting desperate. He told us that the organization would consider putting us on a weekly wage so that we could support ourselves but we were not keen on that idea. Knowing how we had been cheated in the past, Cooper would probably have us working seven days in all kinds of hovels for 10 pounds a week. About a week later Cooper called to tell us that an opportunity had come up for us to play a residency up north for a hundred and sixty pounds a week. We put two and two together and figured it out that it must have been the Top Hat at Spennymoor as we had discussed that with Johnnie Ray there a few weeks ago. Remembering that we had been offered 200 pounds a week, after deducting Cooper's commission of 10% we would have been left with 180 pounds. It was obvious that he was deliberately attempting to take double commission by offering us 160 pounds. We turned it down. A gig came up for us to back Billy Fury on the 17th November. This was good news but by the time that gig would come around we would already have been 25 days without work. I don't know how I got by. I can't remember how much money I had in my pocket at the time. It couldn't have been much, but somehow I got through it. We were all in the same boat. Dave luckily got some session work with Les Baguley who was composing music for a TV film that needed a Chinese feel to it. Then a few days later he got another session, this time with his old mates The Symbols. They were recording a song called the "Best Part Of Breaking Up" which was written by Phil Spector and wanted an organ on the session. Between those two sessions Dave probably made about 15 pounds or thereabouts, so he was better off than all the rest of us. He probably had to lend me a couple of quid to help me out here and there.

17th of November came around and we drove up to Liverpool to play at Dino's Club. To enter the club you had to climb a very long and steep flight of stairs. It was tough work to lug the amps and drums all the way up to the top, and Billy's Marshall PA too, was something to wrestle with. Dave's Hammond, however was a different situation. Dave had made a wooden sled on which the organ was placed. It was held in place by two belts that were lashed around the sled. There was another belt attached to the front of the sled by which it could be pulled. Dave swears that this was his invention as he had not seen any other band with a Hammond that had this kind of set up. As was usual the four of us would pick up the Hammond each of us on a corner of the sled and carry into the club. This time we put it down at the bottom of the stairs. Then we would usually pull it up the stairs with two guys on the front and two pushing from behind. This time Dave told John and Chris that he and I could manage it alone which gave them an opportunity to get some more gear out of the van. Dave and I pulled the Hammond up to the top of the stairs without too much of a struggle. Just as I was changing my hold on the belt to get a better grip, Dave let go at the same time saying "Hold on to this Robbie" as he reached to open the door. The belt slipped out of my hand with Dave and I watching helplessly as the Hammond slid smoothly down the stairs just like a skier on a mountain slope. Time almost stood still with just the roaring sound of the wooden sled against the metal tread plates on the stairs ringing in our ears. It hit the bottom with a huge thud which sent it turning over and over and ending up on its side only a few inches from John Davies who had just come in carrying his bass drum and a tom-tom. Dave cursed me all the way down the stairs, putting all the blame on me. Upon inspection we saw a long split on the side of the organ where the wood had splintered, along with a few smaller fractures. "That's all right" Dave said, "I can fix that, but will the bloody thing work when we plug it in?" We got the Hammond back up the stairs safely this time with the four of us and vowed never to do it any other way again. Placing it up on the stage we manoeuvred it into position and Dave gingerly plugged it in. We all held our breath as Dave engaged the two switches and we heard the beautiful sound of the start up engine in operation. Releasing it after a few seconds Dave nervously ran his fingers over the keys. Hallelujah it worked. Dave proceeded to check out all the draw bars and stops and everything was fine. Dave gave me a glance saying "You're lucky this time Robbie." I accepted fault for the incident and I never said anything, but I thought that it was partly Dave's fault as he had let go before making sure that I had a good grip in the belt. The show that evening went down very well with Billy on home turf, he was born in Liverpool. It also felt great to have some money in my pocket again. We were paid 80 pounds for the gig, which gave us 20 pounds each. The only downside to the gig at Dino's was that someone stole Dave's briefcase from the dressing room. Luckily he had nothing of any great value in it, just some sheets of music manuscript, pens and a few odds and ends. The real lucky break was that Dave's diary that he always kept in the brief case had been left in the van as he had been writing in it on the way to the gig. If that diary had been stolen many of the details of this part of the story would have been lost forever, and Dave admits that if this had happened he probably would have not continued to keep a record of the day by day events.

The following night we played with Billy in Chester. We got set up but found that the Hammond was beginning to act up a bit. We all kept our fingers crossed that it would be all right when we played the set. We were getting closer to Billy as we had now done quite a few gigs with him and we often chatted together in the dressing room. We respected him and looked up to him as he was already an idol when the rest of us were just kids. Before I met him and had only seen him in action on TV, movies and on stage, I thought that he probably had a mean streak in him due to those facial expressions and stances that he portrayed in his act. However he was the total opposite of that. He was always great to be around and never ever gave any hint of meanness or ego. After you knew him for a while you couldn't even imagine seeing him being anything but pleasant. Chris in particular enjoyed chatting with Billy and that night in the dressing room, out of the blue Chris said "Hey Bill, do you have any reefers?" I couldn't imagine why Chris had said this to Billy, and how would he know that Billy smoked reefers and how did he have the nerve to ask this? - I suspected that Chris had most likely indulged in the art of smoking and Dave had mentioned that he had tried it a few times himself and always talked about us clubbing together to get a ten quid deal. For my part I had never been exposed to smoking pot, didn't really know much about it and generally thought that it was something only done by beatniks or weird artists and poets. I didn't even really enjoy smoking cigarettes it was just the in thing to do. In fact it was something that Pete and Roger Holder together with me looked down upon and perceived it as some kind of drug addiction.

Billy leaned back in his chair and with a nervous smile said "No boys I don't have anything on me" to which Chris replied with his cocky little whine "Oh c'mon Bill, c'mon give us one." Billy reached inside his jacket pocket and produced a soft pack of Pall Mall cigarettes and pulled out a rather strange looking cigarette with a piece of carton rolled up in the end to serve as a filter. He handed it to Chris and Chris thanked him. Chris sniffed and said "All right boys let's light this up shall we?" We followed him out to behind the club and in a secluded corner the four of us smoked it together. Billy did not join us. I was petrified and would not have wanted to try it but I knew that I had to hold my own with the rest of the guys and couldn't chicken out. I was scared of what I might experience but as it happened I didn't feel a thing and couldn't see what the big deal was. The only thing that I experienced was the passing of the joint and the pleasant and exotic herbal smell of the smoke which I actually found enjoyable. I asked Chris what had made him ask Billy for a joint. Chris's answer was that he had seen Billy come out of the toilet and recognized that unmistakable odour of marijuana wafting through the air.

Back in the dressing room Billy greeted us with "All right boys?" and we all sat back down and continued to hold a casual conversation with Billy, joking and laughing together. At one point in the conversation Billy asked us if we had ever tried Amyl Nitrates. I thought "What the hell is he talking about?" We shook our heads and he explained that they were generally called Poppers or Snappers and came in small glass vials covered with a net–like covering that you broke under your nose and inhaled. He said that you used it when having sex with a girl and broke it at the point just as you were reaching an orgasm and it was fantastic. He was surprised to find out that we had never tried it. My knowledge of any kind of drug use was virtually non-existent and anyway I just looked upon it as something very weird and really had no interest in it or desire to use it. Looking back and now knowing that Billy had heart problems and Poppers are used to treat Angina attacks it is likely that he probably got them on prescription.

That Sunday the Diamond Twins returned from Singapore with Sonia smuggling in a genuine Rolex watch for Dave which she had strapped to the inside of her leg in her suspender belt. Dave was overjoyed with his most welcomed gift but was not at all happy when Sonia told him that one of the tour musicians had attempted to sexually molest her in her dressing room and she bore the scratches on her shoulder and chest to prove it. Dave was totally infuriated and after finding out the name of the musician vowed to go after him and deal out some justified punishment. Sonia advised against this and said it was better to forget the whole thing. She did not consider pressing any charges against her assailant.

On Monday November 20th Dave and Sonia went back over to see Ronnie King to follow up on the audition that we had performed a few weeks ago. They found out that King was not at all interested in The Tornados but he did say that he felt that he could do something with Sonia. When King started to outwardly make all kinds of inappropriate suggestions to Sonia in front of Dave it became clear what his intentions were and the meeting ended up with Dave and Ronnie King getting into a pushing and shoving contest with Dave and Sonia walking out in a huff. After Sonia's unpleasant experience in

Singapore it was the straw that broke the camel's back. Those events closed any possible opportunities with the Ronnie King Agency and it was just as well.

A day or so later I received a call from my Mother at Dave's house. She was calling from the phone box at the end of the street to tell me that my sister Georgina and her boyfriend Ray were getting married on the coming Saturday November 25th. My mum was hoping that I could come down for the ceremony. I knew that we were scheduled to appear at Wantage Town Hall that Saturday and as Wantage was not too far from Gloucester I decided that I would take the train immediately and attend the wedding. My dad said that I could use his car to drive to the gig. Upon my arrival at Clegram Road I commented on how this was all rather sudden and was told that Georgina was three months pregnant. Ray had asked my Dad a few weeks before to marry Georgina and under the circumstances he had given his consent. My sister had just turned 19 years old and Ray was 23. That Saturday it was a cool autumn day and rained for most of the day. As my father escorted my sister down the aisle at St. Stephen's church just a stone's throw from the Bristol Hotel where I had played a few years ago with The Vendettas, I stood next to my mum and held her hand. I could feel her shaking and saw tear-drops rolling down her cheeks. I spent as much time as I could at the reception which was actually held at the Bristol Hotel and left in the late afternoon to drive to the gig in Wantage.

I didn't see the Bedford outside as I drove up to the town hall and became a little concerned that the boys may have had some trouble with it as it had been acting up again. However I did notice another van parked outside which looked similar to the one belonging to Dave's next door neighbour. I found out that it was indeed that vehicle and that Dave had decided to buy it for a good price. It was much better looking than the old Bedford and much more reliable. We decided that I would now sell the Bedford. The gig went over very well in Wantage although Dave's Hammond was showing some signs of acting up and it was obvious that it would need some work on it as it was beginning to fall apart. That night in the dressing room we were all joking around and with a play on words I came up with the nickname of "Boris" for Chris. I thought of the name Chris and then thought of the name "Christophe" who was the French singer we had worked with in Barcelona. I then came up with Boris Christoff the famous old time opera star and "hey presto" from that day onwards Chris Lethbridge became known as Boris. Being the easy going and comical character that he was Chris did not object and in fact he really quite enjoyed his new name. After the gig I returned to Gloucester and a day or so later I took the train and returned to Bromley.

I got a sinking feeling in my stomach when I sat down in the front room at Dave's for a cup of tea and Dave told me that Heinz Burt had called and offered him a job to play with the Wild Boys again. There was a tour of France coming up and they needed an organist. I asked Dave what he was going to do and he said he didn't know. On top of that he also had another recording session coming up at the end of November with The Symbols. I honestly thought and felt that it would only be a matter of time until Dave would get snapped up by some band along the way. Dave never did leave the band. We had made some good money on the last two gigs with Billy and had about 40 pounds each in our pockets, and with his session coming up Dave did not feel so worried about money and so he was not under so much pressure to look for another band. He had played for Heinz before and knew what it was like, and The Symbols didn't want to add another member to their group; so even considering the uncertain future of The Tornados he decided to go with what he felt in his heart.

There was little going on until the 6th December when we were to do a show with Billy in Norwich. But that didn't matter; we had money in our pockets and didn't need to spend much of it. Boris had found himself a bed sitter and no longer had to sleep outside in the van and John was happy with Debbie in Acton. Dave and I were having fun jamming together in the front room. Sometimes I would pick up Boris' bass and try to play along with Dave on some jazz pieces. We had also put some new songs in our Tornados act. I had been doing some heavy listening to the album John Mayall and the Bluesbreakers with Eric Clapton and so we had put songs "All Your Love" and "Little Girl" into our repertoire. The first few times we played it Dave said it was the best solo he had ever heard me play. After the way I used to butcher the "Tornados" solos with Dave having to let me off the hook by taking over those parts himself, I felt pleased that maybe I was getting somewhere with my guitar playing after all. I think that I had the confidence to play that stuff because that's what I wanted to do. I had so much enjoyed one of the first albums that I bought titled the *Blues Of T Bone Walker.* Back then I found something very alluring about the blues and it gave me a strange feeling to listen to those old blues records. I had never really had the chance to play that kind of music in The Whirlwinds or Saxons and only now in the final months of Joe Meek's last group of Tornados did my opportunity arise. Just like everyone in the UK I was totally awed by the *Sergeant Pepper* album. We chose to do covers of "Lucy In The Sky with Diamonds" and "A Day In The Life." We did these well with Dave doing an excellent job on the Hammond. His interpretation of the discordant crescendo in "A Day In The Life" gave me goose bumps when we played it. At that time I was also astounded by the Jimmie Hendrix *Are You Experienced* album and Bob Dylan's *Blonde on Blonde*. I felt that this was more my kind of music but I could only get away with so much at a time. We also did a very good cover of "A Whiter Shade Of Pale" by Procol Harem. Dave always played it with superb accuracy and it sounded just like the record.

At Norwich we began to introduce some of the new material that we had worked on, which in some ways was changing the feel of The Tornados' show. At these one-nighters there was always an opening band, usually locals. Then we would open up with a half hour set and Billy would close the show. That night I noticed that the opening band did a couple of Hendrix numbers along with some other good material which inspired me to try to get more of that kind of music into our set. There was a DJ there that night who acted as a host for the evening. Backstage before the show he came into our dressing room carrying a large brief case. He told us that he had been asked to give us our payment for the evening. This was great we were actually being paid before the show. After having been through a few situations where we didn't get paid or they said they had mailed a cheque to George Cooper, this was a rare and most welcomed event. "By the way" he said "If you boys need any "Gear" come and see me" and he pulled out a building brick sized clump of what looked to me like cabbage and parsley pressed into a block. We didn't go to see him.

The gig went over well and we were beginning to feel a little better about ourselves as a band. The large gaps of time between the jobs had worn us down and had given us a lot of time for what was usually, negative thinking. Now with the work picking up a little more and with good receptions at the shows the morale of the group had improved and put us all into a "Happy-go-lucky" mood full of fun and frivolity. As we drove out of Norwich well after midnight Dave noticed the gallon of petrol in the back of the van. We always kept a gallon for emergencies, as just recently we had run out of petrol in the early hours of the morning and I had walked for miles in the dead of night to try to find a filling station. "Here boys" said Dave "C'mon lets set the road on fire." Boris pulled into a side street and parked the van. Climbing out with nervous excited giggles, Dave opened up the petrol can and poured most of the gallon down the gutter and just like it had rained the petrol made its way about twenty or so yards down the street. Dave jumped back into the van next to Boris and striking a match he casually threw it into the gutter as we drove off. "Woof!" The petrol ignited and a wall of fire spread twenty yards down the street, brightly illuminating the houses on either side. We sped away with our heads twisted around to watch the amazing light show that Dave had created. We turned the corner with sounds of mischievous, schoolboy laughter escaping from the open window of the van. This laughter suddenly stopped after about a hundred yards when we all saw the police car heading towards us. "Oh shit" we all said in unison. "Take the side streets Boris, they're bound to come looking for us." Only when we were finally outside the city did we begin to feel relaxed and began to laugh and joke again.

Dave and I were woken up the next morning by Dave's mum shouting up the stairs that George Cooper was on the phone. I lay there on the camp bed and waited for Dave to return with whatever news he had. "Get a load of this Robbie boy." Dave announced with that pleased look on his face, "We're rehearsing with Billy on Saturday and playing the gig with him on Sunday at the American Embassy, and George said something about a recording session and sending us on a tour of Israel." Once more things were taking a change for the better and the future for The Tornados was looking a little brighter.

After a good rehearsal with Billy on Saturday we played the gig at the Grosvenor House to a very receptive audience and all in all it was a great gig and we had a lot of compliments from all kinds of people. This was a great boost for us and the overall feeling of the band was good and positive. We were back on track again.

Cooper called again on Monday morning confirming that the recording session was on and we were required to play and perform four songs at Lansdowne Studios. The four songs were to be "Puppet On A String" by Sandie Shaw which Sonia would sing, "Daydream Believer" by The Monkees and "When I'm Sixty Four" The Beatles which I would sing, and we were told that they were bringing in a professional session singer to sing "The Last Waltz" by Englebert Humperdinck. Luckily Sonia knew "Puppet On A String" and had the record, so we got that one off quickly. Dave went out and bought The Monkees 45 so that was just a case of listening to it and getting it down. We also bought copies of the sheet music for the other two songs and got them down in record time, working late into Monday night. I was very familiar with "When I'm Sixty Four" as I had played *Sgt. Pepper* over and over, so that helped things along. We realized that our final rehearsal would be in the studio right before the session. We explained to George Cooper that we needed a bit more rehearsal time due to the short notice and the apparent urgency of the session. George assured us that they had arranged for extra time in the studio to compensate for that.

Early the next morning Dave and I together with Sonia drove off to Lansdowne Studios where we would all meet for the session. It was a nightmare because the van was beginning to act up badly and kept stalling all the way there in the morning rush hour traffic. There were a few times when it was very hard to restart the van and we seriously doubted that we would ever make it to the studio. Luckily, by a miracle, we did make it.

We began to work on the songs and get them finished up while the technicians took time to get everything mic'd up. Luck really seemed to be on our side as we were ready to begin recording not too long after the set-up had been done and the balancing and sound adjustments were made. The backing tracks went down quite quickly without any major problems. Dave changed to the studio piano for "The Last Waltz" and as we did not have a copy of the record we played it in the key that it was written in for the sheet music and by lunch time we were ready to start with the vocals.

Sonia launched into "Puppet On A String" and was about half way through a take when we saw George Cooper, come into the studio along with two Indian gentlemen and an olive skinned guy who looked like he could be from the Middle East. He actually turned out to be from New York and was the agent who wished to book us for the tour of Israel. When the take was over and Sonia came into the control room to hear the playback we were all introduced. The two Indian gentlemen were from Zell records, and the other guy was introduced to us as Danny Ben-Av. The Indians explained that the recordings that we were making were to be released in India on an EP and would be accessible to the poor people who could not afford to buy the original records. It was something that reminded me of the Embassy Records that they used to sell in Woolworth's. Danny Ben-Av didn't say too much at this point but he did seem a bit preoccupied with Sonia and watched her intently as she performed a second take. Both takes were excellent and were mixed together with the song coming out quite well.

When my vocal takes were finished on "Daydream Believer" and I had done my best take-off of Davy Jones we gathered together in the control room. George Cooper announced that we were indeed going on a six weeks tour of Israel as Danny Ben-Av had liked the band and was ready to go ahead. Danny had now loosened up a bit and was talking freely with us. He told us that we all looked like we could use some sunshine. He said that we should start to see some sun a few days into the cruise across the Mediterranean and we should be arriving in Israel sometime around Christmas. This was great news. According to Cooper the pay was decent and we could also look at it as a great holiday in the sun when everybody else in England would be freezing their asses off. We were all totally excited with the exception of John who was a bit quiet and didn't seem to be sharing our enthusiasm. Just to think in no time at all we would be on our way to Israel; this strange place far away in the east.

We were all taking a short break when the "professional session singer" showed up to sing "The Last Waltz." The sound men began to play the track back to him and we handed him the sheet music. He was having a terrible time in pitching the tune and finally said that this had to be the wrong take. It was in the wrong key and you would need a choirboy to sing it. He even had Dave join him in the studio and as Dave played it on the piano he reconfirmed that the song was in the wrong key. For a male voice it was too high to sing in that key and too low to sing when you lowered it an octave. I later found out that he was absolutely correct. We had not learned this song from the record and we had just gone along with it as it was written. The sheet music was in a different key and not like the original record. The session time was ending and as we were breaking down our gear one of George Coopers' assistants approached me. I noticed that he had been having a rather stressed huddle with the Indians. "We need somebody to sing the song; do you think you could give it a try? He asked.

I said that I didn't think so, due to the key. He said that there was no choice at this point, somebody had to do it. They didn't have time to re-record the song, so could I please help them out? I would get paid for the session, just show up and try. I couldn't really say no, so I said "Okay" and made arrangements to meet them at the studio the next morning. That night at dinner Mr. and Mrs. Watts gave me specific directions on how to get to the studio by train and underground. It was great staying at Dave's and the next best thing to being at home as we had the advice and encouragement of our seniors who had seen more years of life than we had. Mrs. Watts in particular was always voicing encouragement to Dave and I. Like Dave, she was a pianist and was responsible for Dave's introduction to the piano.

The Watts' directions worked out fine for me and that morning found me showing up at Lansdowne studios at around 9.30 where I met up with George Cooper's executive, whose name I don't remember. We chatted over coffee and I mentioned that The Tornados were leaving soon for a tour of Israel. He asked me if I had ever tried any

Jewish food and I answered "No." In fact I knew very little about Jewish people or their food. All I knew was that millions of them were slaughtered in WW2. I remembered the documentary war time films that I had watched on the BBC as a kid that showed heaps of bodies being bulldozed into mass graves like garbage. It was horrible to watch and gave me a sick feeling in my stomach. I had also heard the derogatory, prejudicial remarks and racial slurs that you came across in everyday life. All that I had heard was that Jews are dirty and smell of garlic, they love money and will cheat you out of your last cent and most of all that they are very tight with their money. They would never give you a penny. I had been told most of this by co-worker John Devereux when I worked at the Bon Marche department store in Gloucester. The head of our department, Hughie Newton was a Jew of Austrian descent who had supposedly written a book on how he had escaped from a concentration camp in Germany during World War II.and Devereux despised him. I gathered that my coffee partner was probably Jewish so I felt it better to direct the conversation towards the coming session. I mentioned that it was not going to be that easy to sing so early in the morning especially in a key which was virtually impossible to sing in. Anyway we downed our last few drops of our coffee and walked across the road to the studio.

The technicians had already got the mic set up and were just starting to put on the playback when we walked into the studio. We listened through it twice and I was thinking "Jesus Christ, how in the hell am I going to pull this off?" I was trying to pitch it in my head as I listened but it was impossible. When they told me to go into the booth to test the mic I was dreading it. After they were happy with the sound it was my turn to sing along with the track. I tried it in full voice which was all right up until it came to the refrain with me screeching "I had the last waltz with you". It was horrendous and I was embarrassed as hell and did all I could to let the technicians know that it was in the wrong key and impossible to sing. They said that maybe it was the early morning and maybe my voice would loosen up and all I could say was "It's in the wrong key and it can't be sung like this." On the third take I made a real effort to try to figure out a way to pull it off. It was okay until the refrain came around but all at once I moved closer to the mic and in a half falsetto kind of whisper I spoke the words. Within a few seconds after the refrain the machine stopped and it all went quiet. I said to myself "Shit! It probably sounded ridiculous and they're on their way into the booth to curse me out." The two Indian gentlemen had also shown up and together with my coffee partner they approached me as I took off the head phones. "That's it!" They said in unison "You've just got to speak it exactly like you just did and it'll sound great."

After a few more takes we completed the number. As I listened to the play back it occurred to me that in some way I felt I had been influenced by Joe Meek. After all Joe was the master of being able to take a complete and utter abortion of a song and turn it into something at the very least acceptable, or even sometimes turn it into a hit. He would do this by electronic wizardry and or by coaching the vocalist on how to put across the song. I may have also been influenced by Joe's recording of The Blue Rondos "Please Stay" which had been sung in almost a whisper. Joe probably would have liked that kind of approach that I was inspired to give to the song. I got paid my session money, said goodbye to everyone and walked out down to the tube station. I was thinking "Thank God that record will never be released in the UK." I never heard that recording again, and it's just as well. I must have sounded like some adolescent schoolboy whimpering in the moonlight. I think that Englebert Humperdinck would have probably gone into shock if he had heard it, or he may have laughed thinking that it was a joke: which it was.

As I walked in through the front door and towards the kitchen back at Dave's place, Dave walked up to me with a very worried look on his face." John's not coming to Israel, we have no drummer what are we going to do." Dave went on to tell me that he had already been over to George Cooper and had picked up some money for the trip expenses and had also gone over to get the Green card insurance for the van. He had not been home long when John had called with a shocker. Apparently Debbie was pregnant and John was refusing to leave her. Once again we were thrown into a very scary predicament and it was almost impossible to figure out how we were going to get 'round this one. The phone rang and it was Boris. He had already heard the bad news from John but he was in fact the bringer of good news. John had mentioned to Boris that a friend of theirs who had played with Boris in the Alan Walker band in Cheltenham might be able to fit in on drums. His name was Mick Strachan and Boris had spoken to him already and he had agreed to join the band. He was also a very good drummer according to Boris. So it all looked like things were getting better again. The only set back was that we were asked to return the Marshall PA system, so Dave and I drove over and gave it back to Billy. This left us a bit on the downside as we knew that we would not sound as good now, so we just had to put up with it and carry on regardless.

I decided that I would shoot down to Gloucester to pick up some personal things and let my folks know that I was leaving for Israel. I drove down in the old Bedford that was still being parked outside of Dave's place and I picked up some clothing along with my collection of LPs which I kept in a nice wooden carrying case that my dad had made for me. It was painted with black gloss paint and he had put a monogram on the front, R H in golden letters. Boris had mentioned that he would be taking his small portable record player with him so I thought that my L P collection would give us some sounds to listen to when we were not working. I got back to Dave's place Friday afternoon as we were scheduled to leave for Israel on Saturday morning which was the 16th December. Dave answered the front door and led me into the kitchen where he said that Boris was waiting with Mick Strachan. When Boris introduced me to Mick, I had to look twice. Here was this skinny guy about 5′ 10″ with a very bad, spotty complexion, and the biggest, sticking out ears that I had ever seen. To say that he looked like Dumbo the elephant was an understatement. I felt embarrassed and had to look away with concerns of having this weird looking guy in the band. But what was there to do? We had to leave the following morning. Dave and Boris suddenly started to laugh as Mick began to take off the huge fake ears that he was wearing and I laughed too, knowing that they had pulled a good trick on me. I was relieved to see the real Mick and apart from his complexion he looked fine. That evening we spent hours changing the jack plugs on the mics with Dave giving the soldering iron a lot of action. I also found out that Mick Strachan was more than a drummer and could also sing, play the harmonica and acoustic guitar that he had brought along. He serenaded us while we all sat in the living room. His favourite song was "San Francisco Bay." Here we were, The Tornados, on the eve of our departure to the Middle East sitting in the front room at Dave's place in Bromley with a drummer that we had never played with before and once again faced with a situation that we would have to overcome.

At 5am on Saturday morning we set off to pick up Sonia in Maidstone and continued down to Dover. We paid the fare and boarded the ferry to Bolougne. We had been given expense money by Cooper which was supposed to be enough to get us to Marseilles and provide for a hotel there. We decided to change it to Francs while on board and everything was running smoothly until we set foot on French soil. The Customs officers there asked us in French "Vous avez une carnet?" We had no idea what they were asking us, and what was this carnet that they kept talking about? They asked us by means of broken English and gesticulations that they wanted to see the contents of the van and we had to unload all of the equipment out onto the dock. They wrote down all kind of notes and jabbered among themselves and still asked us to produce this carnet. We eventually found out that a carnet was a form of a manifest that contained details and the value of what we were bringing into the country and without that we would not be allowed to proceed. We showed them our tickets for Zim Cruise Lines leaving from Marseilles for Israel on December 18th and implored them that we had to get to Marseilles. They said that they were worried that we might try to sell our musical gear in France. We explained that if we did that we would have no way of fulfilling our contract in Israel as we would have no instruments to play on. Using sign language they motioned for us to put the gear back in the van so we figured that we would be able to proceed. They also told us all to get back into the van. The customs officers walked off into their office and one of them picked up a phone and was talking for sometime. As we saw him end the call we expected that he would wave us through and we would be on our way, but no, he just sat there with his fellow officers and totally ignored us for about an hour.

We had no idea what we could do as none of us knew much French and felt that we could not communicate with them. When we were really starting to get pissed off with the whole thing a Customs car pulled up and an officer got out and entered the Customs office. It looked like they were having some kind of a discussion. Eventually they all walked out together and the new guy started to speak in some kind of English asking about the carnet again. We went through the whole story with him and to our utter dismay he asked us to get all the gear out of the van again. Once again they jabbered away in French until we were told that as we had no carnet we would have to pay a certain amount of money which was far in excess of what we had in our expense money. When we told them that we were unable to pay it they asked to see how much money we had. Dave produced the Francs that we had bought on the ferry explaining that this was to provide petrol, food and accommodation for us to travel to Marseilles. This was followed by another lengthy discussion in French between the officers. We were then told to put back the gear in the van and wait. Once more they returned to the office and seemed to be looking up some information. Eventually they came back out and told us that we would have to pay a fee to transport the gear through France. It looked like they decided that they could take part of the money that we had and took about 15 pounds in Francs from our expense money. They didn't give us any receipt for our payment and most likely divided the money among themselves. We were just happy to get out of there and drove off in the direction of Paris having wasted 4 hours with those assholes in the French Customs. Looking back I really don't know how we were able to undertake this trip through France. We had no idea how long the remainder of our money would last or even if it would get us to the ship, we had a pretty full tank of petrol but how far would that get us?

Well at least it had got us to Paris. The drive from Bolougne to Marseilles was pretty much a straight drive through the centre of France that would take us 16 hours or more.

It was well into the evening when we decided that we had to stop somewhere in Paris to get something to eat. We pulled up outside of a small bistro called "Chez Oscar" or "Oscar's Place." Luckily Oscar spoke reasonable English and he brought us all steak and chips. He was the only person we saw in the bistro. He cooked the food and served it to us, entertained us, and he really was a one man show. The food happened to be good and we enjoyed it. When Oscar presented us the bill at the end of the meal Dave looked at it and said "Bloody 'ell, How much?" It turned out to be pretty expensive for what we had and Dave paid out the money realizing that another chunk of our expense money had gone.

It was getting late when we left the bistro. Dave had driven from Bolougne so I volunteered to take over and drive through the night and get us as far as I could. Mick sat in the front with me as co pilot. We had worked out a route and all you had to do was follow a list of the towns that you had to pass through and it was quite easy. There were no big highways then, like today, but it was all well sign posted and easy to follow but you really couldn't keep up a good speed. As we were leaving Paris I said "Hey boys when we are on our way back home coming through Paris, remind me to throw a brick through Oscar's window." "Okay Robbie we will" replied the sleepy voices from the back seat, "Good night Robbie" and we settled down for the night. It wasn't too long before Mick started to drop off and soon it was just me driving through this dark French night staying awake and alert, driving on the opposite side of the road with the safety of all of us well in mind. The thrill of driving down through the middle of France in the dead of night excited me and at no time did I ever get tired or sleepy.

At around 3am while passing through some nondescript, nameless little French town I spotted a petrol station which was open all night and had a little grocery store attached. I thought that it would be a good opportunity to fuel up and get something to drink. All that they had were different bottles of what I thought must be some kind of white lemonade. I thought it was a bit strange but even so I bought one of the bottles and paid for the petrol. As we drove away I unscrewed the bottle cap and took a swig. "Its bloody water" I moaned "I've just bought a bottle of bloody water." I complained about being ripped off again in France and went on about water being free and that you should not have to pay for it. There was no commercial water industry then as there is today. Who would want to buy water when you could drink it from a water fountain or from your own tap at home?

In the end Sonia said "Well Robbie it's probably some kind of healing water with special minerals from a holy well somewhere and that's why it's sold. It's probably very good for you." Well I guess that I did feel a little better after hearing Sonia's words and drove off into the night again.

I continued to drive until about 10am and although I could have kept going Boris said that as I had been driving for about 12 hours that he would take over and that I should get in the back and have a sleep. After a few more hours and filling up with petrol again we saw that our money was getting low. Knowing that we had enough gas to get us to our destination we decided to spend the money we had left on a few roast beef sandwiches that we shared in a small rural café somewhere along the road. We had already accepted the fact that there was no way that we would sleep in a hotel that night. It was early evening when we finally drove into Marseilles. We eventually found the offices of Zim Cruise Lines but they were already closed. Our intention was to hopefully be able to use their facilities and freshen up but that would have to wait until the next morning. Having no money, nothing to do and nowhere to go we just found a place to park and sat in the van together. I don't even remember if any one of us had to go to the toilet. When it became dark at last we figured that we would just try to go to sleep. Dave and Sonia lay across the front seat and Mick, Boris and I did the best we could to get comfortable in the back bench seat. At one point during the night it got so cold that Dave had to start up the van and put the heater on to give us a bit of warmth. Although we were all very tired we did not get much sleep that night and when day began to break we were all glad to see the sunrise.

We drove back around to the Zim offices and waited until they opened at 9am and told them our tale of woe and asked if we could use their bathroom. When we had all freshened up we asked for directions to the port hoping that we would be able to board the ship and get some rest. We were told that we were not allowed to board until 6pm so we were faced with another day with nothing to do except sit around in the van. We did take a bit of a drive around the city but we were not really in the mood for sightseeing and seeing all the restaurants busy with people sitting outside enjoying their meals was just too much for us to handle. We drove to the port and arrived at dock 15 at 4pm. We had not eaten for more than 24 hours and were absolutely starving. We stood around and watched our van get hoisted up on board the ship by a large crane along with some other vehicles. They were all lashed down and secured. Official boarding time was 6pm but it was 7pm by the time we finally got on and into our room. They had put us all together but Sonia pulled a few strings and was able to get her own room. Needless to say Dave stayed along with her for the voyage. We finally got something to eat when we went to dinner at 8pm. This was pure luxury, a bed to sleep in and "food".

The next day we spent eating and taking it easy wandering the decks and began to settle down. The only bad thing was that we had no money and couldn't enjoy the benefit of the duty free prices in the bar. When we were passing Sicily on the way to our first port of call in Naples, Dave came up with an idea to get some cash. By a stroke of luck he had found his cheque book was still in his suitcase and the Purser was willing to cash a cheque for him for 15 pounds. We divided the money amongst ourselves and promised to pay Dave back when we got paid in Israel. Now things really did improve. We headed straight for the bar and quenched our thirsts. While enjoying our drinks we got talking to an American guy called Dan. He said that he was from Arizona and was travelling to the Middle East. He hung out with us for the voyage and we enjoyed sitting on deck at night looking up at the stars. Dan said that it was unreal as he was seeing the constellations in totally different parts of the sky. Not at all like when he was back home in Arizona.

By the next morning we had landed in Naples. Although the weather was beginning to get a bit overcast we still went ashore just to take a look around. We were approached by several hucksters offering all kinds of wares; watches, cameras, jewellery and God knows what. Before too long the rain began to come down pretty steady and we returned to the ship, ringing wet. There was a kind of night club on deck with a dance floor and a piano so we got permission to rehearse there in the afternoons.

Sonia Diamond, Dave Watts, Robb Huxley - probably taken on the ship going to Israel

The wind was beginning to blow and whipped up the sea as we sailed out of Naples Harbour. We all made our way up on deck and started to unload our gear from the van and carry it over to the club room. We got set up and began to run through our numbers with Mick. Boris was right, Mick was good. He had no trouble with anything and did an excellent job on "Wade In The Water" à la the Graham Bond Organization. We noticed that the ship was starting to pitch a little. Sometimes it was difficult to stay on mic, and outside, things were getting to look pretty grey and soupy. From time to time some passengers and crew members peered in through the windows to see what was going on. At dinner time our utensils were sliding about the table and the waiters were having difficulty in keeping their balance. At one point Boris slid away from the table on his chair. We all had a good laugh but we didn't realize that we were heading into some really bad weather. Just before dinner the purser had come up to us and said that many of the guests on the ship had heard us rehearsing and were hoping that we might play for them that night. Thinking that it would be a good opportunity for extra rehearsal and a good work out for Mick we agreed. With dinner over we went out on deck and over to the club room. The sea looked black and the waves were building with a pretty hard wind blowing.

We had a very good time that night. It was quite a struggle to be able to stand up and play due to the rocking of the ship but the audience enjoyed it we enjoyed it, all kinds of people bought us drinks and by the time we said goodnight and staggered off to our berths the sea was getting to be quite rough. Dave and I paused for a few seconds and held on to the guard rail and looking out across the waves Dave said "Bloody 'ell Robbie" and we made our way downstairs. Throughout the night the weather worsened, we got tossed around in our bunks; Boris was heaving and throwing up so we didn't get a lot of sleep. The sound of the waves pounding the ship got quite scary at times and we could hear water slopping around. The next morning found us with even worse weather. Boris was feeling pretty sick so Mick and I decided to venture out to see what was going on. It was almost as if the whole ship was deserted. The corridors were completely empty. We held on tightly to the hand rails; the ship was really rolling now and it was impossible to walk without that assistance. The air was thick with the smell of vomit and the sounds of people coughing and heaving in their rooms. Up on the main deck they had posted signs on the exit doors that nobody was allowed out on deck. We suddenly saw Arizona Dan staggering up towards us "This is fuckin' unreal man, it's just like being on a ghost ship." There was somebody on duty in the purser's office who told us that there were some pastries available in the dining room but no breakfast could be served due to the bad conditions. We sat down at a table holding on to it so as not to slide away from it and grabbed a couple of sandwiches but there was nothing to drink as any type of liquid would just get spilled. A couple of other people trickled in along with an older American lady. They pecked at the food a bit but didn't stay long. There was nothing to do all day except hang around and try to look out from the spray covered windows at the raging seas. In the late morning Dave arrived in the empty lounge where we were sitting. He looked a bit on the pale side and said that he had been sea-sick but was beginning to feel better especially now that he had made it upstairs. He had seen Boris in our cabin who, he reported was in his bunk and looking pretty green. Dave also said that Sonia was feeling rough and couldn't come up to the main deck. Dave said "Let's take a look outside boys." so we opened up an exit door with a "No one allowed on deck" sign and quickly stepped outside but we didn't dare approach the guard rail. The sound of the storm was deafening, the winds were blowing a gale and we looked in utter awe as we saw 25 foot black waves breaking over the bow of the ship, pounding into the vehicles lashed on the deck almost breaking them away from the belts that had them secured to the deck. The deck was running with water and it looked like that any minute our van would get washed overboard. This violent scenario really put the fear of Christ into us and we quickly returned to the apparent safety of the lounge with Dave declaring that we were all going to die! We spotted a crew member and asked him about the weather. He said that we were ploughing through a force nine storm which had 50 – 55 mph winds with about 23 foot waves. It's what you might call a strong gale. When we asked if we were in danger he said "Oh we'll be all right once we get through this, but I think that this is the worst crossing that we have had in the past 15 years."

That day 21st December 1967 really dragged on. There was nothing to do but sit around as it was almost impossible to stay on your feet. No one was working in the bar so we couldn't even get a drink. We went down to see Boris a couple of times but he was still feeling very bad. We tried to coax him to come upstairs telling him that he would feel better but he refused. He was always on the verge of throwing up and the smell of vomit that had taken over below deck just made him feel worse. I was very lucky and at no time did I ever feel sick or woozy. I attributed this to the fact that I was from a seafaring family. My ancestors, the Huxleys had all been sailors and sailed the old tall ships back and forth from England to China. They owned property in Shanghai and at one time were deemed to be quite wealthy. I presumed that all their experiences of sailing the high seas had been passed down to me and were firmly embedded in my genes. At dinner time nobody showed up except the three musketeers Mick, Arizona Dan and me. There was no hot food only the same kind of stuff that we had for breakfast. It was too dangerous to attempt any kind of cooking in the galley. That night the bad weather persisted with the constant rolling of the ship. Around 2am the ship suddenly listed heavily causing Boris to get thrown right out of his bunk and on to the floor. We stayed in that listing position for what seemed like a few minutes and I thought "Oh no the ship has keeled over" but it suddenly righted itself and we all got thrown in the opposite direction. I will never forget that night.

The next morning it seemed like we were coming out of the storm and things were calming down a bit. People were milling around the decks and there was a long line at the first aid room where a nurse was handing out medicine for seasickness. We had managed to get Boris upstairs and he was given some medication in the form of suppositories. Boris said that he didn't really want to shove one up his ass but knowing that it would help him he reluctantly went off to the bathroom and succeeded with the operation. Although the ship was still rolling things were a bit better and the galley was able to provide food for breakfast along with some coffee which was most welcomed. Dave and Sonia made an appearance and looked like they were in a recovery mode. We were now allowed out on deck so we decided to take a look at the van. The cars were all over the place and every one of them had signs of damage. The van didn't look as if it was damaged but upon closer inspection we did find a few dings and dents. The sky was beginning to clear up but the waves were still on the big side. We stood by the guard rail and looked down to see the stabilizers that were usually below the water line were coming up right out of the water. The club room was in total disarray as we entered in to inspect our gear. Although the amps and drums had shifted a bit they seemed to be intact. The baby grand piano however had rolled across the room and had smashed into the wall and was badly damaged. All things considered however, we did manage to get some rehearsing done in the afternoon. Boris was beginning to feel better but the only problem was that he was plagued with gas and was belching constantly. Each time he burped we could smell the odour of rotten eggs similar to the smell of stink bombs that we used to fool around with at school. We put it down to the suppositories and all tried to keep away from him but that foul smell just hung real heavy in the air. The purser did pay us a visit during the rehearsals telling us that the ship would not be landing in Greece as was scheduled due to the weather being still too rough to enter the port. He thought that it would be a good idea and would help with the morale of the passengers if we could play again that night. We of course consented and enjoyed another evening of performing. We were very well received again and got to talk to some Israelis who tried to teach us a few words in Hebrew. We told them that we would be touring Israel. They asked us the name of our band and we told them that we were The Tornados. They weren't sure what a tornado was so we explained that it was a very strong wind storm. "Aha" they said "Now we understand why we have had all this terrible weather." and we all laughed. The spirit of Joe Meek had really made the presence of his Tornados felt here in the Mediterranean.

The next morning we were able to dock in Cyprus. We got up and decided that we would take a look ashore but were told that the launch had already left at 7am so we were stuck on board once again.

On Christmas Eve 24th December 1967 we were approaching the Israeli port of Haifa. The bad weather had now subsided and the sea was completely flat and calm. The water had a kind of muddy, turquoise look to it. We loaded the gear back into the van, packed our suitcases and waited up on deck taking in the sights of this Middle Eastern port as we approached the harbour. As the ship was being secured at the dock I surveyed the scene. It was a total hive of activity with all kinds of hustle and bustle taking place. The most prominent thing that I noticed was that there were several young people dressed in military uniforms, so much so that I thought that there must have been some kind of emergency or something. The young men were equipped with machine guns and even some of the young girls were carrying rifles. I had never seen anything like this before and I found it fascinating. The girls particularly got my attention. There were blondes, brunettes, short, tall and for the most part very attractive young ladies. Some were very fair skinned and looked like

Europeans, while others were of dark complexion. There were even a few red heads here and there. I must say that the sight of all these attractive young women who also looked in very good shape, carrying weapons and dressed in military uniform was a big turn on.

As we all walked down the gang plank we were met by some of the young soldier ladies who smiled and pointed us in the direction of Customs and Immigration. As we proceeded in that direction we could already see our van being lowered on to the dock. We were systematically ushered from one office to another and were made to sign all different kinds of papers and asked various questions by the immigration officers. They also made us take all of the gear out of the van just like in France. They didn't ask us to pay any money but they did write down all the particulars in our respective passports. All this being accomplished we were released and made our way to the van. Arizona Dan joined us there as we had promised him a ride to Tel Aviv with us. Then we saw a familiar face. It was Danny Ben–Av who approached us and welcomed us to Israel. He said that he had heard that we had a pretty rough trip and hoped that we were all okay. The plan was that we should follow him to Tel Aviv. He was driving a Ford Mustang and we got in behind him and drove out of the port. It was a bright sunny day as I looked out of the van window at the palm trees and Arabic looking buildings that lined the route.

We had just about reached the outskirts of Haifa when all of a sudden we heard a grinding noise coming from the front end of the van. Almost immediately after this one of the front wheels collapsed and became detached causing the front of the van to slump down on one side. Luckily we were travelling quite slowly at the time so nobody was hurt. Danny Ben-Av saw what happened and turned around as we were all piling out of the van to survey the damage. The wheel had come off and we all agreed that it must have been caused by the stress and stain that the van had undergone during the rough voyage. A tow truck was called and the van was towed away to some garage for repair.

There was not enough room for all of us to fit in Ben–Av's Mustang so I ended up waiting with Arizona Dan on the side of the road as we were told that they would send a car to pick us up once they got to Tel

Aviv.

Once I met up with the rest of the band in Tel Aviv, Danny Ben–Av said that we were going over to meet Raffi Shauli and we would be staying at his house until our flat was ready for us to move in to. Raffi Shauli was an Israeli businessman and was the guy who was sponsoring our 6 week tour. We found out that he was married to Mandy Rice–Davies who was a British showgirl who had played a small part in the Profumo scandal that rocked the British Government in 1963. I remember seeing her on the news riding off in a taxi with Christine Keeler who she shared a flat with. Keeler along with Stephen Ward a celebrated osteopath and artist renowned for his portraits of royalty were involved with Mandy Rice–Davies in the sex scandal that brought about the resignation of John Profumo the British Secretary of State for War. There was also considerable involvement with MI5 and British and Russian spy rings. It was almost like a James Bond movie. So here I was in Tel Aviv Israel on my way to meet the notorious Mandy Rice-Davis. After having gone through our brief but scary involvement with the infamous Kray Twins I thought that this one would be a breeze and the thought of meeting her was quite thrilling. We met Raffi out side of his nightclub on Ben Yehuda Street. The name of the club was Mandy's obviously named for his wife. He was from Yemenite descent, good looking and spoke good English. He told us that almost everybody spoke English in Israel and that his English was improved when he worked as a flight attendant for sometime. He said that we were going over to his place and insisted that some of us ride with him in his army style open jeep. He was a gregarious character and was definitely putting on a show for our benefit. I rode in the jeep and at one point at a stop light he deliberately let his jeep roll and bump into the car waiting in front. The driver jumped out of his car and approached us. I thought "Oh no, here we go again" but it turned out that it was somebody he knew; a friend of his. They ended up laughing and shaking hands. It was a lucky occurrence for Raffi as it gave him another opportunity to show off to us.

We all bundled into Raffi's house and were greeted at the front door by Mandy. She welcomed us politely and we all sat down at the dining table. Looking at her as she brought a tray of tea and biscuits to us I couldn't figure out what the big deal was. I didn't think that she looked like anything special. The Israeli girls in their army uniforms were far more attractive. It was not my place to judge her but I also did notice that she acted rather aloof. It was not that easy to make conversation as I'm sure that she knew that we were aware of her notoriety. We were about the same age. She was a year older than me so she was 23 at the time. As she came around with the tea pot she asked me how much milk I wanted. As we used to say at home if you didn't want a lot of milk in your tea I said "Just a drop" and that's exactly what she gave me although I would say it was more of a spot that a drop. She moved on to Boris but then hesitated and returned to me asking if that was enough milk for me. I said that I would like a little more but she told me that she had given me what I had asked for and then poured the exact amount of milk into my tea. After tea we went outside into the garden and stood around talking in the warm sunshine and thinking how happy we were on Christmas Eve to be enjoying the warm weather, while all the folks back home were shivering in the cold.

That night Raffi drove us over to an old part of town which we later found out was the Yemenite Village which was close to the old port of Jaffa. All I could think of was that I was in some far off land right in the spot where the Jaffa oranges came from. He took us to what we thought was a very primitive restaurant. It was an old stone building where we sat outside at a long, rustic wooden table. It was already dark and a couple of lamps suspended from a tarpaulin which served as our roof, provided the light over the table. Raffi disappeared through a door way and quickly reappeared. As we all continued talking we were brought out some orange and grapefruit soda pops by a small dark looking Arab guy. We also got hot pita bread which I originally mistook for poppadums a favourite of ours from the Indian restaurants back in England. The pita bread was served with Hummus which was a paste of garbanzo beans spread on a plate, with a dash of olive oil, a dab of tahini sauce a hot pickled pepper and a sprinkling of paprika. We were instructed to tear off pieces of the pita and use it to pick up the hummus from the plate. We ended up with some steak on the grill with some English style chips followed by some good Turkish coffee. We left the restaurant in good spirits and even though we had no money we had somewhere to sleep and we were being fed.

We woke up on Christmas Day with the sun already up and shining brightly through the lace curtains. As our van was not ready yet and we couldn't rehearse we decided to take a walk down Dizengoff Street which is the main street in Tel Aviv and used to end up at a circle with a fountain in the middle. It was a Monday morning and it was business as usual. The streets were full of traffic and the buses roared by at high speed. We strolled along looking at the shops and the restaurants with everyone sitting outside in the sun under the shade of umbrellas advertising some kind of drink in a language that we couldn't read. All the streets were signposted in Hebrew, English and Arabic so you could find your way around and as we began to find out almost everybody spoke English and the menus in the restaurants were in English too. As we paused by the fountain in Dizengoff Circle I thought about my folks back home in England and how they were probably still asleep or just about to wake up on their frosty Christmas Day; while I was here half way across the world smoking an Israeli brand cigarette in the sunshine with the smell of some exotic food wafting through the air with the aroma of roasted nuts that were being sold on the side walk. On Christmas night Raffi took us down to Jaffa for a meal at a fish restaurant and that was that. Certainly it was a much different Christmas from a year ago when we were stuck up in Newcastle staying in a hovel and playing in empty depressing clubs.

Boxing Day we got our van back with all the musical gear intact. We followed Danny Ben–Av over to Ha Yarkon Street to Mini Mandy's one of Raffi's night clubs. It was located right on the ocean. Danny told us that an Israeli band called The Lions was rehearsing there and we could do our rehearsal after them. They were sitting around with their manager, a guy named Haim Saban when we entered the club and it seemed like they were checking us out, especially our gear. They really took notice when the four of us carried the Hammond in. They were taking a break from their rehearsal and as we were bringing in the last of our gear they got up on stage to continue. We immediately noticed that they had a Marshall PA system, were using Fender guitars, Ludwig drums and what looked like Fender amps. Those amps turned out to be made in Israel by a British guy called Wally Garrett who had been a member of a band called The Sing Sing.

The Lions were a five piece band using lead and rhythm guitars, bass and drums. Each member was also a vocalist. They proceeded to play a few numbers like "California Dreaming", "Dedicated To The One I Love" along with some other pop songs of the day. They had strong voices and they were very good. Their manager Haim Saban, had hand picked them all for their vocal and musical abilities and created The Lions and he stood in the back of the room looking as proud as a peacock. As they broke down their gear and we began to set up ours it really began to look like this rehearsal had been set up so that Haim Saban could show off his super group to this visiting British band, The Tornados.

We knew that The Lions were going to stay around to see what we could do and sure enough they did. We decided to play "Wade In The Water"; the jazzy type instrumental originally done by Graham Bond and Dave really let it all go. We wanted to show them that we were a different kind of band to them. We followed it with "All Your Love" by The Bluesbreakers and when Sonia got up to do one of her numbers they all took notice. It was a pity that our first meeting with an Israeli band turned out to be a "My band's better than your band" situation, all put together by The Lions' manager Haim Saban. After a while The Lions got up and left us to continue our rehearsal undisturbed by their presence as it should have been from the beginning.

Danny Ben–Av showed up as we were winding down the rehearsal telling us that we were to appear in an interview at a local radio station that night and that he and Raffi Shauli were taking us there after dinner. We all arrived at the radio station in the evening. The whole place was filled with men and women all wearing army uniforms but without the customary weapons. We were subsequently told that this radio station was run by the Israeli Army and was called Galey Tsahal. We were to be interviewed by a guy called Abner Rosenbloom who by all accounts was acclaimed to be some kind of expert on pop music. We were told that most of the conversation we would hear would be in Hebrew but we would be asked questions in English and the interviewer would translate our replies to the listeners. About 5 minutes before the interview Abner Rosenbloom came out to meet us. He was a skinny guy with a terrible pock marked complexion with greasy hair. He told us how much he liked "Telstar" and before long we were all seated together in the studio. "Telstar" was used to kick off the interview followed by a lengthy introduction by the host. The only words we could understand were titles of Tornado records and the name Joe Meek which cropped up from time to time. He then asked us to introduce ourselves which we proceeded to do and we all rattled our names off. Boris thought that this would be a good time to pull out a marker and draw an eye on each of the lenses of my eye-glasses. We were asked what it was like to record with Joe Meek so we talked about how Joe was dead and that he had shot himself in the studio. This really got Abner's attention and he continued to translate into Hebrew. At one point in his commentary we suddenly heard the names Clem Cattini, George Bellamy, Alan Caddy, Heinz Burt and Roger LaVern followed by the names Dave Watts, Chris Lethbridge, Mick Strachan, Robb Huxley and Sonia Diamond. Just like magic Abner Rosenbloom brought out an LP by The Tornados with the original group with all their names on it. Although I didn't understand Hebrew I knew what was coming next. "Where are the members of this band, The Tornados" we were asked as he displayed the album cover to us. Our reply in unison was "Oh they're all dead." When he then asked us if they were all killed in the shooting incident at the recording studio and were we there at the time? We all fell about in fits of laughter much to the dismay of our puzzled host. Danny Ben–Av and Raffi Shauli seeing where the interview was going motioned to Rosenbloom to wind it down. It was not in their best interest to let him continue to expose us as being a bunch of phonies. This would have no benefit at all. On our way out of the studio Danny Ben–Av said that we were lucky that Raffi had a lot of pull in the community and was able to shut Abner Rosenbloom up, if not he would have torn us to pieces.

This dispute as to who were The Tornados was not new to us as we had often been asked at gigs where Heinz was or which one of us was Clem Cattini, but this time on the radio it was a bit different so we were glad to get out of there.

We followed Danny Ben–Av along Ben Yehuda Street and pulled up outside of Mandy's nightclub. We found out that the club was located in the basement of a four storey building and you would never really know that it was there until you walked down the stairs and into the club. It was not a big club by any means. There was a small dance floor surrounded by booths and tables, they had a pretty good bar and also served food there. Raffi ushered us in and told us to order whatever drinks we wanted as they would be on the house, which was just as well as none of us had any money anyway. The heavy sound of soul music filled the air and was accompanied by a sound sensitive light system. The blackness of the club was pierced by all kinds of coloured lights flickering and pulsating along with the beat of the music and a huddle of swaying and writhing bodies danced away on the dance floor. Mandy Rice–Davies acted as a hostess and walked the club with a gin in her hand passing from table to table, smiling at the guests. While talking to Danny Ben-Av I mentioned that I was interested to notice that the club did not play pop music but soul music. At that time in England we were pretty much done with soul music and the psychedelic era was at its beginning with Jimi Hendrix at the forefront. I asked Danny what type of music did Israeli kids like. He said it would be best to ask somebody from a local group and suggested that we might look for a Canadian guy who was the singer in a band from Tel Aviv called The Churchills.

He was usually in the club and after a brief search Danny found him. We were introduced to him and he told us that his name was Stan Solomon. Mick, Boris and I introduced ourselves and told him that we were part of The Tornados from England. He said that he heard that we were in town and that we might be doing some gigs together with his band. We asked him about the Israeli music scene and if soul music was the in thing at that time. He told us that The Churchills were basically a pop band and that he just did a half hour set of soul music. He said that bubble gum pop music was about all the kids liked and that Mandy's was the only place that you would hear soul music all night. He said that the half hour set of soul music he did was about as much as the audiences could take. He asked what we played and we told him. They will probably expect you to play all the hits that they hear on the radio, but you should just say "Fuck that shit" and play whatever you want.

Stan was about 20 years old, about 5 feet 6 in height with brown hair and a freckled complexion. When I first saw him I thought that he looked a bit like Davy Jones from The Monkees. He remarked upon my glasses with Boris' eyes drawn on them, which I had apparently forgotten about and said "Hey! Are you guys stoned? If you wanna get high I've got some great Lebanese hash." Boris' and Mick's eyes lit up and said they would take Stan up on his offer. Mick said that we were supposed to be moving into a flat in a couple of days and we would invite him over. At that time I was unaware of how much involvement and influence Stan Solomon would have in the next 25 years of my life.

We played our first gig in Israel at the Club Casablan on 29th December. It was located in Jaffa and the stage was so small that we just set up the gear on the dance floor and played like that. We did two 45 minute sets. We played quite well and the audience seemed to be responsive, but it did feel a bit strange. We found that the audience did like to come up and talk to us. They spoke English with heavy accents and usually asked if we were from Liverpool or did we ever play with Cliff Richard. It was hard to figure out if they liked our music or not.

The next day Raffi told us that he would be taking us over to our flat which was in Tel Aviv and was on King David Street. He also mentioned that we had been booked to do a tour with two other Israeli bands but that had been cancelled at the last minute. King David Street was a pretty respectable street lined on each side with apartment buildings all about 4 storeys high. Our flat was on the 4th floor and Raffi led the way as we lugged our suitcases up the stairs It was a spacious three bedroom flat with hardly anything in it. The floors were made of stone tiles and the place echoed as we spoke and walked from room to room. Dave and Sonia took the master bedroom while Mick, Boris and I chose the larger of the other two rooms. We pushed an extra bed into the room so the three of us hung out and slept together in the same room with our three beds positioned around the walls. We put Boris' little record player on a chair with my box of records underneath and that would be our little corner of the world for the next two months. As Raffi handed us two sets of keys he said "By the way there's no electricity in the flat but I'll get it on for you in a day or so." Luckily there was hot water of sorts as the building had solar heating panels on the roof which were and still are very popular in Israel. After what we had been through since we left England to be a couple of days with no electricity was bearable so we put up with it. Raffi also came up with some money for us. He said that we would only be able to get paid half of what we were supposed to get for the next few weeks as the tour had been cancelled and we would have to wait until his new club would open up. It would be called The Cheetah.

With a bit of money in our pockets we drove down to the Jaffa Market and bought some food and knives and forks, although I don't remember that we ever cooked anything there. That's because there was no stove in the flat. Raffi did show up with a Primus camper's stove but that wasn't much use to us. That afternoon Arizona Dan showed up at the flat. He said that he had asked about us at Mandy's and had been told where to find us. We invited him to come with us that night as we were doing a 20 minute spot at the Casablan. Before we all left he brought out a hash pipe and we all took some good tokes. In Dave's diary for 31st December 1967 he has written, "Did a 20 minute spot, stoned out of our minds."

On New Years Day we drove over to the Casablan packed up the gear and took it over to the Mini Club and got it set up. We played a 30 minute spot there that night and enjoyed it. Mick Strachan was doing a very good job on the drums and he kept us in good shape. Sonia was going over well with her songs and we were getting tighter as a band. The audiences in the Casablan and the Mini were not kids and we were received reasonably well. It would be a lot different once we got out into the kids clubs. After the show we were invited over to Raffi's place for a few drinks. Mandy was there and had just got ready to go down to Mandy's. We had a little chat with her and she asked us how we were finding things in Israel and we said "Okay" and that was about it. As she was leaving she said "Come on over to the club, dinner and drinks are on the house." We didn't need any more encouragement and took Mandy up on her offer. We all had steak dinners and the alcohol was flowing freely especially the gin which Mandy drank and encouraged us to do the same. She made sure that our glasses were always full. With the pulsating music and the flashing lights we were all having a real good time. We stumbled out of the club at about 2 in the morning and made our way to King David Street to our flat and groped our way around in the dark and finally found our beds. We still had no electricity.

At our rehearsal at the Mini the next day Danny Ben-Av asked Dave if he would let The Lions use his Hammond on a recording session. Apparently Dave had the only Hammond in the country and together with his Leslie Speaker system it was very desirable. Dave said that it would be okay and rightfully so. Our PA was a piece of shit and we had been able to use The Churchill's Marshall on our gigs so Dave thought that it was fair. We continued to rehearse the following day at the Mini. Danny Ben-Av showed up and told us that a photographer was coming over to shoot some publicity shots and The Churchills were coming over for the shoot. They showed up when we were still rehearsing and we could see that they were watching us in everything we did. They looked a bit younger than us and talked among themselves. Although we could not understand their language we could see that they seemed to be a happy go lucky, full of fun, bunch of kids. When the photographer arrived we went outside and down to the beach. It was a nice day but a bit breezy so the sea was quite choppy. We all posed by the shore on the sand and the rocks and we all walked out on a small jetty where the waves were breaking over it. The photographer said he loved to get shots with the waves breaking behind us. This was fine but we were getting soaked and before long we were all wringing wet and returned to the Mini looking like we had just jumped into the ocean. We saw The Churchills had changed into their stage suits which were floral printed waiter's uniforms with vests and frilly shirts. The band wore red ones while Stan Solomon wore the same but in blue. They all disappeared for the photo shoot and returned in about 20 minutes all wet and talking excitedly.

I had another chance to talk with Stan Solomon and invited him to come over to the flat that evening. He showed up with a kilo of hash in a carry–on bag and Boris rolled up a big joint which we smoked sitting in the darkness of the flat. Dave came in with Sonia and Dave took a few tokes. Sonia sat with us but she didn't ever smoke but when she started to burst out in fits of laughter we figured that she had got high just from the smoke that filled the room. Stan told us that he was currently staying with Churchills' drummer, Ami Treibich at Ami's parents' home but was not feeling comfortable there. We said that he was welcome to stay with us at the flat as we had lots of room and a spare bed for as long as we would be in Israel so he took us up on our offer and from that moment on he stayed with us. When we all finally woke up the next day we were all hungry but there was nothing to eat in the flat so we decided to walk down to the corner of King David and Ibn Gvirol Street. There we found a small coffee shop and right next door was a nice little restaurant called Bar-El. Dave and I remembered that just down the street from Joe Meek's studio in Holloway Road was a small transport café called Charlie's Restaurant so we christened Bar–El as Charlie's and as the food was very good, affordable and the owners were nice we continued to eat there regularly. This first meal that we ate at Charlie's took what little money we had left so we knew that we would need to speak to Danny or Raffi as we were absolutely broke. That afternoon we decided to take a drive down to Jaffa for something to do. We pulled up to the outdoor market which was full of all kinds of stalls and shops with the vendors hawking their various wares. Dave said that it reminded him of Petticoat Lane in the East End of London and for a lark Dave and I climbed on top of the van with an old pair of trousers that we found behind one of the seats and started shouting at the passers by offering the pants up for sale. Before we knew it we were surrounded by dozens of people who were all curious to find out what all the noise was about. The crowd was getting bigger by the moment as people seemed to appear out of nowhere. Soon the van was completely surrounded by a mass of people and when we heard the sound of a police siren approaching, we decided it was time to get out of there. The only problem was that we couldn't move the van. Boris and Mick were in fits of laughter while Sonia was looking a bit worried. Dave said "Bugger this, lads" and got behind the wheel and with his hand firmly planted on the horn managed to force our way out through the crowd. As we pulled off we could still see all kinds of people who were running down the side streets coming to see what the commotion was all about. One thing we found out about Israel was that even the smallest, out of the ordinary occurrence attracted hundreds of people. The Israelis were a very inquisitive bunch of people. Later that afternoon Raffi Shauli showed up at the flat and handed out some more money to us. He brought a guy with him dressed in army fatigues, saying that this was a friend of his from the army and that they were going to fix the electricity. They disappeared up on to the roof and hot wired the electric. Now we were bathed in luxury and had power, it was a wonderful day. We hooked up Boris' little record player and soon the sounds of Jimi Hendrix and The Beatles *Magical Mystery Tour* filled the flat.

Over the next few days as we were not working we hung around with Stan and spent the evenings smoking, talking listening to music and having fun with Stan's cassette recorder. Boris would sit up higher than us on a couple of cushions and conduct the all Australian Farting Contest in which we featured Dave Watts as a surprise contestant from England, who knocked out Big Jim Asshole in a most exciting final. Dave's expertise in the ability to fart at will really shone through and for an encore Dave farted to the riff of "Sunshine Of Your Love." Stan and I also started to write poetry. We wrote most of it in my note and song book that I carried around, and still have. We wrote all kinds of stuff in it, some funny, some serious, some stupid, and some about what was going on in our lives at that time. We were writing so much and knocking ourselves out that Boris got irritated and ridiculed us, but in the end he said that we bastards were really quite lucky as we would be able to look at all that nonsense years in the future and be able to be reminded of those days in Israel. He got that one right for sure.

We were all having a good time, getting high, going down to eat at Charlie's, listening to music; Mick started to disappear late at night and we knew he was going down to Mandy's, he told us he had met a girl down there, Mona. The only downside was that we were still not being paid what we were contracted for. As it was there was not much that we could have done about it. We were thousands of miles away from home so we just couldn't say "Fuck it let's go home" it wasn't that easy. We didn't have enough money to get us through France and back to England anyway. We played a gig at the Mini Club and at the end of the evening, on our way out; we took twenty five tins of assorted food from the kitchen. We thought that we would take part of the payment that they owed us in food. We bought a can opener and cooked the food on the small primus stove in the flat.

The following day there was a scare and the whole country was on the alert. We tried to find out from Ben-Av what was up and we were told that there could be another war coming up as there was some kind of trouble down at the border with Egypt. We thought "Lovely, not only are we not getting paid properly but we're going to be caught up in a war." Luckily we were never affected by anything that may have occurred there.

Things began to get a bit strange when we were walking back from Charlie's in the evening and we started to notice what turned out to be bats flitting around in the twilight. There were large flocks of them diving in low over us. We thought that there was a plague of bats upon Israel. That night a big storm blew up followed by seventy to eighty mph winds over the next few days. When the weather got back to normal we were glad to be able to get out and about again and drove down to the Mini Club to get the gear ready as we were told that we would be playing the opening show at the Cheetah club on the 16th January. To Dave's horror he found that two keys had been broken off the Hammond. At first we presumed that something had fallen on the organ and snapped the keys off but there was no evidence of that. The keys were broken off in the mid range of the keyboard and Dave said that some bastard had done it on purpose to screw us up. We couldn't figure out why somebody would have done that. We didn't look upon The Tornados as being some kind of threat to anybody or to the other bands as we played a different kind of music to them, but we did feel that there was some kind of rivalry between the groups there and that we had been caught up in that. Presently The Churchills roadie showed up and when asked he said that nobody had been in the club for the past two days due to the stormy weather. The janitor in the club also confirmed that. So it was a complete mystery but we did come to the conclusion that we were the victims of sabotage. We broke down the gear and loaded it into the van and decided to drive over to Wally Garrett's place and although his business was guitar amps he was able to help us and glued the keys back onto the keyboard. Luckily the keys held well and Dave was able to play again with no difficulty. That evening back at the flat Stan came in and told us that there had been a tragedy in The Churchills' band. Their bass player's mother had been run over by a bus and killed and the band was in a state of shock. The bass player's name was Michael Gavrielov and he was a founder member of the band. As expected he was distraught but had said that he would do his best to show up for the gigs that were coming up.

The next day being the 16th we went over to the Cheetah club in the afternoon to set up the gear and do a sound check. The club although quite spacious was really no more than just a large bare room with a few tables and chairs scattered here and there. There was no kind of decorative adornment on the walls but there was at least a pretty good sized stage on which we could stand, and we were able to fit all of the gear on too. Danny Ben-Av showed up and during a break from the sound check Danny told us that they wanted to do something special for the opening night. He went out to his car and returned with a Hussar's army uniform, a plumed helmet and a sword. He said that I should wear this for the opening night and that I should be seen entering the club in the full regalia. I was not that excited about making a spectacle of myself and said that I didn't think that it was necessary and anyway we were not Sergeant Pepper's Lonely Hearts Club Band. Boris said "Oh come on Robbie you can do it" and under pressure from everybody I had no choice and consented to wear the uniform. When I tried on the jacket it reminded me of a picture I had seen showing Jimi Hendrix wearing one similar so I felt a bit better and decided that I would back comb my hair that night and puff it up à la Jimi Hendrix.

When we showed up at the Cheetah Club that evening there was a sizeable crowd milling around outside. To our surprise it was mainly made up of young guys. For the most part they were all dressed in a similar way which meant that they were wearing very low cut pants with wide belts, floral or plaid shirts and pointed shoes. There was no evidence of long hair styles in fact everyone looked like they could have been French or Italian. This was probably due to the crowd being made up of Israelis that were mostly of dark skinned Moroccan ethnicity. They surrounded our van as we pulled up outside of the club and tried to peer through the windows to get a look at us. The roadie that we had met at the Mini Club showed up out of the blue and began shouting at the onlookers. We could not understand what he was yelling but it looked like he was ordering them to move back and let us get out of the van. He spoke to us in English and told us that his name was Yoshko and that he worked for Haim Saban and Yehuda Talit and was there to watch over us. Yehuda Talit was The Churchills' manager and as we were exiting the van they showed up and watched from the sidelines as we made our way into the club. I got a lot of looks from the crowd as I got out of the van in my uniform looking just like I had left the movie set of some epic Napoleon filming. I felt a bit awkward with the heavy helmet balanced precariously on my head and using the sword like a walking stick I made my way through the crowd. Sonia got a few whistles from the guys and I heard the words Beatles and Liverpool shouted around. Once inside the club I had to get that helmet off my head and teased my hair up once more. As we were checking out the gear and tuning up I noticed that Michael Gavrielov from The Churchills had come in and was sitting over on the side with his girlfriend. We decided to walk over to him and offer our sympathy for the terrible loss of his mother. He forced a smile as we shook hands. He told us that he had come to see us play so that he could take his mind off things for a while. By the time we were ready to begin the scheduled two forty-five minute sets only a few people had trickled into the club. We thought that they were just waiting for us to start but after we had played the first few numbers only a fraction of the people that had been gathered outside entered the club. During the course of the evening our audience grew a little more but overall the attendance was disappointing. After the show we drove back to the Mini Club and stashed away the gear and decided that we would rehearse over the next few days and clean up some of our numbers.

Danny Ben-Av showed up with Raffi Shauli just as we were perfecting the discordant build up in "A Day In The Life" by The Beatles. They said that they had to talk to us so we all sat around one of the tables and lit up some cigarettes. When we discussed the poor attendance at the Cheetah Club Danny said that the kids outside waited until we started to play and as they didn't recognize any of the songs that we were playing they wouldn't come in. Danny pulled out a handful of 45s from his briefcase and said that we were to learn those numbers. We sifted through the discs on the table and saw that it was a collection of songs that all the other groups in Tel Aviv were playing. The ones I remember were "The Letter" by The Box Tops, which had been a big hit in '67 and stayed at number one on the Billboard charts for a month and won several awards including *Cashbox Magazine's* Record of the Year; "San Francisco" (Be sure to wear flowers in your hair) by Scott McKenzie which had been a top ten hit in the USA in '67 and was recognized as the anthem for the Hippie Movement; "L.S.D" some obscure record that had been a hit in Israel, and they said that Sonia must sing "Respect" by Aretha Franklin. We agreed to the fact that these were great hits but why should we play them? We had been brought to Israel as The Tornados and to appear as such, for what we were, and what we played, this would just lump us in together with the rest of the Israeli groups. Why bring The Tornados all the way from England to play the same songs as everybody else when you might as well just play the record in the club or have a local band play it. We just about threw up when we were suggested to play "Here We Go Loop De Loop, Here We Go Loop De Lie". We had seen The Lions play it at their rehearsal and thought that it was a silly number. During the subsequent conversation it became clear that the Israeli kids could only appreciate bands by comparing how they played the same songs. If a band played music that they had never heard they considered the band to be crap and would not think twice about coming into the club, and that was why the attendance was poor at The Cheetah. Raffi Shauli said that if the attendances didn't go up they wouldn't make any money and we wouldn't get paid. At this point we knew that we had no choice in the matter and agreed to perform the numbers. We got them all down over the next few days. A verse from "Rockin' In Jerusalem" a song I wrote remembering the trip to Israel sums it all up.

Well when we got out on the road we didn't go down so great,
They said that they wanted to hear all the songs that were in the Hit Parade,
And Danny Ben-Av told us boys you gotta understand,
We want you just to sound like any other Israeli Band.
So we said goodbye to Graham Bond and The Blues Breakers too,
If you're going to San Francisco, you better take the Letter with you.
So we swallowed hard and learned the songs and played 'em note for note.
And wished to Christ we could take "em all and shove 'em down his throat.
We're ROCKIN' IN JERUSALEM;
we're ROCKIN' IN JERUSALEM TONIGHT.

I thought back to the conversation that I had with Stan Solomon at Mandy's Club regarding the music scene in Israel and he had been right, we did get asked to play the hits. He said that the kids basically didn't like him or the soul music that he sang and he was looked upon as an interruption in The Churchills' set by the audience. Stan refused to sing any of the hits and so got away with it by just performing a half hour set and letting The Churchills' take care of all the hits. He said that he got hassled regularly by guys in the audience asking him to sing some pop song or other. They always asked him why didn't he sing this or why didn't he sing that?

We had very little trouble getting off the songs, we took the records back to the flat and played them on Boris' little record player. We did the numbers well with Dave's Hammond playing giving us an edge over the Israeli bands. Sonia did her best with "Respect" but she was not a soul singer. She had a great powerful voice and always sang perfectly but she couldn't belt it out like Aretha.

During those rehearsals we blew one of the speakers in the Vox columns. Our audio system was pretty lame as it was so it had to be replaced and we had no money for a new speaker. Dave and Boris found that the speakers in the Mini Club's system were the same size as ours so they promptly disconnected one of them and replaced it with our blown speaker. Boris sniffed and said "Fuck these assholes, they're screwing us with the money so they owe us on this one." On the drive back to the flat we noticed that the van was beginning to suffer from its diet of Israeli petrol which Dave said was a pretty bad quality.

On the 20th January it was time to return to The Cheetah again. This time we opened up our set with the new numbers and lo and behold the people began to come into the club and we had an audience. Once we had used up the new additions to our repertoire it was a little different when we had to play the songs that they didn't know. When we could see that the audience was getting irritated we would have to repeat some of the new songs to keep them happy. We must have played "The Letter" to the point of embarrassment, but they would keep asking for it and all we wanted to do was play, keep them happy and hopefully get paid. After our 90 minute spot at The Cheetah a blond guy by the name of Michel came to escort us over to the second venue which was the club at Bat Yam (Beautiful Sea). The club was in some ways a bit similar to Mandy's in the respect that it was down in a basement located in a shopping centre. There were street vendors everywhere with portable grills cooking shish kabob and steaks that they were stuffing into pita bread. The heavy aroma of spices, onion and garlic hung in the air and if you didn't know where the club was you could easily miss it. Unlike Mandy's, Bat Yam's audience was made up of kids from mid to late teens. It was a struggle to get the Hammond down the stairs into the club. There was no problem with the rest of the gear as we used The Churchills' amps and they used ours. The air in the club was thick. There was no air conditioning and we felt that we were walking into a sauna. It was a long narrow room with a very low ceiling and when we got up on the stage there was very little room above us. Dave said" You better not jump up and down Robbie you'll bang your bloody head on the ceiling." I guess that we went down okay. We sprinkled the new songs throughout our set and managed to keep the crowd's attention for the ninety minute set. We were all pouring with sweat and felt drained from the heat and lack of fresh air. Mick was beginning to look a bit weird about half way through the evening. He was looking like he was in some other world and his face bore an anxious expression. "It must be the heat" I suggested to Boris as we both looked back at Mick as he slouched over the drums. "Nah!" answered Boris, "He ate a chunk of hash earlier and he's tripped out."

Danny Ben-Av showed up at Bat Yam at the end of the night and looked happier than usual. In fact he was pleased about the attendances at the clubs and said 'You see, if you play some of the music they know everything is okay." He also told us that we would be working four out of the next five nights.

The second gig was at a club called The Cocos which was a Spartan looking kind of place located in an area mostly made up of factories. It was a warm humid night and we showed up around dusk. We got out of the van and the first things we noticed were huge rats that were scurrying everywhere seemingly unaffected by human presence. They would dart in and out looking like black shadows in the night which you were not quite sure if you had seen or not. Sonia was terrified and we all had the creeps so we hurried inside and up the stairs. The place was practically unadorned. It was just a big room similar to The Cheetah with a stage that was just about big enough for the band and there was a small concession which sold orange pop, grapefruit pop and white lemonade. At these kinds of clubs we always got bugged by guys insisting that they help us carry the Hammond into the place. Everybody and his brother wanted to get a hand on it somewhere. When we would arrive at the entrance door it was a competition to see how many of them could get in without paying pretending that they were with the group. We soon got wise to this and on future occasions the roadie Yoshko would yell at everybody to stand back when we carried the Hammond in.

Well we did actually get paid the following morning when Danny Ben-Av came by the flat. This was the first time that we had been paid correctly but we were working almost every night to get it. When we did get to see Stan here and there we talked about our gigs and Stan talked about his gigs with The Churchills and we would all go down to Charlie's to eat at lunch time. That night we played in a dance hall just outside of Tel Aviv called Petah Tikva. We arrived there in the afternoon to set up the gear and get everything ready and then just had to hang around the place for a few hours. The place got pretty packed out that night with the dance floor full of kids. There was a local curiosity there in the form of a dark skinned little guy who was almost like a midget except that he didn't have short stunted legs; he had a very short body and apparently no neck. He could have passed for the hunchback of Notre Dame but was better looking. When the floor was filled with dancers he would circulate among them hopping around and from time to time he would leap up into the air so high that we could see him above the heads of the people. He always wore a huge grin on his face and it delighted everybody to watch him especially us, as we could see everything very well from up on the stage which was very high in comparison to the hall. In fact it was higher than the average person that would be standing on the dance floor. As usual there was the group of young guys that were always gathered together right in front of the stage. They were looking up at us, especially Sonia from where they stood and they were continually smiling and we thought that they must really be enjoying the show. They would often call Sonia to come to the edge of the stage like they wanted to ask her something and generally encouraged her to stay up front. Sonia took it that she was going over well and continued to dance around in her sexy flaring mini skirt. All at once a big, burly tough guy who turned out to be a bouncer burst through the crowd and began to set about the half a dozen young guys that were in front of the stage he smacked them all across their heads like an angry father and pushed them all out of the club; at the same time indicating to Sonia that she should move back on the stage. The guys up front had all been looking up Sonia's dress and getting a real good view. Sonia blushed a little stood back from the edge of the stage and we got through the rest of the show without further incident.

We drove 4 hours the next day to somewhere up near Nazareth to play at a cinema with The Lions and some other Israeli band. On the way there I couldn't stop thinking about "Jesus of Nazareth" as we were taught at school and church and thinking of Nazareth as some far away place in the world that you would never ever see; and here I was driving towards it. As was usual there was a big crowd of people outside the cinema when we arrived and Yoshko was barking at everybody to stand back and got us through the crowd and into the cinema. We were beginning to understand the different scene that we were experiencing there in Israel. Guys used to shout "Hey Johnny you know Liverpool" but they pronounced it "Libber Fool" and we used to crack up. Some of them would come right up to you and sing a line from a song like "Gimme a ticket for an Aeroplane" or "Lucy is this guy that I love" which was meant to be "Lucy In The Sky With Diamonds" Backstage at the cinema we hung around with The Lions and another band that looked like they were just kids. They were called The Monsters and they were a three piece band, guitar, bass and drums and they opened up the show. The guitar player had very long hair even by European standards and it was red. We were told his name was Gingie Land. The bass player was a kid of about 17 and the drummer a kid of 16, Yakie Yosha and Moti Levi. They were like what you might call a garage band today. They had something different about them and although I couldn't understand a word they were saying to the audience I could see that they were getting a reaction. They sang all their songs in English. Gingie Land did all the vocals. Later he told us that he was born in the USA and his parents had immigrated to Israel when he was a kid.

The Lions did a very good show and played well but I couldn't help feeling that because of the way that they were dressed in their stage clothes I expected them to at any moment, throw down their instruments and turn into a trapeze act or start walking on the High Wire. But the kids liked them and they went down well with a set of music that was definitely aimed at the audience. The highlight of their show was when the bass player, Danny Shoshan gave his bass over to the lead singer and went on to do a few soul numbers and really put on a big, dramatic show in the style of James Brown. He had and still has a very rich powerful voice. Here we see something similar to what was happening in The Churchills, with Stan Solomon doing his 30 minutes of soul music hoping to be something different and special and hopefully cause some kind of a sensation. Soul music was the medium which Israeli bands used, to try to break away from the norm. In England it was what we called Underground music or Psychedelic music all mixed in together with a good helping of blues. As The Tornados at that time we were beginning to take the road of breaking away from the normal pop scene. It showed in our repertoire with "All Your Love" and "Little Girl" that we covered from John Mayall and The Bluesbreakers, a definite blues influence, and 'A Day In The Life" and "Lucy In The Sky With Diamonds" from The Beatles which was all part of the emerging Psychedelic era. I was already planning to include some Hendrix numbers in our set when we would get back to England.

When the evening was coming to a close and the gear was being put into the vans The Tornados and The Lions stood around and chatted together. We were standing in a dimly lit passageway and I was hanging with The Lions' drummer Moshe. He produced a flashlight from somewhere and asked me to shine it on the wall, which I did and he proceeded to create shadows on the wall displaying various animals and caricatures at the same time giggling like a small child. He just about had me giggling along with him. I asked Lions' bass player, Danny if Moshe was tripping out on acid or something and Danny said "No, he's always like that, that's the way he is." I thought "Wow, that's weird." Throughout the evening I noticed that Dave had been talking to Danny Ben-Av and as we were just about to get in the van Dave came up to me and said that Ben-Av had offered him and Sonia a ride home with him in his Mustang or "Ben-Avmobile" as Boris called it. We followed them back and somewhere deep inside of me I felt that something was afoot. That event would contribute to the final break up of Joe Meek's last group of Tornados.

Finally we got a day off although much of it was spent sleeping after getting back to the flat just before daybreak. Stan and I began to hang out together on the time off. I turned him on to Hendrix and The Blues Breakers which we listened to on Boris' record player. We continued to write poetry during our smoking sessions and bit by bit we began to sing and play together in the big empty living room at the flat. It was good to sing and play there as the room had a natural echo due to the stone floors and lack of any furniture. It wasn't long before we had a couple of songs written.

That night down at Charlie's restaurant we got to see the paper man. Apart from Stan and I he was the only other customer in the restaurant. He sat in the corner and ate his food just like a ritual. Over the next weeks we would continue to study him and got to strike up conversations with him. He was probably in his late sixties, with a bald head and always wore the same white shirt. We asked him why he mixed up his foods in certain ways and why he put ice in his hot tea. He gave us an elaborate explanation why people should not eat anything that is too hot or too cold. He told us that he was lucky to be alive as in the war for independence in the forties his house was destroyed by a bomb blast. He was asleep at the time on the second floor and he was blown into the street and landed still lying in bed. We all had a good laugh. Whenever he stood up he would have these large wads of something in the back pockets of his trousers and would be continually searching for something on the floor or in the corner behind his table. Our Persian waiter Maurice took a delight in telling us that those wads were just pieces of plain paper and that one time the paper man had been hit on the head and robbed. The robber must have thought that his victim was carrying his life savings around in his back pockets. According to Maurice the robber when finding out that his booty was nothing more than pieces of plain paper, he threw them at the paper man screaming "What the hell is this?" Later the paper man confirmed that the story was true and when asked why he carried the plain sheets of paper around he said "You never know when you might need a piece of paper for something." At that point we revealed to him that we called him the paper man and he was quite amused by that. He said that we should all stuff our pants pockets with paper and carry signs around saying "We are the paper men of Tel Aviv."

Back out on the road again the next day we drove up to the ancient city of Akko or Acre as it is written in English. It is located on the coast a little to the north of Haifa and is a historical city that dates back some 4,000 years. We played a half hour set there in a small club. As what seemed to be the norm, there was a group of vendors with their little stands set up around the entrance to the club. As we were leaving Dave, for a lark, reached out and picked up a few peanuts from a tray that an Arabian looking guy was holding and continued to walk to the van. As we were getting into the van the Arab guy came running up to us and screaming and shouting he pushed a pistol in Dave's face. Danny Ben-Av was quick to react and immediately consoled the vendor and paid him some money to get rid of him. He walked away muttering and probably cursed us out in Arabic. Ben-Av warned Dave to be careful as it was unwise to play those kinds of tricks on Arabs. He told Dave that he could have been shot or killed. Dave was visibly shaken as nobody had ever stuck a gun in his face before. On the drive back to Tel Aviv at around 2am Dave, now recovered from his run in with the Arab guy, spotted a banana plantation on the side of the road. He asked Boris to pull over and ignoring Sonia's pleas for him to be careful he ran over to a tree and broke off a whole bunch of bananas. It was such a large bunch that he had a job to carry it to the van. He threw it in the back on top of the gear. Over the next few days we ate so many bananas that we got sick of them in the end. Not only that, the bunch was infested with insects that became real pests in the flat. We also found out from Michel our escort who when he saw the bananas in the flat told us that we had taken them from a Kibbutz which usually had armed guards on patrol and anyone caught stealing could have been shot on sight. So in theory Dave could have been shot twice on that day.

We all hung around the flat on our day off. Boris' record player was kept in use, my Beatles EP. *Magical Mystery Tour* was often on the turntable and Dave got rid of the squawking birds that had been annoying us constantly in the trees outside our windows. He went downstairs and finding a house brick he hurled it up at the birds in the tree which scared the shit out of them and they flew off in a squawking flock and settled in another tree across the road where they proceeded to annoy somebody else. The only thing that Dave had miscalculated was that a car was parked directly under the tree. The house brick tumbled down and landed smack on top of the car.

We watched from the window and saw Dave, who realizing what he had done swiftly turned around and came bounding up stairs back to the flat, quickly closing the door and disappearing into his bedroom. A little later on when I was sitting alone in the empty living room strumming on my 335 Dave and Sonia came in and we did a little three part harmony together as we often did. At one point Dave said "Listen Robbie I've got to tell you something. The other night on the way back when we drove with Danny Ben-Av he told me that they wanted to build, what he called, an English style band in Israel and asked me if I would like to stay on here and play the Hammond." Dave said that it was something to do with The Lions and he didn't know what to do. It was clear to see that there was a lot of work here but he felt that he couldn't leave us, mainly me and Son, and said that he didn't want to go along with it unless I could play in the band too. Chris and Mick kept talking about getting back to England so I began to feel that sometime in the next couple of weeks that some situation would arrive. I felt that Dave was probably going to go for it in the end and if I was not considered for the band, then should I leave with Boris and Mick or stay in Israel hoping for something? It was an insecure and worrisome feeling that gradually came over me. It was just another one in a series of stressful events that had taken place in the past five months; starting with the departure of the Holder brothers. Being on our second bass player and second drummer who had only been with us a matter of weeks it seemed like we were not that tight fit group any more. Although I tried to deny it I just knew and felt that a change was bound to come.

Later on when Stan and I were writing some poetry I told him about what Dave and I had talked about and that I didn't know if I should stay in Israel or return to England. Stan immediately told me to stay. He said that we could make a band together or he would get me into The Churchills. He knew that two of the band members were due to be called up for their national service in the Israeli Army and that would be a good time to get me into the band. Although Stan's words gave me some feeling of hope I still felt worried; and inside I was hoping that I could still stay with Dave and get into the "British Style" band that Danny Ben-Av was talking about. I didn't realize it at the time but this bid to get Dave into the "British Style" band which would turn out to be The Lions Of Judea" was coming from their manager Haim Saban. We played again at Bat Yam after our day off. It was the second time that we played there. Just like the first time we had all the people in the front continually calling out the names of the songs they wanted to hear. It aggravated me and during the set I was developing an angry attitude. If only they would just listen to what we wanted to play. People would come up to the stage when you were singing a number and start to pull on your trouser leg to get your attention expecting you to stop singing and talk to them. At the end of the show I was admonished by the club owner and Danny Ben-Av for making rude gestures on stage. I guess the use of my middle finger was unacceptable.

We enjoyed a couple of days off. Mick, Boris, Stan and I hung out all day long in that little bedroom. We sat on our beds and listened to music while Boris rolled up the joints. Stan and I were still writing a lot of poetry and it was just pouring out of us. We would often collapse on the floor with laughter at things that we had written. From the moment that Stan and I met we had been creative and that creativity was to continue throughout our short career in music together. During the day Dave and Boris went down to fetch a few things from the van and came upstairs looking puzzled. Dave said that it was freaky as when he and Boris went to the van which was parked outside they found it running with the doors locked and no key in the ignition!

We decided to do some more rehearsals over at Mini Mandy's on the 29th January just to brush up as we were due to play at The Cheetah on the 30th. We were also waiting to get paid and Danny Ben-Av kept putting us off and coming up with nothing. We had a big row with Raffi and Mandy when we went over to see them about getting paid. They had no money to pay us and we walked out in a huff. At the gig that night Danny Ben-Av met us after the show and invited us over to Mandy's for a peace talk. Throughout the night we went through a back and forth thing with them where we complained that we were not getting paid on time, and that for the amount of work that they were getting out of us we should be paid even more money.

They in turn hit us back with "Well your PA system was not powerful enough and we had to rent a Marshall PA for you." And it went on and on all night long with Ben-Av becoming nastier and meaner by the minute. It finally erupted into a full fledged shouting match with even Mick who was a real quiet, soft spoken guy, raising his voice and putting in his two cents. It was not a good feeling so when Sonia who was getting upset by the big fight with Danny Ben-Av said that she wanted to leave, we all got up. Raffi asked us not to leave so we continued to converse in a restrained manor. Raffi said he would get our pay for us by February 1st and we ended up parting under friendlier circumstances. We were assured that we would be paid so with some feeling of accomplishment we walked out of Mandy's into the daylight at 7am. We were all in bed by 7.30. At 11.30 we were woken up by a loud banging on the apartment door. As I stirred from my deep sleep it sounded like distant cannon fire. Realizing that it was the front door I stumbled out of our room and bumping into Dave in the process, we both discovered that it was Yoshko shouting "Come on, come on, and wake up everybody's waiting outside." We looked out of the front window and there parked outside was a 60 seater coach. He told us we were driving to Tiberias which would be about 4 hours from Tel Aviv and we were doing a big show with The Lions and The Churchills. We couldn't believe that Stan was still asleep in his room as he must have known about the gig and why wasn't he awake? We woke him up and he said "Oh shit that's right we're all playing together in Tiberias, I spaced out." He dragged himself out of bed and said that they would just have to wait until we all got ready. After our traumatic night at Mandy's and our lack of sleep The Tornados finally got themselves awake and ready and trooped downstairs with Stan lighting a cigarette and bringing up the rear. The Lions and Churchills were all on the bus along with a roadie by the name of Little Tony. He was huge to say the least. He was 6 foot six and big all over with a large ugly scar on his cheek. He had greasy, black hair, a bad facial complexion but contrary to his appearance he was really quite pleasant and spoke reasonable English. We drove over to the Cheetah to get the Hammond and whatever gear was needed and drove north to Tiberias located on the shore of the Sea of Galilee. The bus ride was fun. It almost felt like we were on a Magical Mystery Tour. Once again it was exciting for me to know that we were on our way to the very special place where Jesus is said to have walked on the water. As bands we did not intermingle that much but from time to time one band member may have struck up a conversation with a member of another band. I had a chat with Danny Shoshan, Lions' bass player. We talked mainly about music. I told him to listen to a guy called Jimi Hendrix, Danny was basically into soul music and had the kind of voice that could pull it off. He confessed that he was not happy with most of the music that The Lions played and preferred to play a harder style of music and that was why he did his soul feature act to end The Lions' set. We really didn't get to talk to The Churchills much, but Stan did come over for a chat here and there. The Churchills were younger than The Lions and Tornados by about three or four years. They seemed to be fun loving and they laughed and joked together, but we couldn't understand what they were saying. One of them spoke English with a South African accent. Stan introduced him to us as Selwyn. He was born in South Africa but his family immigrated to Israel. As of that time we had not seen The Churchills perform but had heard a lot from Stan. I was interested to see how they were.

We pulled into the town of Tiberias which dates back about 2000 years and is located on the eastern shore of the Sea of Galilee. Although a lake, its size is so great that you could imagine it as being a sea. We looked across it and could see the smoky outlines of mountains in the distance. Michael of The Churchills who Stan had brought over to talk to us explained that those mountains were in Syria and that the Syrians were their enemies. It seemed like we were gradually descending into the town and in fact we were. Tiberias is situated 200 meters below sea level. We had the luxury of staying in a hotel that night and we all bundled into the place and took to our rooms. Boris, Mick and I had a room together and after we settled down I decided to take a walk around the place. At the end of a long corridor I could hear sounds of laughter and as I approached the open door I could here Stan Solomon's voice and peals of laughter. It was Stan who was parading around the room wearing Little Tony's trousers (The group

Roadie) which were about 100 sizes too big for him with the waist band coming up almost to his chin. Little Tony was taking a shower and Stan had the Churchills in fits particularly Selwyn who was actually in tears. I was invited in to join in their frivolities and accepted. Stan formally introduced me to The Churchills after the laughter had died down and Little Tony had come out of the shower wondering what all the noise had been about.

One by one I met and shook hands with The Churchills. They were Ami Trebich, on drums, Haim Romano lead guitar, Selwyn Lifschitz guitar and vocals, Michael Gavrielov bass and vocals and "Churchill" who was actually a guy called Yitzhak Klepter lead and rhythm guitar. Michael explained that when Yitzhak was at school he was kind of chubby and had been given the nickname of Churchill by his school mates due to a resemblance to Sir Winston Churchill and that's how they had come up with the name "Churchills."

They opened up the show that night and I stepped out into the audience to take a look. Well they were basically a carbon copy of what all Israeli groups were playing at that time but I did notice that what they played they played very well. Selwyn did a nice job of knocking off "The Letter" and "Live For Today" and they did a very good job of backing Stan on his half hour set of soul music. They not only played well but gave a good vocal backing to his numbers. I thought that their outfits were a bit dated and blasé but on the whole they were a very good band. We went on after The Lions to close the show and half way through our second number the power went off. Apparently this was a regular occurrence in this area and was more or less tolerated by every one. We thought that it would be the end of everything and that we would all go back to the hotel. Not so; the whole audience sat and waited around with us for over an hour till the power came back on again when we restarted our set and finished up the evening.

February 1st was "Payday", we drove over to the Mini Club to collect our money, and met with Danny Ben-Av, Raffi Shauli, and a guy called Sasson who in due course we found out was either an accountant or he was from the Income Tax people. It was never quite clear. He presented us with some papers to sign and informed us that we owed the Israeli government taxes and they were deducting 250 Lira, at that time about 30 pounds, from our pay. There was nothing that we could do about that. We just took our money and left presuming that it had been some kind of a fiddle and we had lost out again.

February 3rd came around - it was the first anniversary of the Holloway Road tragedy. It is doubtful if any of us even realized the significance of that day. The name of Joe Meek probably never even entered our minds. There was so much going on. There we were thousands of miles away from England in the Middle East having to adjust to a different kind of audience and culture. The possible break up of The Tornados was definitely looming upon the horizon and the future was filled with uncertainty. I had no idea what was in store for me and still didn't know for sure what Dave's situation was with The Lions. It was a worry to me and was always in the back of my mind. I had spoken to Boris and Mick again as to what they thought about the situation and they were still adamant that they would leave Israel and the sooner the better. If Dave did go to The Lions then I would definitely be on my own with this one. Stan Solomon remained supportive toward me and still promised that he would get me into The Churchills. We had just written our first song together and there was a definite creative thing going on between us.

As far as February 3rd 1968 went it was just another day in Tel-Aviv. We played a double between The Cheetah and Bat Yam. It was a very hot and sticky night with the air thick and humid. It was unbearable in the clubs; we were absolutely dripping with sweat and completely out of energy. It was hard to breathe to say the least. Although it was just another day in Tel Aviv it was the last gig that Joe Meek's "end of the line" Tornados would ever play. Exactly one year to the day that Joe Meek shot and killed Violet Shenton and then, himself The New Tornados played their final gig and faded into oblivion.

+++

Robb's story continues in Israel and that will be published later...

In the meantime Robb's website www.robbhuxley.com has several chapters on the post Tornados years in Israel and you can contact him via the site. You can also view videos there including The Saxons "Saxons War Cry" and "Click-Ete-Clack." Also the complete contents of Robb's album *Lost Songs Of The Sixties* are available to listen online at the site.

In 2006 Robb paid a visit to the UK and visited Joe Meek's grave

19305717R00177

Printed in Great Britain
by Amazon